SPANISH PHONOLOGY: DESCRIPTIVE AND HISTORICAL

SPANISH PHONOLOGY: DESCRIPTIVE AND HISTORICAL

I. R. Macpherson

MANCHESTER UNIVERSITY PRESS

BARNES & NOBLE BOOKS · NEW YORK

© Manchester University Press 1975

Published by MANCHESTER UNIVERSITY PRESS
Oxford Road, Manchester M13 9PL

UK ISBN 0 7190 0788 7

British Library Cataloguing in Publication Data
Macpherson, Ian, Richard
   Spanish phonology.
   1. Spanish language – Phonology
   I. Title
   461'.5   PC4726

   ISBN 0–7190–0788–7

Text set in 8/10 pt IBM Press Roman, printed and bound
in Great Britain at The Pitman Press, Bath

CONTENTS

PART I: DESCRIPTIVE PHONOLOGY

PART II: HISTORICAL PHONOLOGY

LIST OF FIGURES AND TABLES

FIGURES

TABLES

PREFACE

This book is intended to serve as a general introduction to the phonetics and phonology, both descriptive and historical, of the Spanish language. Until now, to the best of my knowledge, there has been no introductory course in English available. For the descriptive phonetics of Spanish, the student has been able since 1918 to consult Tomás Navarro's *Manual de pronunciación española* and, more recently, Quilis and Fernández's *Curso de fonética y fonología españolas* and J. B. Dalbor's *Spanish Pronunciation*; for a study of the history of the language and of historical phonology he has had available principally Rafael Lapesa's *Historia de la lengua española,* W. J. Entwistle's *The Spanish Language* and Ramón Menéndez Pidal's *Gramática histórica española.* With the exception of Quilis and Fernández, and Dalbor, these were designed primarily as works of reference, with their information presented in a form suitable for leisurely consultation.

In order to fill a gap which in my belief has existed for a long time, I have here combined into one volume an introduction to Spanish phonetics and phonology approached from a descriptive point of view in the first part and from a historical point of view in the second. It has not been my aim to present the material in any formalistic way, but arranged in what I believe in the light of my teaching experience so far to be a manageable order – roughly speaking, the straightforward material comes first in each part and the more complicated follows. The method of presentation of this introductory course is thus comparable to the method adopted in most courses designed to teach a foreign language: the basic elements are presented first, the finer detail later. A course constructed in this way is often less than ideal as a reference work: I have tried to compensate for this by providing, on pp. 169–81, comprehensive subject and word indexes to the material contained in the main body of the text.

My justification for the order in which the information is presented – since it may well be objected that what is 'easy' for one may well be found 'difficult' by another – is that the order of presentation is not something which has emerged overnight, but has evolved slowly during constant revision and reworking of a course taught to undergraduates over a period of ten years, a process aided considerably by the criticisms and suggestions both of those undergraduates and of fellow teachers of the subject. I make no claim that this introductory textbook covers exhaustively any aspect of the subjects with which it deals; I should like to think, however, that I have been able to introduce the basic information and terminology without serious omission in a way which is intelligible to elementary students without offending the standards of professional linguists. I trust too that the test, with its suggestions for further reading, its exercises and its bibliography, will be sufficient to provide both a basic framework and a stimulus to further reading and study.

My indebtedness to the many scholars who have written on the Spanish language or on some individual aspect of it will be evident throughout. I have not acknowledged in full detail every aspect of the text which depends, either wittingly or unwittingly, upon the massive contributions to knowledge of A. Alonso, D. Alonso, M. Alvar, E. Alarcos, V. García de Diego, W. J. Entwistle, Y. Malkiel, R. Lapesa, A. Martinet, R. Menéndez Pidal, M. K. Pope and T. Navarro. To do so would not have been practical, but I have tried to draw attention, in the text or in the notes, to any special indebtedness, and the reading list which follows each chapter should provide a clear indication of the scholarly works consulted. I should like to express my gratitude to Dr G. B. Gybbon-Monypenny, of the University of Manchester, who converted my poor sketches into illustrations fit for publication, and to my colleagues and friends in the University of Durham, in particular Mrs A. Squires of the English Department, who have patiently allowed me to pick their brains during the writing of this book. I am especially indebted to the late Professor J. W. Rees and to Professor H. Ramsden, of the University of Manchester, to Professor P. Russell-Gebbett of The Queen's University, Belfast, and to Professor I. D. L. Michael of the University of Southampton, all of whom have read sections of the typescript, corrected much detail and made valuable suggestions for improvements. To my teacher, J. W. Rees, for the example of dedication and scholarly meticulousness which he set me in my early postgraduate years, I shall always owe an incalculable debt.

INTRODUCTION: AIMS AND METHODS

TERMINOLOGY

The terms *linguistics* and *philology* are both in general use to describe the
study of language which is 'scientific' in approach – that is, which is worthy
of scholarly attention and which is guided by the desire for exhaustiveness,
consistency and economy in its methods of description and analysis. Of
these, the term *philology* has in recent years shown signs of falling steadily
from favour, largely because in British usage it has come increasingly to imply
only one particular branch of linguistic study – the study of language in its
process of evolution: **historical philology. Linguistics**, on the other hand,
appears to be gaining in favour as a general term, both to describe the study
of languages as systems **(descriptive linguistics)** and also to describe their
historical development **(historical linguistics).**

Spanish is a **Romance** language. That is to say, it is one of a number of
languages that have evolved principally from Latin. The linguist who devotes
himself to the study of the Spanish language may be concerned either with a
descriptive study of Spanish as a self-contained system **(Spanish linguistics)**
or with a comparative study of Spanish in relationship with other Romance
languages **(Romance linguistics).** The term **Hispanic linguistics** is commonly
used to describe the narrower comparative study of all the languages and
dialects (Castilian, Catalan, Portuguese, Aragonese, Leonese etc.) which
evolved from Latin in the Iberian Peninsula, together with their subsequent
development in other parts of the world. In this manual we are chiefly
concerned with the narrowest of the three areas of study described, that of
Spanish linguistics.

The principal fields of linguistic study are **phonetics** (the study of sounds),
phonology (the study of the patterns and organization of a language in terms
of the sounds which it contains), **morphology** (the study of word-forms),
syntax (the study of sentence-structure) and **semantics** (the study of meaning).
The present volume is concerned solely with phonetics and phonology.

Within each of the fields indicated the linguist who is concerned with the
Spanish language may emphasize either the study of Spanish functioning as a
system at a given moment in time and in a given place (a **descriptive** or
synchronic study) or the study of Spanish in its process of evolution from
Latin (a **historical** or **diachronic** study). In the first part of this manual we are
concerned with synchronic study – a description of the Spanish sound
system as it exists today; in the second part we are concerned with diachronic
study – the process by which the sound system of modern Spanish evolved
from Latin.

The linguist must also form some clear idea of the complexities of his task. A term like *the Spanish language* is of course an abstract idea. It is obvious to the most casual observer that no two individuals speak in an identical way and that a generalization made about the speech of one man may be quite untrue of the speech of his neighbour. The most common method of dealing with the difficulty is the one employed here. The speech of educated persons from one part of the country or one section of the population is taken as the 'norm': thus it is the French of the educated Parisian and the 'Received Pronunciation' (*RP*) of those educated at English public schools which is generally taught as a foreign language in schools throughout the world. In Spain it is **Castilian**, the speech of an educated minority in New Castile, which has acquired prestige as the 'standard' language and which is taught to foreign learners of 'Spanish'. Accordingly, the linguistic system described in both parts of this manual is that of Castilian. Attention is drawn throughout, however, to the principal dialectal variants of pronunciation which are to be found both in the Peninsula and in Spanish America. For the sake of convenience the term **Spanish** is used when statements are made about the language which are true for the majority of speakers; the term **Castilian** is generally reserved for use on those occasions when it is desired to draw attention to the fact that a linguistic feature is peculiar to that geographical area.

SYSTEM OF REFERENCE

A full bibliography and list of works consulted appears on pp. 161—8. Works referred to are listed in alphabetical order by author, followed by date and place of publication of first edition or the edition consulted, whichever is relevant. This bibliography is intended to have two functions: to provide full references to works which are mentioned in the main text and to provide suggestions for further study.

Each chapter ends with a brief list of suggestions for further reading. Articles quoted in this list are normally referred to by author, date of publication, and page reference either to the whole article or part of it. Books are treated in a similar way, with reference to the pages, chapters or paragraphs particularly relevant. References in the text and notes are made simply by author and date of publication.

Because of the great size of the field covered — the bibliography includes items which range from bulky dictionaries and works on General Linguistics to short specialized journal articles which deal with one small detail of interest to Hispanic scholars — the bibliography has had to be highly selective. Specialists in General Linguistics, phonetics or dialect geography, for example, will not find it adequate for their special needs, but I trust that the university students for whom it is designed will find enough in it to encourage them to read further in areas of the subject which attract their interest. Not all books and articles included in the bibliography are referred to in the text; this in no way represents a judgement on their relevance or value.

DIACRITICAL MARKS

[̟] advanced variety: *cacha* **ká̟t͡ʃa** *valle* **bá̟ʎe**

[̠] retracted variety: *salvo* **sá̠lβo** *caja* **ká̠xa**

[̨] open variety: *teja* **tę́ja** *rico* **r̄į́ko**
cojo **kǫ́xo** *burro* **bų́r̄o**

[.] close variety (vowel): French *pré* **pṛe** V.L. *tēla* **tẹ́la**

[̬] voice: *rasgo* **r̄ás̬ɣo** *juzgar* **xuθ̬ɣár**

[̥] breath: *verdad* **berðáð̥** *ciudad* **θjuðáð̥**

[̪] dental articulation: *bastar* **bas̪tár** *alto* **ál̪to**
antes **án̪tes** *conde* **kǫ́n̪de**

[•] interdental articulation (cons.): *alzar* **aḷθár**
conciencia **koṇθjéṇθja**

[´] palatal articulation (cons.): *quepa* **ḱépa** *guindo* **ǵíndo**

[˜] nasalization: *mano* **mãno** *niño* **nĩɲo**

OTHER CONVENTIONS

– syllabification: *un ojo* **ú-nó-xo**
| breath group
‖ major pause
´ stress: *palo* **pálo**
: long vowel: C.L. CĀRUM **ka:rum** C.L. FLŌREM **flo:rem**

PHONETIC SYMBOLS USED FOR THE TRANSCRIPTION OF SPANISH AND OLD SPANISH

See tables 1–2. The following points, which apply to both tables, should be noted:

1. The phonetic symbols which appear in columns I and II are the only symbols used in phonetic transcriptions in this book.
2. The phonetic symbols in column III are discussed in the main text, but are not used in phonetic transcriptions.
3. Symbols which appear in the last column appear in the works of other scholars, but are not used or discussed in any detail in the text. The only exception to this is the symbol **z**, which does not appear in Part I, but is used in Part II to designate the voiced alveolar sibilant of Old Spanish (see 13.10).

[*continued on p. 6*

TABLE I   PHONETIC SYMBOLS USED FOR THE TRANSCRIPTION OF SPANISH

I PHONEMES	II ALLOPHONES	III ADDITIONAL ALLOPHONIC SYMBOLS FOR NARROWER TRANSCRIPTIONS	IV ALTERNATIVE SYMBOLS USED BY OTHER PHONETICIANS	
(a) VOWELS				
/i/ as in *fino* fíno	j as in *bien* bjén	į as in *baile* bái̯le, *voy* bói̯	y	ŷ
	baile bái̯le	j̃ as in *mayo* mãjo, *la hierba* la jérβa	y	ŷ
	mayo májo	ʒ as in *mayo* máʒo, *pollo* póʒo	y	ĵ
		d̃ʒ as in *mayo* mádʒo, *pollo* pódʒo	ž	z̃
			dž	
	ɟj as in *yerno* ɟjérno		y	dŷ
/e/ as in *pera* péra			ɟ	
/a/ as in *casa* kása	w as in *fuera* fwéra	u̯ as in *causa* káu̯sa, *reuma* r̃éu̯ma		
/o/ as in *tomo* tómo	*causa* káwsa	w̃ as in *hueco* w̃éko, *las huertas* laṣ wértas		
/u/ as in *puro* púro	*hueco* wéko			
(b) CONSONANTS				
/p/ as in *pata* páta				
/b/ as in *vara* bára	β as in *ave* áβe		ɓ	ɓ
/t/ as in *tapa* tápa				
/d/ as in *dar* dár	ð as in *nada* náða		đ	ɗ
/k/ as in *casa* kása				
/g/ as in *gato* gáto	ɣ as in *lago* láɣo		ǥ	ǥ
/f/ as in *fama* fáma				
/θ/ as in *cera* θéra				
/s/ as in *paso* páso	ṣ as in *rasgo* raṣɣo		ż	ż
/x/ as in *mujer* muxér	ɡ̥ as in *juzgar* xuɡ̥ɣár		ẓ	

TABLE 1 (contd.) **PHONETIC SYMBOLS USED FOR THE TRANSCRIPTION OF SPANISH**

I PHONEMES	II ALLOPHONES	III ADDITIONAL ALLOPHONIC SYMBOLS FOR NARROWER TRANSCRIPTIONS	IV ALTERNATIVE SYMBOLS USED BY OTHER PHONETICIANS
/t͡ʃ/ as in *chico* t͡ʃíko			/c/ /ĉ/ /t̃ʃ/ /š̃/
/r/ as in *caro* káro		ř as in *para* pářa	ɾ
/r̄/ as in *carro* kár̄o			/rr/
/l/ as in *palo* pálo			
/ʎ/ as in *calle* káʎe			/ʎ/ /l'/ /ʒ/
/m/ as in *cama* káma	m̩ as in *confuso* komʃúso		m̥
/n/ as in *mano* máno	ŋ as in *cinco* θíŋko		ṇ
/ɲ/ as in *año* áɲo			/n̥/ /n'/

TABLE 2 **ADDITIONAL PHONETIC SYMBOLS USED FOR THE TRANSCRIPTION OF OLD SPANISH CONSONANTS**

I PHONEMES	II ALLOPHONES	IV ALTERNATIVE SYMBOLS USED BY OTHER PHONETICIANS
/ts/ as in O.Sp. *çena* t͡séna		/ŝ/
/dz/ as in O.Sp. *dize* díd͡ze		/ẑ/
/ʒ/ as in O.Sp. *mejor* meʒór	d͡ʒ as in O.Sp. *jueves* d͡ʒ wéʒes	/ž̂/ /ẑ/ dž ɟ
/ʃ/ as in O.Sp. *exe* éʃe		/š̂/
/h/ as in O.Sp. *fecho* hét͡ʃo		
/z/ as in O.Sp. *casa* káza		

4. The type of Spanish taken as a basis for the phonetic transcriptions used in this manual is Castilian Spanish, the language of the educated speakers of New Castile.

PHONETIC SYMBOLS USED IN THE TRANSCRIPTION OF ENGLISH

VOWELS AND DIPHTHONGS

ij	as in *bead* bijd	ɜ	as in *bird* bɜd
ɪ	as in *bid* bɪd	ə	as in *about* əbawt
ɛ	as in *bed* bɛd	ej	as in *day* dej
æ	as in *bad* bæd	ɜw	as in *no* nɜw
ɑ	as in *bard* bɑd	aj	as in *eye* aj
ɔ	as in *bog* bɔg	aw	as in *now* naw
ɐ	as in *board* bɐd	ɔj	as in *boy* bɔj
u	as in *good* gud	iə	as in *beer* biə
uw	as in *food* fuwd	ɛə	as in *bare* bɛə
ʌ	as in *bud* bʌd	uə	as in *moor* muə

SEMIVOWELS

w   as in *wet* wɛt, *away* əwej
j   as in *yes* jɛs, *beyond* bijɔnd

CONSONANTS

p	as in *pet* pɛt	s	as in *set* sɛt
b	as in *bog* bɔg	z	as in *zeal* zijl
v	as in *live* lɪv	ʃ	as in *ship* ʃɪp
t	as in *tin* tɪn	ʒ	as in *pleasure* plɛʒə
d	as in *day* dej	t͡ʃ	as in *chin* t͡ʃin
ð	as in *then* ðɛn	d͡ʒ	as in *jam* d͡ʒæm
k	as in *cut* kʌt	r	as in *red* rɛd
g	as in *give* gɪv	l	as in *lamb* læm
f	as in *fat* fæt	m	as in *met* mɛt
h	as in *hat* hæt	n	as in *net* nɛt
θ	as in *thin* θɪn	ŋ	as in *sing* sɪŋ

NOTES
1. English phoneticians adopt a wide range of methods for marking the stress on phonetic transcripts of English words, none of which corresponds to the most common Spanish system of writing an acute accent over the stressed vowel or diphthong. In order to avoid confusion, the stress accent on English words is left unmarked throughout this book.
2. The method of transcribing English vowels and diphthongs which is used here was first proposed for IPA trancriptions by A. D. Schoch (1907). It is a system which has subsequently been adopted by a number of writers, including L. Bloomfield (1935), G. L. Trager (1935) and W. Jassem (1952).

Its most characteristic features are the consonantal representation of the second element of the diphthongs in *day, eye, boy, no, now,* and the way in which the syllabic nuclei of words such as *bead* and *food* are represented qualitatively, as diphthongs. The system is described by D. Abercrombie (1964) on pp. 88–9, and summarized on p. 92. It is adopted here with some modification. In place of Abercrombie's **a, e, i, o, ε**, the symbols **ʌ, ε, ı, ɐ, æ** represent the vowel sounds of *bud, bed, bid, board, bad.* This allows the symbols **a, e, i, o** to be reserved exclusively to represent the Spanish vowel sounds of *casa, pera, fino, tomo.*

3. The type of English taken as a basis for the phonetic transcriptions used here is **Received Pronunciation** for which the initials *RP* are used throughout. 'This is an accent which can be heard from speakers originating in any part of England, but still local in the sense that it is virtually confined to English people and those educated at English public schools' (B. Strang, 1962, 21). The term has been current since the middle of the nineteenth century, and is now universally used.

OTHER CONVENTIONS AND ABBREVIATIONS

CONVENTIONS

Latin words. These appear in capital letters, whether the word is Classical, Vulgar or Late Latin: CĬRCA, V.L. MARTĔLLU, L.L. FŬNDA etc. For Latin nouns and adjectives the form usually given is the accusative (without final -M, which regularly falls in polysyllables), this being the case which has commonly survived into Spanish.

Quantity. The length of Classical Latin vowels is indicated by a superposed hook ˘ for short vowels, or dash ¯ for long vowels: VĔNIRE, VĪGĬNTĪ etc. In phonetic script Classical Latin short vowels are unmarked and long vowels are followed by a colon: VĔNĪRE **weni:re**, VĪGĬNTĪ **wi:ginti:** etc.

Stress. The stressed syllable of an individual word or group of words is conventionally marked with the acute accent ´ in transcriptions of Vulgar Latin and Spanish only. The accent is not used in transcriptions of English, nor (since there is no clear evidence that Classical Latin contained an expiratory accent) is it used in phonetic representations of Classical Latin.

Use of italics and bold type. In the examples quoted throughout the book italics are used to indicate the normal orthography of a word *(mayo)* and bold type indicate its pronunciation **májo.** An italicized letter or letters indicates a graph *(d, ch);* a symbol or symbols in bold type indicates a pronunciation **ð, t͡ʃ.**

ABBREVIATIONS

C.L.	Classical Latin
V.L.	Vulgar Latin
L.L.	Late Latin
O.Sp.	Old Spanish
M.Sp.	Modern Spanish
RP	Received Pronunciation ('standard' English)
*	hypothetical form
>	'becomes'
<	'derives from'
/ /	phonemic script
> ø	'is lost'

PART I: DESCRIPTIVE PHONOLOGY

1 PHONETICS AND PHONOLOGY

1.1 'Speech, as phoneticians well agree, consists of a continuous stream of sound within breath groups; neither sounds nor words are separated consistently from one another by pauses, but have to be abstracted from the continuum' (Pike, 1943, 42). As members of a language community, certain groups of people accept certain sounds and sequences of sound (speech-chains) as conventional methods of representing certain meanings.

1.2 For the purposes of linguistic description, the continuous stream of sound can be analysed into smaller units or **segments** according to one of two principal criteria. If the continuum of sound is examined with particular regard to its **substance,** the linguist seeks to subdivide it into segments which are generally referred to as **speech-sounds**. These speech-sounds can then be described as objectively as possible according to the movements of the lips, tongue and other organs of speech which produce them, and such descriptions can be made in fairly absolute terms. An analysis of substance made in this way can be described as a **phonetic** analysis. If, on the other hand, the linguist turns his attention to the **structure**, rather than the substance, of the continuum which he is examining, he may discover that many of the 'sounds' of the language which he is describing, although differing in detail, can usefully be considered as a group or family when their ability to distinguish one word from another is taken into consideration. He may then describe these families of sounds according to the ways in which they contrast with each other, drawing attention to such differences or similarities as convey meaning – i.e. are **functional** – in the language which he is describing. An analysis of form made in this way will result in a **phonological**, or **phonemic**, description.

PHONETICS: SPEECH-SOUNDS

1.3 Most of the sounds which make up a speech-chain are deliberately and consciously articulated. The speaker adjusts his speech-organs to a succession of definite positions, and since the parts of the body mainly responsible for the production of speech-sounds are fairly easy to observe either directly or indirectly, by means of x-ray photography or laryngoscope, the speaker's actions and the position of his lips, tongue and other speech-organs can be described and classified accurately.

1.4 The speech-sounds described in this way are, given the nature of language, somewhat arbitrary segments. In the first place, the transition from one speech-sound to the next in a speech-chain is by no means a sudden one; the characteristic individual sounds of a language are linked in speech by a series of transitions, or glides, as the speech-organs move smoothly from the final position of one sound to the initial position of the following one. As a result, the point of separation between one speech-sound and the next has of necessity to be taken at some point on the glide which is convenient for the purpose of phonetic analysis. Second, since there is practically no limit to the number of speech-sounds which can be produced by human beings, and since there are few natural divisions within the range of sounds in human speech, the phonetician has constantly to make personal decisions about the degree of accuracy he wishes to achieve. These decisions may depend upon a large number of factors, the most common of which are the particular purposes of his analysis.

1.5   Depending on his purpose at the time, the phonetician may choose a 'broader' or a 'narrower' method of phonetic transcription to record the sounds of the language he is studying. A **broad transcription** is most commonly understood to be a form of phonetic script which uses the smallest number of symbols and marks which will represent the language being studied without risk of ambiguity. This can be achieved only by introducing a number of conventions: for example in broad transcription of Spanish the symbol b may be used to represent all occurrences of the letters *b* and *v* in normal orthography, but only after establishing the convention that its value is that of fricative β in some environments and of plosive b in others (8.4–6). In a comparative study the symbol t may be used to represent the sounds written *t* in both Spanish and English, provided that the convention is first established that in English words the symbol represents an alveolar stop and in Spanish words a dental stop (8.7 n. 1). A more **narrow transcription** may be devised, which dispenses with some of these conventions by introducing extra symbols or marks to indicate finer distinctions: for example, whereas in a broad transcription the symbol l might indicate all varieties of the Spanish lateral sound except for the palatal ʎ of words like *calle*, a narrower transcription would mark the differences between the alveolar lateral of *palo*, the dental lateral of *alto*, and the interdental lateral of *alzar* (9.4–6). In a comparative study of Spanish and English, it would also be necessary to devise a further symbol ł to denote the 'dark' or velar *l* found in English *noble, health, pulpit* (9.4). A narrow transcription is a form of transcription which uses more than the minimum number of symbols and marks necessary to avoid ambiguity. The additional symbols and marks may be introduced either for greater precision within one language or for a more accurate comparison of two or more languages, and it will be obvious that there is practically no limit to the degree of 'narrowness' which could theoretically be achieved.

PHONOLOGY: PHONEMES AND ALLOPHONES

1.6   The principles underlying broad transcriptions are closely related to the concept of the **phoneme**. The reason why all sounds written *b* and *v* in normal Spanish orthography can be represented by just one phonetic symbol in broad transcriptions is that the distinction between the plosive sound phonetically transcribed **b** and the fricative sound phonetically transcribed β is never a **functional** one. All sounds written *b* or *v* are bilabial consonants in Spanish. When either *b* or *v* is initial in a breath group or follows a nasal consonant, the air-flow is completely stopped for a moment at the lips and the bilabial consonant is realized as a plosive **b**. In all other circumstances there is no complete stoppage at the lips, and both *b* and *v* are realized as a fricative β. But the distinction between the plosive and the fricative sounds of *b* and *v* is not a functional one, in that it never has the effect of differentiating in meaning between otherwise identical sequences of sounds in Spanish; the precise nature of the sound depends entirely on its **phonetic context** (the speech-sounds which immediately precede and follow it). Thus **v** will normally be realized as a plosive in *vagar* **bayár** and *quieren vagar* **kjérem bayár**, but as a fricative in *quiere vagar* **kjére βayar** and in *para vagar* **para βayár** (8.4–5). The replacement of **b** by β in differing phonetic contexts makes no difference whatsoever to the meaning of *vagar*: whatever variety of voiced bilabial is used, the sense is the same. In this case it can be said that **b** and β, the pair of speech-sounds which can be phonetically distinguished, belong to the same **phoneme** and are positional variants, or **allophones**, of that phoneme. In a given speech system, the occurrence of one rather than another of the phonetic variants of a particular phoneme depends entirely on the position of that phoneme in a sequence of speech-sounds. If as a further test we remove the first segment in the string of sounds represented in writing by *vagar*, and replace it by a bilabial sound **p** in which the vocal cords do not vibrate, the meaning of the string of sounds is altered: *vagar* 'to wander' becomes *pagar* 'to pay' and it can be deduced that the sounds represented in orthography by *v* and *p* are members of different phonemes (8.6).

1.7 In order to distinguish in writing between speech-sounds (phonetic units) and phonemes (functional units), it has become conventional to enclose symbols representing phonemes between oblique lines. This convention is followed throughout. The conclusions which can be drawn from 1.6 could thus be expressed in this way: /p/ and /b/ are phonemes of Spanish; /b/ has two allophones, **b** and β, of which the former occurs when the sound written *b* or *v* is initial in a breath group (see 5.2) or after a nasal, and the latter is its realization elsewhere.

1.8 An initial step in isolating the phonemes of a language is to contrast pairs of words which are phonetically identical, ideally, in all but one feature. If we consider a pair of words, *paso* and *vaso*, which are phonetically identical in all but the first sound feature, we could deduce that /p/ and /b/ are different phonemes in Spanish because they **contrast** in this environment. In the word *paso*, the phoneme /p/ occurs in the initial position, where it is in contrast with /b/, /k/, /r/, etc. *(vaso, caso, raso)*; the phoneme /a/ occurs in the second position, where it contrasts with /i/, /u/, etc. *(piso, puso)*; the phoneme /s/ occurs in third position, where it contrasts with /l/, /r/, /b/, etc. *(palo, paro, pavo)*; the phoneme /o/ occurs in final position, where it contrasts with /a/, /e/ *(pasa, pase)*. If such a contrast involves a difference in meaning, the phonetic feature is established as **distinctive**, or **functional**. The distinctiveness or contrast between phonemes is generally taken as their ability to differentiate one sequence of sounds from another: pairs of words, like *paso* and *vaso, paso* and *piso, paso* and *palo, paso* and *pasa,* which are used to test this ability to differentiate between words, are known as **minimal pairs.**

9   Phonetic units like p and **b** which are capable of differentiating one form from another are said to be **distinctive.** Phonetic units like **b** and β, which do not appear in the same context and which never have the function of distinguishing different words, are said to be in **complementary distribution.** Sounds in complementary distribution are members of the same phoneme. In some instances, however, it will prove impossible to predict which of two allophones a native speaker would use in a particular phonetic context, and such unpredictable differences are considered to be instances of **free variation.** For example either the allophone **w** or the allophone **gw** might be heard in words such as *huerta* **wérta** or **gwérta** and *hueco* **wéko** or **gwéko** (7.5 n.1); in these words the allophones occur in the same environment but are interchangeable. In these circumstances the speech-sounds **w** and **gw** are as non-distinctive as were **b** and β in the earlier examples, and they are treated as members of the same phoneme /u/, freely variant in this environment.

10   **Neutralization.** In certain phonetic contexts the contrastive function of two or more phonemes may be neutralized. In Castilian Spanish the phonemes /s/ and /θ/ may appear in initial, intervocalic or final position in a word, and wherever they appear their function is distinctive: *segar/cegar, coser/cocer, os/hoz.* The phonemes /r/ and /r̄/ are only distinctive, however, when they occur in an intervocalic position: *coro/corro, quería/querría, vario/barrio.* When the sound written *r* occurs elsewhere, its precise phonetic nature varies, but it does so in a purely mechanical way: a rolled vibrant r̄ appears in *rey* r̄ej, *honra* ónr̄a, *Israel* ir̄aél, a flapped vibrant r (or with some speakers a fricative sound ɹ in *arte* árte, *pronto* prónto, *decir* deθír. For distinctive purposes, the number of vibrations given to the consonant by an individual speaker becomes immaterial in these circumstances, where /r/ and /r̄/ never contrast; the appearance of one or the other is controlled automatically by the phonetic context. The substitution of /r/ for /r̄/, or vice versa, only produces a change of meaning in otherwise identical strings of sounds when the /r/ or /r̄/ occur in an intervocalic position. This phenomenon, whereby the distinctive features of phonemes become irrelevant in certain contexts, is known as **neutralization.** For the term **archiphoneme,** used in this connexion by linguists of the Prague school, see E. Alarcos (1965), 49–51. Prague-school phonologists define the phoneme as the sum of its relevant features. The archiphoneme can consequently be regarded as the sum of the relevant features common to two or more phonemes, and is commonly transcribed with the capital symbol corresponding to one of the members: thus *rey* is transcribed as Réj, *Israel* as iRaél, *decir* as deθíR.

11   Whereas the description of a speech-sound in terms of articulatory phonetics would be valid for that sound in any language in which it occurred, any statement made about phonemic differences is valid only for the language for which it is made. To illustrate this, it can be shown that the phoneme /d/ in

Spanish has allophones d and ð, heard in *doy* dój and *no doy* nó ðój
respectively (8.8–10). In English, d and ð are not allophonic variants but
separate phonemes /d/ and /ð/ which distinguish between otherwise identical
sound-sequences: *den* dɛn and *then* ðɛn, *load* lɜwd and *loathe* lɜwð, *breed*
brijd and *breathe* brijð. Similarly ŋ is in Spanish a positional variant of the
phoneme /n/; velar ŋ is heard normally only before velar consonants, as in
ganga gáŋga, *banco* báŋko, *ángel* áŋxel *gran cosa* gráŋ kósa (9.11). But in
English /n/ and /ŋ/ are separate phonemes, which distinguish between
minimal pairs such as *sin* sin and *sing* siŋ, *ran* ræn and *rang* ræŋ, *tons* tʌnz
and *tongues* tʌŋz. It will be obvious that allophones are grouped into
phonemes not by their nature but by the way they function in the system of
the particular language to which they belong.

1.12   The phoneme can be described in general terms as a group or family of sounds
in a given language which functions as a unit of contrast, but although most
linguists have been able to agree that the phoneme is an essential component
of a linguistic system, few have been able to agree on a definition.
W. F. Twaddell (1935), chs. 2 and 3, offers a convenient grouping of many
early definitions and sets up a procedure (ch. 5) for defining it as an
'abstractional fiction'; N. S. Trubetzkoy (1935 and 1939), K. L. Pike (1947)
and D. Jones (1950) are among others who have since devoted monographs
to the subject. The difficulties involved in defining the phoneme, however,
are, as is sensibly observed by B. Malmberg (1964), 85, often more theoretical
than practical: 'Anyone who knows a language well is hardly ever in doubt
about whether a difference is phonemic or not. A naive speaker is not usually
conscious of any other phonetic differences than the phonemic and so does
not feel the need to incorporate non-phonemic differences in writing.
Alphabetic writing presupposes a phonemic analysis of the language, but not
an analysis of non-distinctive phonetic features.'

1.13   **FURTHER READING.** D. Abercrombie (1964), Part I; (1967), ch. 5.
E. Alarcos (1965), I. 1–2. L. Bloomfield (1935), chs. 5–8. J. B. Dalbor (1969),
chs. 1, 2 and 5. A. C. Gimson (1962), ch. 5. D. Jones (1950), chs. 1–20.
J. Lyons (1968), chs. 1–3. B. Malmberg (1964), 74–122. A. Martinet (1964),
chs. 1–3. K. L. Pike (1943), chs. 3 and 4; (1947c), ch. 4. A. Quilis and
J. A. Fernández (1964), ch. 1. R. H. Robins (1964), 1–20, 82–86, 121–37.
E. Sapir (1921), chs. 1 and 2. N. S. Trubetzkoy (1935 and 1939).
W. F. Twaddell (1935), chs. 2 and 3.

1.14   **EXERCISES ON CHAPTER 1**
1. How many speech-sounds can be distinguished in each of the following
words? *Siquiera, lechuga, querella, cohete, taxista, guerrero.*
2. Devise three sets of minimal pairs (e.g. *copia/cofia*) to illustrate that the
sounds written *p* and *f* are phonemes of Spanish.
3. From the following sets of minimal pairs, what evidence can be deduced
about the phonemic status of the sounds written *s, g, j,* and *ch* in Spanish?
*Coser/coger, puso/pujo, vaso/bajo, oso/ocho, peso/pecho, caja/cacha,
marchen/margen.*

4. In Spanish the distinction between the sounds written *m* and *n* is maintained when these sounds occur between vowels, but neutralized when they occur in an absolutely final position in a word. Devise examples to illustrate this.

5. The phoneme /ʎ/ (written *ll*) is of restricted occurrence in Spanish. Consider whether (*a*) it may begin a word, (*b*) it may end a word, (*c*) it may begin a syllable, (*d*) it may end a syllable. In which of these positions is the opposition /ʎ/–/l/ distinctive?

2 THE ORGANS OF SPEECH

2.1 Although the term 'speech-sound' is in common currency, there is no organ in the human body which is reserved solely for the purpose of producing speech. That is to say, no single component of the body is specifically designed for the purpose of talking. Parts of the body such as the lungs, the larynx, the tongue, the teeth and the lips, which are used to produce the sounds of language, each have other and biologically more essential duties to perform in connexion with the refuelling and maintenance of the human machine. Speech among human beings is thus a secondary function which makes use of organs which initially evolved for purposes other than that of communication; such organs are commonly, if somewhat inexactly, referred to as the organs of speech, and it is helpful in a study of phonetics to have some idea of their position and function. The diagrams and explanations in this chapter contain all that should be necessary for the purposes of this book.

2.2 The **respiratory system** contains the lungs, which, as their primary function, ensure a supply of oxygen to the blood, and which also provide the fuel for speech in the form of air, which is drawn in rapidly and released more slowly. In the speech process air may be expelled either through the mouth or through the nose, or through both together, and during its outward journey the speaker can interfere in various ways and at various points with its smooth passage. Figure 1 shows the main parts of the throat, mouth and nose which may be involved in the process of speech.

2.3 The **phonatory system** is formed by the **larynx**, a valve which is capable of defending the lungs against the entry of a foreign body or of enclosing air within the lungs to assist in muscular effort by the arms or the abdomen. As an organ of speech the larynx, which is situated at the top of the windpipe, represents the first point at which the outward passage of air can be controlled. The larynx contains the **vocal cords**, which are rather like two lips or bands of elastic tissue mounted horizontally in the windpipe. These normally lie apart when we breathe in and out, leaving a space (the **glottis**) between them through which air can escape freely. They can be brought together at will so as to touch and block the air flow completely (see **glottal stop**, 3.17 n. 1); they can be brought close together, but not so close that they begin to vibrate, in which case the diminished force of the air-stream which passes between them produces an effect known as **whisper**. They may also be brought still closer together and air forced between them. In this last case the passage of air causes the vocal cords to vibrate rapidly, rather like reeds in a musical instrument, as often as 800 times per second, in a series of clicks. These clicks come in such rapid succession that the ear interprets them as a musical note, varying in

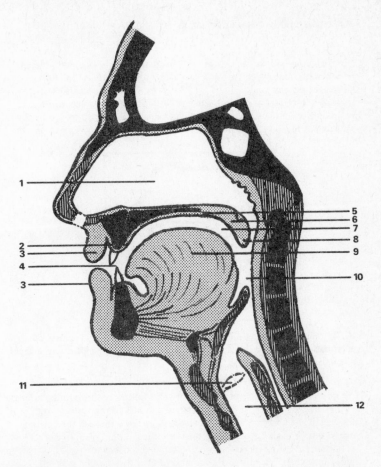

FIG. 1   THE ORGANS OF SPEECH. 1 nasal cavity, 2 alveolar ridge, 3 lips, 4 teeth, 5 hard palate, 6 soft palate (velum), 7 mouth cavity, 8 uvula, 9 tongue, 10 pharynx, 11 vocal cords, 12 windpipe.

height according to the speed of vibration – the more rapid the vibration the higher the note. This musical note, whether high or low, is known as **voice** (3.15–16). Consonants which are produced with the vocal cords vibrating (e.g. *m, g*) are called **voiced** consonants; consonants produced with the vocal cords at rest (e.g. *f, p*) are **voiceless** or **breathed** consonants.

The air current, either vibrating or not, according to the action of the vocal cords, now passes through an area in the throat immediately behind the mouth and known as the **pharynx.** Here the air current is subject to further modification according to the shape taken up by the upper cavities of the pharynx and mouth; these cavities act as the main resonators of the note produced in the larynx.

2.5   The **articulatory system** consists of the mouth, the tongue, the teeth, the lips and the nose, all of which are also connected with the primary functions of smelling, eating and swallowing. From the pharynx, air may be allowed to escape either through the mouth alone or through the nose alone, or through both mouth and nose simultaneously. These operations are controlled by the **soft palate,** which in the normal lowered position (fig. 2) allows air to pass on

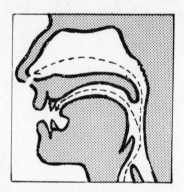

FIG. 2   THE SOFT PALATE LOWERED. Position of the soft palate during the pronunciation of a nasal vowel. The oral passage is open and the air escapes through both mouth and nose.

both sides, into the mouth and nasal cavity (the normal position for breathing, and for nasal vowels), but which can be raised to make firm contact with the back wall of the pharynx, when it prevents air escaping through the nose and forces it out through the only remaining exit, the mouth. This is its normal position for most English and Spanish vowels and consonants (fig. 3); if the contact made between soft palate and back wall of the pharynx is slightly relaxed, however, some air may escape through the nasal cavity as well as the mouth, so that a partially nasalized sound is produced.

2.6   The roof of the mouth, or **palate,** separates the mouth cavity from the nasal cavity and can be divided into three principal areas (fig. 4). These are, from front to back, the **alveolar ridge,** the **hard palate** and the **soft palate** or **velum.** The alveolar ridge is the hard part of the gums immediately behind the upper front teeth, where the roof of the mouth is convex. Consonants such as English *l* in *lake,* Castilian *s* in *soy,* pronounced with the tip of the tongue against this ridge, are alveolar consonants. The remainder of the roof of the mouth is concave in shape; the front part, which can be explored with the tip of the tongue, is the hard palate; consonants made by bringing the tongue close to this part of the roof of the mouth, like English ʃ, spelled *sh* in *ship,* or d͡ʒ, spelled *j* in *jump,* and Spanish t͡ʃ, spelled *ch* in *chico,* or d͡j, spelled *y* in *yo,* are palatal consonants. Further back in the mouth the palate becomes soft;

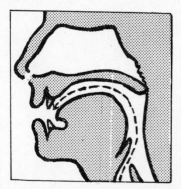

FIG. 3 THE SOFT PALATE RAISED. Position of the soft palate for the pronunciation of the open central vowel **a**. Air is allowed to escape through the mouth only.

consonants such as *g* in English *got,* Spanish *gota,* which are made by raising the back of the tongue towards this soft palate or velum, are velar consonants. The soft palate can be moved upwards or downwards by means of a sort of hinge at the point where it joins the hard palate and when it is fully raised its rearmost part, the **uvula**. makes firm contact with the back wall of the pharynx and prevents air expelled by the lungs from reaching the nasal cavity.

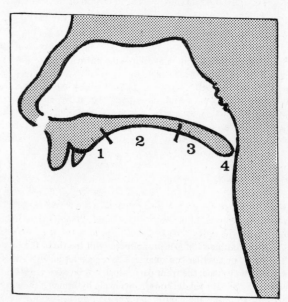

FIG. 4 THE PALATE. 1 alveolar ridge, 2 hard palate, 3 soft palate (velum), 4 uvula.

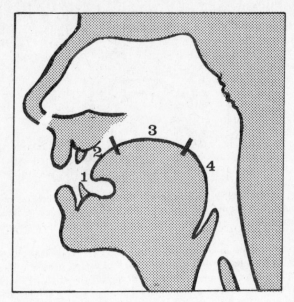

Fig. 5   THE TONGUE. 1 tip, 2 blade, 3 front, 4 back. .

2.7   The tongue is the most mobile of the speech-organs. Unlike the palate it has
no obvious natural divisions, but for the purpose of descriptive phonetics it is
convenient to think of it as divided into three major parts (fig. 5). When the
tongue is at rest, the part which lies opposite the soft palate is the **back**, the
part which lies under the hard palate is the **front**, and the part which lies under
the alveolar ridge is the **blade**. The most forward part of all, which is included
in the blade, is the **tip**. The tip of the tongue is extremely flexible, and can be
made to touch any part of the mouth from the teeth to the forward part of
the soft palate; the front and back of the tongue can be raised to touch the
hard and soft palate respectively, or to adopt any intermediate position.

2.8   The upper front teeth play only a small part in the pronunciation of English;
they are, however, more important for Spanish, since both Spanish *t* and *d*
(e.g. in *tanto, dando*) are made by stopping the breath with the tip of the
tongue against the upper front teeth. Consonants made in this way are **dental**
consonants. The lower teeth are fairly unimportant in speech.

2.9   The most forward of the organs used in producing speech are the lips. The two
lips may be compressed firmly together to produce consonants such as *p* or *m*
(bilabials); the lower lip may be brought up to touch the upper teeth in the
production of a consonant such as *f* (labiodental). Or the lips may be kept
apart, either flat or rounded, or drawn in or pushed out to varying degrees, so
as to contribute towards the characteristic timbre (3.5) of the vowel and
consonant sounds of a language.

0   The vocal cords, the lips, the tongue and the soft palate are all movable organs, while the teeth, the gums, the hard palate and the nasal cavity are fixed. The sounds of speech are produced by adjusting a movable organ – an **articulator** – towards a fixed organ, or by bringing together two adjacent movable organs. Since the speech processes are carried out quickly, the adjustment of the articulators in sequence has to be effected equally quickly, and one of the most common causes of phonetic variation and change is the failure or inability of a speaker to effect – in the correct sequence and at speed – all the adjustments which he is required to make.

1   When two adjustments overlap the effect is known as **assimilation.** An example of **contextual assimilation** is the frequent voicing of final *s* in a Spanish syllable when a voiced consonant follows; in *ellas* the final consonant is voiceless: éʎas; but in *ellas duermen* éʎas̬ ðwérmen the vocal cords, anticipating the position they will occupy for the *d* of *duermen,* may begin to vibrate an instant before they should, so that the *s* is articulated as a voiced consonant. In the phrase *con uso* kon úso the speech-organs normally take up their positions for an alveolar nasal *n;* in *confuso,* however, if the lips and teeth are already in position for the labiodental *f* as the *n* is being pronounced, the result is the labiodental nasal m̩: kom̩fúso. This type of assimilation, which is caused by an overlapping of adjustments and leads to a sound being articulated in a special way in some phonetic contexts, is a characteristic feature of modern Spanish pronunciation.

12   **FURTHER READING.** D. Abercrombie (1967), ch. 2. J. B. Dalbor (1969), ch. 5. A. C. Gimson (1962), ch. 2. C. F. Hockett (1955), paras. 1–166. D. Jones (1958), paras. 12–29; (1960), ch. 3. A. Martinet (1964), 2.11–2.15. T. Navarro (1965), paras. 8–11. J. D. O'Connor (1967), ch. 2. K. L. Pike (1943), Part II; (1947c), Part I. A. Quilis and J. A. Fernández (1964), ch. 2. R. H. Robins (1964), 88–90. E. Sapir (1921), ch. 3. B. M. H. Strang (1962), paras. 24–27.

13   **EXERCISES ON CHAPTER 2**
1. Make a copy of fig. 1, and label on it the parts of the palate indicated in fig. 4 and the parts of the tongue indicated in fig. 5.
2. Three different kinds of sound may be produced in the larynx. What are they?
3. What sounds of English and Spanish are made with the soft palate lowered?
4. Which of the initial consonants in the following words are made with the tip of the tongue on the alveoles? *sueño, gama, roto, lodo, cama, nada.* Which part of the roof of the mouth does the tongue approach or touch to produce the remainder of the initial consonants in these words?
5. What do the sounds written *p* in *pata* and *m* in *mata* have in common? How do they differ? What do the sounds written *d* in *data* and *n* in *nata* have in common? How do they differ?

3 CLASSIFICATION OF THE SOUNDS OF SPANISH

3.1   In phonetic terms a **vowel** may be described as a continuous voiced sound, in the formation of which air passes through the pharynx and mouth without audible obstruction. In the formation of some vowels air is allowed to pass through the nasal cavity as well as through the mouth. **Semivowels** are gliding sounds, voiced and rather weakly articulated, which have some of the characteristics of vowels and some of the characteristics of consonants (7.1–9). Other sounds are generally described as **consonants**, which may be voiced or voiceless. Consonants include all sounds which are formed by means of an obstruction or narrowing of the air passage in the mouth – e.g. **b, k, g; f, l, s** – and those produced when air is allowed to escape only through the nose – e.g. **m, n**.

3.2   The phonetic distinction between vowel and consonant is in practice less clear-cut than it might appear from 3.1, and its validity has been questioned by a number of linguists, who point among other things to the existence of such paradoxes as partially or fully 'voiceless vowels' such as the first vowel in English *potato* or the final vowel of French *entendu,* and to the difficulties involved in defining the term 'obstruction'. Problems arise in the case of some English pronunciations of **l** and **r**, which have been traditionally described as consonants but which in the terms of the definition are much more like vowels. In Spanish the phonemes /i/ and /u/ also present problems. If, in the articulation of the vowel-sound **i**, the front part of the tongue is progressively raised towards the palate, there comes a point at which the friction of air can be heard, and the 'consonantal' sound **j** of *majo* **má-jo** is produced. Similarly, if the back of the tongue is progressively raised towards the velum in the production of the vowel-sound **u**, there comes a point where the 'consonantal' **w** of *ahuecar* **a-we-kár** is produced. In spite of such considerations, however, it is usually helpful for linguistic purposes to draw a distinction between vowel and consonant where this is practicable, and Spanish (unlike English) is a language in which a fairly clear-cut distinction can be drawn between vowel and consonant on both phonetic and linguistic grounds.

3.3   Some sounds are more 'perceptible' or sonorous than others, in that they have greater inherent carrying power and can be heard at a greater distance. It will be immediately evident that the sound of **a**, articulated normally, can be heard at a much greater distance than that of **p, t, k** or **f**. Perceptibility is an inherent quality: it depends on the size, shape and openness of the resonance chamber formed by the mouth. The concept of perceptibility is closely linked to the concept of prominence, but prominence is an accidental quality. The most prominent speech-sounds are usually the most perceptible, but prominence can be given to a speech-sound by other devices, such as articulating it at greater length, at a higher pitch (3.6) or with increased stress (3.8). It need not necessarily follow that the most perceptible sound in a word or syllable is the most prominent, although in Spanish this is usually the case.

.4   If the sounds of Spanish are classified according to their inherent quality, the five most perceptible sounds are, in order of perceptibility, **a. o, e, u, i,** and all conform to the description of a vowel given in 3.1. If linguistic criteria are taken into account as supplementary or alternative evidence, this classification is confirmed: only these (and slightly more open, or more closed, or nasalized positional variants) may form the nucleus of a Spanish syllable; only these may by themselves form a Spanish word: *a* (preposition), *ha, he* (from *haber*) *e, y, o, u* (conjunctions). On the basis of both phonetic and linguistic evidence Spanish can be said to have five, and only five, vowel phonemes. All other phonemes of Spanish are consonantal in type.

VOWELS

.5   **Timbre.** The characteristic quality, or **timbre**, of a vowel depends upon the shape of the open passage above the larynx. This passage forms a sound-chamber which can be altered in size and shape according to the positions taken up by the lips and tongue; with each alteration of shape, so the **timbre** of the sound produced by the vibration of the vocal cords is modified. As a consequence, a very large number of vowel sounds is theoretically possible and a trained ear is capable of distinguishing well over fifty different vowels. In practice, however, languages make use of comparatively few of the total number of possibilities for communication purposes, and the untrained speaker of English or Spanish normally listens only for the distinctive (phonemic) differences in vowel quality which serve to distinguish one word from another. He may well be aware that vowel sounds do vary in timbre from one speaker to another, and put these variations down to such factors as differences in social status or regional origin; it is rare for variations in vowel quality to lead to mutual unintelligibility between two native speakers of the same language.

.6   **Pitch.** The rate of vibration of the vocal cords in the larynx depends on the degree of tension, and this has an effect on the pitch of the vowel. The greater the rate of vibration of the vocal cords, the higher the musical note, or pitch, of the sound will be. In languages such as English or Spanish, pitch is generally treated as a subsidiary feature of the sounds produced, rather than as an integral part of them; in both languages, despite numerous individual and personal variations, regular sequences of different pitches characterize different kinds of utterance, and these are known collectively as **intonation**.

.7   **Lip position.** The quality of vowel sounds is to some extent dependent on the positions taken up by the lips, which may be **rounded** (for **o, u**), **spread** (for **e, i**), or **neutral** (for **a**). The position taken up by the tongue is, however, the main criterion used for classifying vowels.

3.8   **Stress.** Stress is a generic term for the relatively greater breath force exerted
in the articulation of part of an utterance. In English and Spanish, stress is an
inherent part of the articulation processes of the language. In an isolated
word, one vowel is normally articulated with greater breath force than the
others: cf. the *a* of *tomar, árbol, ánimo, cántamelo.* In a rhythm group (5.2),
many words may be uttered unstressed or with a lesser degree of stress:
cf. *pero no me dijo nada,* which has only three stressed, on *nó, díjo* and
náda, while *pero* and *me* remain unstressed.

3.9   Vowels and classified according to:
(a) The height to which the tongue is raised in the mouth.
(b) The part of the tongue which is raised highest in the mouth.

3.10   Classified according to tongue height, vowels which are articulated with a high
tongue position − i.e. with part of the tongue raised close to the palate − are
known as **close** vowels. Examples: Spanish *i* in *chico,* Spanish *u* in *mula.* Those
articulated with the tongue as low as possible in the mouth are open vowels.
Example: Spanish *a* in *caro.* The term **half-close** is used to describe vowels
articulated with the tongue in a position between the two extremes, but more
close than open. Examples: Spanish *e* in *pera,* Spanish *o* in *tomo.*

3.11   Classified according to the part of the tongue raised highest, vowels articulated
with the front of the tongue towards the hard palate are front, or palatal,
vowels. Examples: Spanish *i, e* in *chico, pera.* Those articulated with the back
of the tongue raised towards the hard palate are called back, or velar, vowels.
Examples: Spanish *o, u* in *tomo, mula.* Spanish *a* as in *caro,* with the centre of
the tongue very slightly raised, is a central vowel.

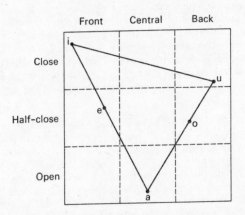

FIG. 6   THE VOWELS OF SPANISH. The diagram is a schematic
representation of the mouth cavity, with the lips to the left and the soft
palate to the right, as in previous figures. Thus i is a close front vowel; u is a
close back vowel; e is a half-close front vowel; o is a half-close back vowel;
a is an open central vowel.

.12   The classification of the five principal Spanish vowels can be represented in diagram form, as in fig. 6.

SEMIVOWELS

.13   In the formation of some kinds of sound the air-stream escapes centrally and its passage is narrowed by an articulatory organ or organs. Sounds of this type, like the first element of English *well yellow*, Spanish *huelo, hielo*, or the sounds written *y, w* in English *ray, cow*, or *y, u* in Spanish *rey, causa*, are generally known as **semivowels;** the terms **frictionless continuant** and **approximant** are also used. The most common semivowels have tongue positions as high as or higher than high vowels and are not capable of forming the nucleus of a syllable; they are sounds which are vowel-like in nature but which function as consonants. Spanish w, as in *huelo, huérfano*, is formed with the vocal cords vibrating, the lips closely rounded and the back of the tongue raised high towards the soft palate, and can be defined as a **labiovelar semivowel.** Spanish **j**, as in *hielo, hierático*, is formed with vocal cords vibrating, the lips spread and the front of the tongue raised high towards the hard palate, and can be defined as an unrounded palatal semivowel.

CONSONANTS

.14   For descriptive purposes, a consonant is classified according to three principal points of reference.
1. By describing the action of the vocal cords. This divides consonants into two major groups – voiced and voiceless (breathed).
2. By describing the point of articulation, and classifying the sound according to the organs with which it is articulated.
3. By describing the manner of articulation, according to the way in which the consonant is produced by the speech-organs involved.

.15   **Action of the vocal cords.** The voiceless consonants of modern Spanish, those made with the vocal cords drawn apart so that air can pass freely between them without vibration, are k as in *caso*, t as in *todo*, p as in *pata*, s as in *solo*, f as in *fama*, t͡ʃ as in *chopo*, θ as in *cera*, and x as in *junto*. Modern Spanish has eight voiceless consonants; all other consonants are voiced. It should be noticed that for every voiceless consonant there is a corresponding voiced consonant which has the same place and manner of articulation, but which has voice substituted for breath – for example g corresponds to k, d to t, b to p. Languages do not necessarily contain complete sets of pairs: whereas English v as in *vast* and d͡ʒ as in *gin* are the voiced versions of f as in *fast* and t͡ʃ as in *chin*, and form part of the regular phonemic structure of the language, Castilian Spanish has f and t͡ʃ sounds, as in *fama, chopo*, but no v or d͡ʒ sound (although both are to be found in the dialects). It is also true that, in general, voiced consonants are pronounced with less energy than voiceless consonants. This is particularly striking when Spanish voiceless x, pronounced with strong breath force in words like *gente, ajo, mujer*, is contrasted with its voiced counterpart ɣ, pronounced very weakly in *lago, migas, trigo.* The term **fortis** is used by some linguists to describe consonants produced with strong breath force, and the term **lenis** to describe those produced with little force.

3.16   The quality of voice can be tested in one of two fairly simple ways. If both hands are placed over the ears and a long *m* sound spoken, the action of the vocal cords will produce a loud buzzing in the ears. By ceasing to pronounce the *m* (devoicing), and just breathing hard through the nose with the lips still closed, the vibrations disappear. Voice has been turned off. The experiment can be reversed by saying *s* with the hands over the ears: there will be no buzzing sound. The effect of turning on voice (voicing) will be to produce *z*, and a loud series of vibrations. Alternatively the fingers can be placed on the neck at the side of the larynx and the vibrations produced by the voiced sounds felt through the tips of the fingers.

3.17   **Point of articulation.** For the purposes of Spanish there are seven main classes of sounds which have to be distinguished under this heading. These are:
1. **Bilabial:** articulated by a complete or partial stoppage with both lips. Examples: Spanish b in *bata, rumbo, voy, enviar.*
2. **Labiodental:** articulated by the lower lip against the upper front teeth. Examples: Spanish f in *fama, frente, difícil, ráfaga.*
3. **Interdental:** articulated with the tip of the tongue just protruding between the upper and the lower teeth. Examples: Spanish θ in *cera, zapato, placer, brazo.*
4. **Dental:** articulated by the tip of the tongue against the upper teeth. Examples: Spanish t in *tema rata*, Spanish d in *duende, dando.*
5. **Alveolar:** articulated by the blade or tip of the tongue against the alveolar ridge. Examples: Spanish l in *lago, palo,* Spanish n in *nota, tono.*
6. **Palatal:** articulated by the front of the tongue against the hard palate. Examples: Spanish ʎ in *llamar, lleno, pollo,* Spanish ɲ in *ñoño, caña, uña.*
7. **Velar:** articulated by the back of the tongue against the soft palate. Examples: Spanish g in *golpe, ganga,* Spanish x˙in *jota, ojo.*

NOTES
1. A further category – **glottal** – has to be distinguished for English, in order to describe sounds articulated in the glottis. Aspirate **h** is a glottal sound, as is the glottal stop ʔ, formed when the glottis is closed completely, the vocal cords are brought together, air compressed behind them and then released suddenly as the glottis is opened. In dialectal English ʔ is frequently used as a substitute for t in unstressed positions – *Tottenham* toʔnəm, *that one* ðæʔ wʌn, and it sometimes appears in *RP* when a word which normally begins with a stressed vowel is particularly emphasized (Jones, 1960, 150–52). The glottal stop is also used occasionally in *RP* to separate successive vowels between which no natural glide develops, as in *Anna acts* ænəʔ ækts, and may be used by some speakers as a means of distinguishing between what would otherwise be ambiguous expressions: *some mice* səm majs but *some ice* səm ʔajs.
2. In the case of palatal and velar consonants it is sometimes necessary to make finer distinctions between sounds, according to the position on the palate or velum where the passage of air is partially or wholly stopped by the tongue.

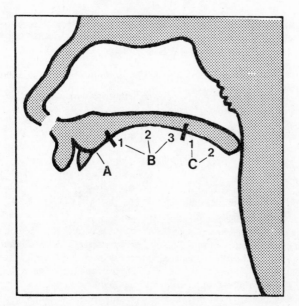

FIG. 7 DIVISIONS OF THE PALATE. A alveolar ridge; B hard palate:
1 pre-, 2 central, 3 post-; C soft palate: 1 pre-, 2 post-.

The terms **prepalatal, central palatal, post-palatal, prevelar** and **post-velar** are
available to indicate these finer distinctions (fig. 7).

18   **Manner of articulation.** Classified according to their manner of articulation,
the sounds of Spanish fall into six main categories. These are:
1. **Plosive.** Also known as **stop** or **occlusive** consonants. Formed by
completely closing the air passage somewhere in the mouth, resulting in an
accumulation of breath which is then allowed to escape with some violence.
Examples: Spanish b in *bata*, d in *duende*, g in *gato*.
2. **Fricative.** Also known as **spirants** or **continuants.** Formed by narrowing the
passage through which air is allowed to escape, so that the air produces audible
friction on its way out. Examples: Spanish f in *fama*, β in *haba*, ð in *nada*,
ɣ in *lago*, x in *dijo*.
3. **Affricate.** Formed initially as a plosive consonant. The initial stoppage is
then followed not by an explosion of breath but by a gradual relaxation into a
fricative sound. Examples: t͡ʃ in *chico, macho,* d͡j in *yo, yerno*.
4. **Lateral.** Formed by an obstacle being placed in the centre of the mouth, so
that air escapes at one or both sides. Examples: l in *lago, pelo,* ʎ in *llamar,
calle.*
5. **Vibrant.** (a) **Rolled** or **multiple.** Formed by a rapid succession of taps.
Examples: Spanish r̄ in *carro, perro.* (b) **Flapped** or **single.** Formed by one
single tap. Examples: Spanish r in *caro, pero.*

6. **Nasal.** Formed when the velum is inert and there is a complete closure in the mouth, so that air can escape only through the nose. Examples: Spanish m in *madre, cama,* Spanish n in *nada, tono.*

NOTES
1. Lateral and vibrant consonants are sometimes classed loosely together under the term of liquids *(líquidas);* even more loosely, linguists writing in Spanish frequently use the term *continuas* as a synonym for *líquidas* **rather than** *fricativas.* The term **sibilant** is used to describe the hissing sounds s, z, ʃ, ʒ, t͡ʃ, d͡ʒ.
2. Sounds produced when the soft palate is raised, so that air escapes only through the mouth, are described as **oral** or **buccal** sounds; sounds produced when the soft palate is lowered are described as **nasal** sounds. In the second case, air may be allowed to escape exclusively through the nose (e.g. **m, n**) or through nose and mouth simultaneously (e.g. the nasal vowels ã, ẽ, õ).

3.19 By considering the points of reference discussed in 3.15, 3.17 and 3.18, the individual consonant sounds of Spanish can be differentiated and described in words. For example, the *t* of *tapa,* articulated with the vocal cords at rest, with the tip of the tongue on the upper front teeth, and a complete closure of the air passage, can be described as a **voiceless dental plosive;** the *g* of *lago,* produced with the vocal cords vibrating, the back of the tongue raised towards the soft palate, and a narrowing of the air passage, can be described as a **voiced velar fricative.** Occasionally a further verbal distinction may have to be made. The sounds represented by *r* in *pero* and *rr* in *perro* are both **voiced alveolar vibrants,** but the first is **flapped** or **single** and the second **rolled** or **multiple.** Both the *s* of English *soup* and the *s* of Spanish *supo* are **voiceless alveolar fricatives:** the English sound, however, articulated with the blade of the tongue against the alveolar ridge and the front raised towards the hard palate, can be further defined as blade-alveolar or predorsal. The Spanish sibilant, with the tip of the tongue curled back on the alveolar ridge, can be further defined as **retroflex** or **tip-alveolar** – the terms **apical** and **cacuminal** are also used by some writers to describe Castilian s.

3.20 **FURTHER READING.** A. C. Gimson (1962), chs. 3–4. D. Jones (1958), paras. 31–57; (1960), chs. 5–9. T. Navarro (1965), paras. 12–25. A. Quilis. and J. A. Fernández (1964), ch. 3. R. H. Robins (1964), 95–116. B. M. H. Strang (1962), paras. 28–33.

3.21 **EXERCISES ON CHAPTER 3**
1. In the following words identify (*a*) the half-close vowels, (*b*) the front vowels, (*c*) the back vowels: *pezonera, tiritón, sincronismo, muchedumbre, rudimento, deducir, bigotudo, hormiguear, nervosidad, zorrería.* Which vowel does not appear on your list? Describe it.
2. Which sounds are voiced in the following words? *Nevar, paje, gallina, físico, dorado, viscoso, chapeta, bajamar, corteza, luchador.*
3. In what feature are the initial consonants alike in the following pairs of words? *Tejo, dejo; nata, lata; coma, goma; bata, mata; ñaques, llagas.*

4. In what feature are the intervocalic consonants alike in the following pairs of words? *Haba, hada; vale, valle; cama, caña; mira, mirra; toco, topo.*

5. Give one example of (*a*) a voiced bilabial plosive, (*b*) a voiceless labiodental fricative, (*c*) a voiced palatal lateral, (*d*) a voiceless interdental fricative, (*e*) a voiced palatal nasal.

4 PHONETIC TRANSCRIPTIONS

4.1   The basic principle common to the large number of phonetic alphabets which have so far been designed is that one and only one symbol is assigned to each distinctive sound of the language which is being represented. By doing so the phonetic alphabet aims at providing, in so far as it is possible, an unambiguous method of representing pronunciation in a written form.

4.2   The phonetic alphabet becomes essential in practical work in phonetics because of the inconsistencies in the standard orthographical systems employed by most languages. Conventional English spelling, like that of French, is notoriously unpredictable. One sound may be spelled in a variety of ways – compare the spelling of the French vowel o in *mot, tôt, beau, chevaux*, or that of the English diphthong aj in *time, sly, high, eye, aye, aisle, pie, height*. Or one spelling may be pronounced in a variety of ways – compare *-lle* in French *fille, ville* or *-ough* in English *enough, thorough, through, cough, bough, dough, thought*. In contrast to English or French, Spanish orthography is largely phonetic; nevertheless it possesses certain eccentricities. The velar fricative sound x is written g in *gente, ingenio*, but *j* in *jota, mujer;* the graph *c* of *coro* represents a sound quite distinct from that of the *c* of *cero*. A phonetic alphabet which provides separate symbols for each sound (x for the g of *gente, jota,* k for the *c* of *coro,* θ for the *c* of *cera*) aims at eliminating ambiguities of representation.

4.3   The phonetic symbols and marks used throughout this book are those recommended by the International Phonetic Association, as set out in its *Principles* (1949) and in Jones and Dahl (1944). They are used in accordance with the Association's principles.

4.4   The International Phonetic Alphabet was first published in *The Phonetic Teacher* in August 1888, and has been subject to constant revision and modification since then. It consists, in so far as is possible, of the ordinary letters of the Roman alphabet, each one assigned to a distinctive sound, and supplemented by a number of symbols borrowed from the Greek alphabet or specially designed for the purpose. Since there is clearly a limit to the number of totally distinct symbols which it would be practicable to introduce, the Association has allowed for the use of diacritic marks which can be added to the basic symbols of the phonetic alphabet to represent more minute shades of sound, and to make more narrowly allophonic or more comparative (4.8) transcriptions than would otherwise be possible.

4.5   Partly because IPA was devised before much was known about phonemic principles, the alphabet contains a number of slight inconsistencies. For example, the Spanish phoneme /n/ has a number of allophonic variants, among them ṇ, found before a dental consonant, as in *antes,* ṋ, found before an interdental consonant, as in *lince,* m̩, found before *f,* as in *confuso,* and ŋ, found before a velar consonant, as in *cinco.* IPA conventions, whereby separate symbols are allocated for labiodental m̩ and velar ŋ, but whereby diacritical marks have to be employed to designate dental ṇ, and interdental ṋ , might suggest that whereas m̩ and ŋ are separate 'sounds', ṇ and n are simply less common variants of the more common alveolar n. In fact, in Spanish all four are positional variants of the phoneme /n/ (9.13). Affricate sounds also provide problems for which no completely satisfactory solution has been found. IPA offers a choice between representing such sounds by special but awkward and unfamiliar symbols (e.g. ɟ, ʃ, ʒ) or by digraphs (e.g. d͡ʒ, t͡s, d͡z), with or without ligatures, which are more familiar and more typographically satisfactory, but which, because they appear to be made up of two independent phonemes, could lead to a false impression of the phonetic composition of the sounds they represent.

.6   In spite of these limitations, the International Phonetic Alphabet, because its conventions have been very carefully defined and widely accepted over a long period of time, and because it is now in use by phoneticians in most parts of the world, remains an extremely useful tool. The only other phonetic alphabet which is commonly used for the transcription of Hispanic languages is that published in the *Revista de Filología Española* (1915); this has, however, the same kind of inconsistencies as the IPA, with the further disadvantage that is hardly known outside Spain and Hispanic studies, and is extremely difficult to use for other languages.

.7   For these reasons the alphabet and conventions adopted in the present book are those of the International Phonetic Association. It is, however, possible to transcribe phonetically any language in a number of different ways, all in conformity with the IPA alphabet and conventions, "for there is no such thing as *the* IPA transcription of English in the sense of an officially sanctioned variety" (Abercrombie, 1964, 13). Equally, there is no such thing as *the* officially sanctioned IPA transcription of Spanish. A transcription which is made by using letters of the simplest possible shapes – i.e. the most romanic letters – can be described as a **simple transcription.** If that transcription makes use only of the minimum number of letters necessary to distinguish without ambiguity all words of different sound in the language being represented, it can be described as a **simple phonemic** transcription. After establishing a set of conventions which govern the circumstances in which, for example, the speech-sounds g and ɣ occur, a simple phonemic transcription would represent both by one single symbol g.

.8   The system used here is not **comparative.** A comparative transcription does not aim at using letters of the simplest possible shapes. In order to draw attention to the differences between the flapped *r* of Spanish *para* and the fricative *r* of English *round,* a comparative transcription of English might adopt the symbol ɹ for each occurrence of the fricative sound. The symbol ɹ would thus have the advantage of being more specific, and of providing a visual reminder in the text of the nature of the English sound without the need for previously established conventions. It would do this at the expense of introducing into the transcription a letter which is complex in shape, less distinctive at a glance, and less satisfactory typographically than the alternative r. It would be possible to establish a comparative system of transcription for English and Spanish which made clear in the text the specific differences between English and Spanish consonant sounds. Such an enterprise, however, would result in the use of so many exotic letters and diacritical marks in the transcription of each language as to make phonetic transcriptions of both languages a printer's and user's nightmare.

4.9   If a system departs from the principles of a simple phonemic transcription by making use of more than the minimum number of letters required to represent the phonemes of the language, selecting the most typographically simple additional symbols and diacritical marks, it can be described as a simple allophonic transcription. Some, but not necessarily all, of the phonemes will be represented by more than one different symbol. The system recommended and employed in this book is of the simple allophonic type. Thirty-three symbols are used, of which twenty-three represent the phonemes of Castilian Spanish, and a further ten – j, d͡ʒ, w, β, ð, ɣ, θ̬, s̬, m̩ and ŋ – represent the most common allophonic variants of the phonemes /i/, /u/, /b/, /d/, /g/, /θ/, /s/, /m/ and /n/. The thirty-three symbols which appear in simple allophonic transcriptions throughout this book are listed in columns I and II of Table I on p. 4. If the need for phonemic transcriptions should arise, these may be made by using only the twenty-three phoneme symbols in column I of that table. More narrow allophonic transcriptions may be made by introducing some or all of the additional symbols and diacritical marks listed on pp. 3 and 4. For a detailed account of the principles governing phonemic, comparative and allophonic transcriptions see D. Abercrombie (1953, and 1964, 16–22) and D. Jones (1960), appendix A.

4.10   **FURTHER READING.** D. Abercrombie (1953), 32–34; (1964), Part I. *Alfabeto fonético*, in *RFE* (1915), 374–6. P. Delattre (1966). International Phonetic Association, *Principles* (1949). D. Jones (1958), paras. 58–67; (1960), ch 10 and first appendix. D. Jones and I. Dahl (1944). T. Navarro (1965), paras. 31, 253–7. A. Quilis and J. A. Fernández (1964), xxvii–xxx and app. 1. R. H. Robins (1964), 91–5. A. D. Schoch (1907), 80–84. G. L. Trager (1935), 10–13.

5 THE SYLLABLE

1   The phonetician, in order to describe and compare the sounds of different languages, analyses speech by dividing it up into a series of segments which can be classified into various categories. Consequently the study of articulatory phonetics can leave the dangerously false impression that language consists of a finite number of individual speech-sounds, linked together in sequence to form words, which are then pieced together in the same fashion to form sentences.

2   In the spoken language, speech-sounds are run together into an unbroken stream of movements, with no break or pause between them. These sequences of sounds are called **rhythm groups** (or alternatively **breath groups** or **phonic groups**), which may be short or long, and can vary from a single syllable like *sí* or *yo* to a comparatively long statement like *Llevo más de dos años aquí en el norte de España.* If what the speaker has to say is too long to utter in one single rhythm group, he pauses at the end of the group before continuing with the next, sometimes taking breath as he does so. The slight pause made between two rhythm groups which are closely linked grammatically is conventionally marked / :

    Estuve tres días en Madrid / capital de España.

The longer pause made between two rhythm groups less closely connected, as at the end of a sentence, or at a colon or semicolon, is conventionally marked ||:

    Estuve tres días en Madrid / capital de España ||| Lo pasé bien ||

A compound or complex sentence is built up with a series of rhythm groups, separated by a series of short or long pauses:

    El año pasado / cuando viajaba por España / pasé tres días en Madrid ||
    pero no me gustó tanto como Córdoba / que me pareció una ciudad
    encantadora ||

3   In every rhythm group, whether it is a single word or a phrase, one or more sounds can be heard to stand out more perceptibly than the others. The most perceptible (sonorous) sounds of Spanish are the vowels (3.3—4), and a word like Spanish *sí* which has only one such sound has only one syllable. The noun *silo* **sí-lo** has two syllables, the group *un silo* **ún-sí-lo** has three, the group *un gran silo* **úŋ-grán-sí-lo** has four, and so on. The Spanish syllable may be described as a single vowel or a group of sounds which contains one vowel, as defined in 3.1; that vowel may stand alone or form the most prominent part of a diphthong or triphthong (5.9 ff.). In general terms, however, the syllable

has proved extremely difficult to define; for an excellent analysis of the
problems and a tentative solution, see Abercrombie (1967), ch. 3.

5.4   Every rhythm group consists of a continuous undulation in prominence, which
       can be visualized as a wavy line with 'peaks' at the most prominent sounds
       and 'troughs' at the least prominent. Thus the rhythm group *me compré un
       gran silo* can be seen to have six peaks of prominence, and therefore six
       syllables:

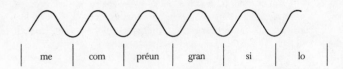

| me | com | préun | gran | si | lo |

or:

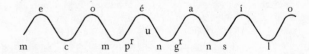

In each syllable the vowel forms the **nucleus,** and other elements (semivowels
or consonants) form the syllabic **margins.**

5.5   The syllable is the basic rhythm unit of Spanish, and one of the most
       characteristic features of the spoken language is that all the syllables in a
       rhythm group, whether stressed or unstressed, tend to follow each other at
       more or less evenly spaced intervals of time. Consider the sentence:

       Juan no sabe lo que dijo Pepe.

       The sentence forms one rhythm group of ten syllables:

       Juan-no-sa-be-lo-que-di-jo-Pe-pe

       It contains five stressed syllables:

       Juán-nó-sá-be-lo-que-dí-jo-Pé-pe

       But the five stressed syllables, although pronounced with greater muscular
       force and therefore more prominent, are neither longer nor shorter in duration
       than the five unstressed syllables; each syllable of the ten is equally clear-cut
       and takes up approximately the same length of time. The result is an even
       pattering rhythm which to English ears sounds rather like that of a machine-
       gun; this type of rhythm unit can be called **syllable-timed** (K. L. Pike, 1946,
       34–5; D. Abercrombie, 1967, 96–8).

5.6   The syllable-timed rhythm of Spanish contrasts sharply with the **stress-timed**
       rhythm of English. In English speech, it is not *all* the syllables but only the

stressed syllables which tend to be evenly spaced in time. Compare the similar timing and stresses of the following pairs of sentences:

(a)   *Bóth   léft súddenly*
(b)   *Bóth of them léft súddenly*
(c)   *The cát's   góne*
(d)   *The cáterpillar's góne*

In each pair of sentences, unstressed syllables have been added without materially altering the time-spacing between the stresses: the effect of adding two extra syllables to (a) is simply that in (b) the phrase *both of them* is pronounced approximately within the time-limit previously allocated to *both*, and the effect of adding three extra syllables to (c) is that in (d) the phrase *the caterpillar's* is pronounced approximately within the time-limit previously allocated to *the cat*.
Now compare:

(e)   *níne   bíg   bláck   cáts*
(f)   *nínety   enórmous   vermílion   cúrtains*

The lapses in time between the stressed syllables of (f) are either equal to or only very marginally greater than those between the stressed syllables of (e), despite the fact that the phrase is six syllables longer. The extra syllables are crushed up more closely together, and the time devoted to the stressed syllables correspondingly shortened.

7   This hurrying of syllables into short time-limits is partly responsible for the loss or obscuring of many unstressed English vowels. By contrast, the even time-spacing of syllables in Spanish tends to operate against the shortening or slurring of vowels. One of the greatest problems for native English speakers is to make the transition from the "Morse-code" rhythm of English to the "machine-gun" rhythm of Spanish (L. James, 1940, 25) — in other words, to switch from a stress-timed to a syllable-timed rhythm. The type of phonetic transcription adopted in this book, which lays emphasis on the syllabic divisions of the rhythm group, provides a constant visual reminder of the syllabic nature of Spanish. In phonetic transcripts syllable division is conventionally marked -.

8   A syllable which ends in a vowel (e.g. Spanish *no, la, me, si)* is described as **open,** and the vowel is **free.** A syllable which ends in a consonant (e.g. Spanish *tal, son, los, red*) is **close,** and the vowel is **blocked.** Spanish has a strong preference for open syllables (B. Malmberg, 1948, 99—120).

9   The nucleus of the Spanish syllable is its most perceptible sound, which is always a vowel. The vowel may form a syllable by itself, as in *a-mo, ta-re-a,* or as the more prominent part of a diphthong, as in *ai-re, oi-go;* it may also be combined, alone or as part of a diphthong, with one or more consonants: *re-don-do, fra-ter-nal, cui-da-do.* The following are the conventions which determine the syllabic structure of Spanish.

5.10   A single consonant occurring between vowels is always grouped with the vowel which follows it: *pe-ra, ma-lo, Za-mo-ra, pa-ta-ta.* The diagraphs *ll, rr* and *ch* represent single speech-sounds, and are treated as single consonants: *po-llo, ca-llar, tie-rra, po-rrón, ha-cha, le-cho.*

5.11   Two consonants occurring between vowels present two possibilities:

(a) Twelve pairs of consonants, all of which have *r* or *l* as the second element, combine readily and are never separated. Both consonants are grouped with the following vowel. The twelve pairs are:

br	*cr*	*fr*	*gr*	*pr*	*dr*	*tr*
bl	*cl*	*fl*	*gl*	*pl*		

Examples:

ca-bra	*a-cre*	*ci-fra*	*ti-gre*	*ci-prés*	*la-drón*	*a-trás*
vo-ca-blo	*bu-cle*	*ri-fle*	*si-glo*	*so-plar*		

(b) In all other groupings of two consonants the consonants are separated, with the first closing the preceding syllable and the second beginning the following syllable: *bur-la, san-to, par-te, des-pen-sa, es-ce-na, es-tu-fi-lla.*

5.12   Three or more consonants occurring between vowels also present two possibilities:
(a) When the last two consonants of the group form one of the twelve pairs described in 5.11, this pair begins the following syllable and the remainder close the preceding syllable: *lum-bre, san-gre, in-fla-mar, abs-tru-so, ins-truc-tor.*
(b) In all other groupings of three consonants the third consonant begins the following syllable and the first two close the preceding syllable: *cons-pi-rar, abs-te-ner, pers-pi-caz.*

5.13   These rules apply uniformly throughout the rhythm group. As a result, a single consonant which occurs between vowels begins the following syllable, and syllabic division may not correspond to word division: *el-hijo: e-li-jo; sus ojos: su-so-jos; en aquellas épocas: e-na-que-lla-sé-po-cas; los pies en el agua: los-pie-se-ne-la-gua.*

5.14   Occasionally, two like consonants come into contact in a rhythm group or, as a result of composition, internally in a word. In these situations they may be pronounced, in carefully enunciated speech, as one long, or **geminate**, consonant in which the closure or obstruction is held momentarily before release. This geminate consonant in part closes the preceding syllable and in part begins the following syllable:

> *innato* i^n-ná-to
> *un niño* ú^n-ní-ɲo

To indicate the fact that this lengthened consonant is not quite twice as long as a consonant in the syllable-initial position, the first part may be represented by a symbol above the line in phonetic transcripts:

innovar i^n-no-βár	*los suelos* lo^s-swé-los
con nata ko^n-ná-ta	*dos sílabas* dó^s-sí-la-βas
obviar o$^\beta$-βjár	*ciudad de plata* θju-δáδ-δe-plá-ta
el lado e^l-lá-δo	*diez celtas* djé$^\theta$-θél-tas
aquel lago a-ké^l-lá-γo	*un cantar regional* úŋ-kan-tá^r-r̄e-xjo-nál

The pronunciation of such geminate consonants depends, however, on a conscious effort towards 'correct' pronunciation by the individual speaker, and does not easily fit into the system of a language which has a certain repugnance for geminate consonants; in normal speech the two consonants are pronounced as one, in which case the distinction between some pairs of words is obscured:

son nombres, son hombres **só-nóm-bres**
el loro, el oro **e-ló-ro**
las salas, las alas **la-sá-las**

5.15 (a) If two of the vowels *a, e, o* come together in any order they normally constitute separate syllables: *jaleo* xa-lé-o, *azahar* a-θa-ár, *creen* kré-en, *paella* pa-é-ʎa, *oasis* o-á-sis, *aéreo* a-é-re-o.

(b) If a stressed *i* or *u* comes into contact with *a, e* or *o*, the two vowels always constitute separate syllables: *hacía* a-θí-a, *paraíso* pa-ra-í-so, *baúl,* ba-úl, *gradúa* gra-δú-a, *buho* bú-o, *reuno* r̄e-ú-no.

5.16 **Syneresis.** Within a word, two vowels may appear in succession and be pronounced in separate syllables (5.15). In such circumstances the vowels are said to be in **hiatus**. In popular speech and in rapid educated speech, however, hiatus is not always preserved, and frequently vowels which should constitute separate syllables are run together to form a single syllable. This feature is known as **syneresis.** Syneresis occurs most readily when two unstressed like vowels come together: *neerlandés* ner-lan-dés, *nihilista* ni-lís-ta, *alcoholismo* al-ko-lís̰-mo: it is rather less frequent when one of the like vowels bears a stress accent: *azahar* a-θár or a-θa-ár, *alcohol* al-kól or al-ko-ól, *leer* lér or le-ér. Less commonly still, two unlike vowels which come into contact may form a single syllable: *cohete* koé-te or ko-é-te *teoría* teo-rí-a or te-o-rí-a, *real* r̄eál or r̄e-ál, *caen* káen or ká-en. When one of those vowels is *u* or *i* it becomes a semivowel in syneresis: *aun* áwn or a-ún, *baúl* báwl or ba-úl *ahí* áj or a-í. Whether groups of vowels are pronounced in hiatus or syneresis is not a linguistic feature which can be reduced to a convenient set of rules: the more uneducated a speaker, the more he will tend to practise syneresis; the faster an educated speaker talks, the more he too will practise syneresis; syneresis is a regular and completely accepted feature of Spanish verse. Syneresis also depends to a considerable extent upon the position of the word in the rhythm group. It is rare when the contiguous vowels occur in a word which is the emphatic word of a rhythm group or comes at the end of a rhythm group: *vea para que lo crea* bé-a-pa-ra-ke-lo-kré-a, *es necesario leer* és̰-ne-θe-sá-rjo-le-ér. In other situations, particularly when the word in question is completely unemphatic, syneresis may be found: *el peor de todos soy yo*

el-peór-ðe-tó-ðos-sój-jó, *deseaba hablar con usted* de-seá-β̵a-β̵lár-ko-nus-té,
voy a pasearme bó-ja-pa-seár-me, *pensaba leer un libro* pen-sá-β̵a-le-rún-lí-β̵ro.

NOTES
1. When the vowels *e* and *o* are combined in syneresis there is a strong
tendency in substandard and dialectal speech for the first vowel in the
combination to be pronounced as the glide j: *teoría* tjo-rí-a, *real* r̄jál, *peonada*
pjo-ná-ða, *teatro* tjá-tro etc.
2. For a more detailed treatment of syneresis, see A. M. Espinosa (1924) and
T. Navarro (1965, paras. 133–52). For *synalepha*, the combining into one
syllable of vowels belonging to different words which come together in a
rhythm group, see also these references and 7.15–21.

5.17   **Combinations of vowel and semivowel.**

(a) Vowel plus semivowel form a diphthong, which is a single syllable: *causa*
káw-sa, *aire* áj-re, *peine* péj-ne, *boina* bój-na, *deudo* déw-ðo.
(b) Semivowel plus vowel form a diphthong, which is a single syllable: *hacia*
á-θja, *dueño* dwé-ɲo, *idiota* i-ðjó-ta, *antiguo* an-tí-ɣwo.

NOTE
In the groups *iu, ui, uy,* it is the first element which normally becomes a
semivowel: *ciudad* θju-ðáð, *cuidado* kwi-ðá-ðo, *muy* mwí, *juicio* xwí-θjo.

(c) Semivowel plus vowel plus semivowel form a triphthong, which is a single
syllable: *liáis* ljájs, *acentuáis* a-θen-twájs, *miau* mjáw, *guau* gwáw.

5.18   The syllable which bears the main stress accent in a word or group of words is
the **stressed** (or **accented** or **tonic**) syllable, and in phonetic transcriptions the
most prominent vowel in the stressed syllable is conventionally marked with
the accent ´; *pata* pá-ta, *hipótesis* i-pó-te-sis, *veinte* béjn-te, *me lo da* me-lo-ðá.
The remaining syllables of the word or group are **unstressed** (or **unaccented** or
atonic) syllables; these are normally left unmarked.

5.19   With few exceptions, Spanish has a stress accent on one syllable of each
word. The commonest stress pattern in the language is for the penultimate
syllable of a word to bear the stress; words which end in a vowel, *n* or *s*
are naturally stressed on this syllable, and are **paroxytones**: *firme* fír-me,
terminan ter-mí-nan, *comes* kó-mes. This type of ending is known in Spanish
as a **terminación grave** or **llana** or **paroxítona**. Words which end in consonants
other than *n* or *s* are naturally stressed on the final syllable and called
oxytones: *tomar* to-már, *pared* pa-réð, *capaz* ka-páθ. This ending is known in
Spanish as a **terminación aguda** or **oxítona**. When the accent falls upon the
antepenultimate syllable of a word, a written accent on that syllable is
obligatory: *pájaro* pá-xa-ro, *frívolo* frí-β̵o-lo, *húmedo* ú-me-ðo; such words
are **proparoxytones**, and the ending is known in Spanish as a **terminación
esdrújula** or **proparoxítona**. The orthographic conventions of Spanish require
that any word in which the stress pattern does not correspond to these
conventions must bear a written accent on its stressed syllable: *tomó* to-mó·

afán a-fán, *venís* be-nís; *alcázar* al-ká-θar, *difícil* di-fí-θil; *cómetelo* kó-me-te-lo
cántasela kán-ta-se-la. The only words which normally bear two stress accents
are adverbs which end in *-mente: fuertemente* fwér-te-mén-te, *rápidamente*
r̄á-pi-ða-mén-te.

NOTES
1. The words *período, cardíaco, alvéolos, océano* are most commonly
pronounced as paroxytones: pe-rjó-do, kar-ðjá-ko, al-βe-ó-los or al-βeó-los,
o-θe-á-no or oθeá-no. Exceptionally, the accent on these words is not written
on the syllable now most commonly stressed.
2. In the scansion of poetry the prosodic conventions of Spanish require that
a **terminación aguda** (actually one syllable) and a **terminación esdrújula**
(actually three syllables) each count as two syllables at the end of a line of
verse or a half-line which is clearly marked by a pause or caesura.

5.20 The principal categories of word normally unstressed in a rhythm group are:

(a) **The definite article:** *el hombre* e-lóm-bre, *la niña* la-ní-ɲa, *las casas*
las-ká-sas. The indefinite article is normally stressed both in singular and in
plural forms – *un hombre* ú-nóm-bre, *una niña* ú-na-ní-ɲa, *unos libros*
ú-nos-lí-βros – but *unos, unas* may be unstressed when used in the sense 'about',
'approximately': *unos quince días* u-nos-kín-θe-ðí-as, *unas veinte poesías*
u-nas̯-β éjn-te-po-e-sí-as.

(b) **Weak pronouns:** *me lo da* me-lo-ðá, *se la comió* se-la-ko-mjó, *se me perdió*
se-me-per-ðjó, *nos saluda* nos-sa-lú-ða, *les habla* le-sá-βla.

(c) **Weak possessive adjectives:** *mi-propósito* mi-pro-pó-si-to, *nuestros abuelos*
nwes-tro-sa-β wé-los, *su libro* su-lí-βro.

(d) **Prepositions:** *para las siete* pa-ra-las-sjé-te, *hasta luego* as-ta-lwé-ɣo,
con tiempo kon-tjém-po, *desde Londres* des̯-ðe-lón-dres.
(e) **Conjunctions:** *Juan y Pepe* xwá-ni-pépe, *seis o siete* séj-so-sjé-te, *no lo dijo*
él sino su padre nó-lo-ðí-xoél-si-no-su-pá-ðre, *hasta que salieron* as-ta-ke-sa-
ljé-ron, *para que nos sentemos* pa-ra-ke-nos-sen-té-mos, *aunque me digas que sí*
awŋ-ke-me-ðí-ɣas-ke-sí.

(f) **Relative pronouns:** *la chica que vi* la-t͡ʃí-ka-ke-βí, *el pueblo adonde vamos*
el-pwé-β loa-ðon-de-βá-mos, *la casa en la que vive* la-ká-saen-la-ke-βí-βe,
la manera como lo dijo la-ma-né-ra-ko-mo-lo-ðí-xo.

(g) **Titles used with Christian names** (*don, doña, fray, San, Santo* etc.):
doña Maria do-ɲa-ma-rí-a, *San Juan de la Cruz* saŋ-xwán-de-la-krúθ, *Santa
Teresa* san-ta-te-ré-sa.

5.21 Consonants which appear in the syllable-initial position are generally
articulated with strong breath force, and are strongly resistant to change or
effacement. Consonants which appear in the syllable-final position in Spanish
are generally weakly articulated, and particularly subject to change or

effacement (8.15–20, 8.27 n. 2, 9.4 nn. 1–3, 9.7, 9.9 nn. 1–3 etc). It is among consonants in the syllable-final position that phonemic differences which are valid elsewhere are most liable to become neutralized (9.14).

5.22 **FURTHER READING.** D. Abercrombie (1940); (1967), chs. 3 and 6. I. B. Dalbor (1969), chs. 6, 23, 31. A. M. Espinosa (1924), 299–309. A. C. Gimson (1962), 5.4–5.42. E. Haugen (1956), 213–21. L. James (1940). B. Malmberg (1948a), 99–120. T. Navarro (1965), paras, 26–30, 68, 133–56. K. L. Pike (1946). A. Quilis and J. A. Fernández (1964), chs. 6 and 12. R. H. Robins (1964), 137–41. R. P. Stockwell, J. D. Bowen and I. Silva-Fuenzalida (1956), 641–65. M. Swadesh (1947), 137–50. G. L. Trager and B. Bloch (1941), 223–46.

5.23 **EXERCISES ON CHAPTER 5**
1. Divide into syllables: *hollín, soplo, atlas, atrás, carretera, isleño, inhabitado, asombroso, ombligo, gordiflón, peligro, ancho, gigantesco, dañable, enronquezco, ennegrecido, transbordador, pitillo, obscurantismo, transcribir.*
2. Divide into syllables: *náufrago, obstruir, inspiración, maizales, tarea, cuartillas, experiencia, obstruccionista, pueblo, salvaguardar, continúa, aúlla, coherente, traiga, techo, diurético, fui, diedro, enmohecer, meandro.*
3. Mark the stressed syllables in the following rhythm groups: *el catedrático no se dio cuenta;* *¿es muy grande vuestro hijo? don Pedro nos compró una casa; a mí no me han dicho nada; fuimos a despedir a la amiga de Pepe, la cual volvía a Madrid; vamos a considerarlo más detenidamente; lo hizo bajo el mando de don Juan; yo no lo sabía, pero ya no importa; mi amigo me ha dicho que hay muchos que creen estar enamorados sin estarlo.*
4. Divide the following rhythm groups into syllables, and mark the stressed syllables: *la devoción al agua no debe sorprender a nadie; hay países en donde la mendicidad desvergonzada sigue siendo problema; al lado del cura, doña María se sintió feliz; dos años más tarde, los suecos se marcharon todos; yo lo que quiero decir es que lo tomo con azúcar.*
5. Identify each of the following words as an oxytone, paroxytone or proparoxytone, and explain the presence of the written accent where there is one: *fumífero, proceridad, gigantazo, también, caballería, procedencia, sinónimo, rezabais, cacao, descortés.*

6 SPANISH VOWELS IN GREATER DETAIL

6.1 The Spanish vowel system is outstanding for its uniformity of timbre. Spanish is a language which, compared with English or French, has few vowel phonemes, and the Spanish vowels are very clearly defined and not easily confused one with the other. The timbre of a vowel – its most distinguishing quality – depends on the shape of the mouth as breath is allowed to escape with the vocal cords vibrating; this is governed partly by the position of the lips, but principally by the position of the tongue. Lip and tongue positions for each of the five Spanish vowel phonemes are well defined, and strikingly uniform from one sound-context to another.

6.2 It is possible to detect slight variations in the timbre of each of the five vowels according to the nature of the sounds which surround it: for example, the *e* of *teja* is rather more open than the *e* of *tela,* the *i* of *rima* rather more open than the *i* of *lima,* the *a* of *pausa* rather more velar than the *a* of *pasa,* but the variants are not distinctive. On no occasion does the substitution of one variety of a Spanish vowel for another in the same phonetic context serve to distinguish one word from another. Only the five vowels *a, e, i, o, u,* can create such a distinction: thus *paso, peso, piso, poso* and *puso,* where the phonetic context for each vowel is identical, are distinguished in meaning only by the nature of the vowel which forms the nucleus of the first syllable. Spanish has five, and only five, distinctive vowel phonemes; each of these phonemes, however, may have allophonic variants in particular and restricted circumstances.

6.3 Unstressed vowels tend to be pronounced, especially in rapid speech, with less muscular tension then those in stressed syllables. The unstressed *e* of *húmedo, valeroso,* is generally a more relaxed, less tense, sound than the stressed *e* of *pera, meta.* Since the relaxation of the vowel follows automatically from its unaccented position, there is no need to mark each unstressed vowel individually in a phonetic transcription; provided that each stressed vowel is marked ´ (5.19), it follows automatically that all vowels between major stresses are unstressed and consequently liable to a slight relaxion in muscular tension.

6.4 Spanish being a syllable-timed language, all vowels have approximately the same duration. It is possible for vowels to be lengthened in Spanish, for stylistic reasons or for reasons of emphasis, but vowel length in Spanish does not affect meaning as it may do in English, where the length of the vowel, accompanied by a tendency towards diphthongization, can be a major factor in distinguishing between otherwise identical sequences of sounds: cf.

should	ʃud	*shoed*	ʃuwd
pull	pul	*pool*	puwl
full	ful	*fool*	fuwl

6.5   Spanish has no nasal vowel phoneme, but in certain circumstances a vowel may be slightly nasalized in contact with nasal consonants:
(a) When it comes between two nasal consonants. Examples: *mano* mã́no *niño* nĩ́ɲo, *ñoño* ɲṍɲo.

(b) When it is in an initial position in a rhythm group, and followed by a nasal consonant: Examples: *once* ṍnθe, *andar* ãndár, *infeliz* ĩɱfelĩ́θ.

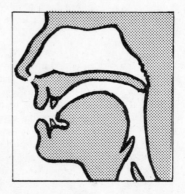

FIG. 8   a

NOTE
Interior in a rhythm group, Spanish vowels are not nasalized when followed by a nasal consonant: *fuente* fwénte, *tanto* tánto, *es insaciable* es insaθjáβle.

DETAILED DESCRIPTIONS

a

6.6   **Open central vowel a.** This is the most open and the most perceptible of any sound in Spanish. The lips are held wide apart, in a neutral position, and the tongue lies low in the mouth, with the centre very slightly raised. Spanish **a** is a central vowel, which is considerably more open than the usual *RP* pronunciation of *a* in *pat* pæt, *chat* t͡ʃæt, and both shorter and more forward than the usual *RP* pronunciation of *a* in *far* fɑ, *class* klɑs, *half* hɑf, *ask* ɑsk. Examples: *fama* fáma, *caro* káro, *patata* patáta, *saber* saβér. See fig. 8.

NOTES

1. **a̠.** When *a* precedes a palatal consonant, the semivowel j, or the front vowel i, it is attracted slightly towards the point of articulation of the following sound, and itself becomes slightly palatalized. The diacritical sign ₊ can be placed under the vowel to indicate a degree of palatalization. Examples: *cacha* ká̠t͡ʃa, *valle* bá̠ʎe, *año* á̠ɲo, *mayo* má̠jo, *aire* á̠jre, *país* pa̠ís.

2. **a̠** When *a* precedes a velar consonant, the semivowel w, or a velar vowel, it is similarly attracted towards the point of articulation of the following sound and may become slightly velarized. The diacritical sign ‿ can be placed under the vowel to indicate a degree of velarization. Velarization is most common when a precedes the consonants l and x and the vowels o and u. Examples: *salvo* sá̱lβo, *caja* ká̱xa, *ahogar* a̱oɣár, *caos* ká̱os, *bauprés* ba̱wprés, *aún* a̱ún.

u

6.7 **Close back vowel u.** Spanish u is pronounced with close lip-rounding and the back of the tongue raised high towards the soft palate. The timbre is similar to the u of French *rouge* and *RP rule* ruwl, but the vowel is much shorter than either of these, there is no tendency towards diphthongization as in *RP*, the lips are pushed well forward, and the lip-rounding is rather more close than for the first element of *RP* uw. Examples: *puro* púro, *dudar* duðár, *abertura* aβertúra. See fig. 9.

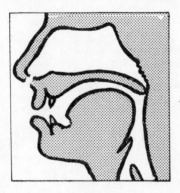

Fig. 9　u

NOTE

u̞. A slightly less close u, with the lips less forward, lip-rounding less close, and tongue position slightly lower (but not as low as for the short u of *RP full* ful, *good* gud) is found before x, before and after r̄, and in close syllables. Examples: *lujo* lú̞xo, *burro* bú̞r̄o *rudo* r̄ú̞ðo, *surco* sú̞rko, *gustar* gu̞stár, *puntero* pu̞ntéro.

i

6.8 **Close front vowel i.** Spanish i is pronounced with spread lips and the front of the tongue raised close to the hard palate. The timbre is similar to the i of French *vie, ici* and *RP tree* trij, *beak* bijk, but the duration is much shorter than that of *RP* ij. Examples: *pico* píko, *caudillo* kawðíʎo, *limón* limón, *sirena* siréna. See fig. 10.

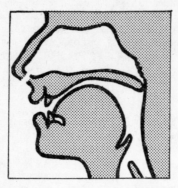

FIG. 10   i

NOTE

ḷ. A less close i, with the tongue position slightly lower (but nevertheless nearer to the close position of Spanish i than to the half-close position of *RP* ı in *fit* fıt, *think* θıŋk, *rich* rıtʃ). The allophone is found in the same phonetic contexts as open u̯ (6.7 n.). Examples: *hijo* íxo, *pirrico* pḭ́r̃iko, *rico* ŕ̃iko, *vista* bí̯sta, *barril* bar̃íl̯.

o

6.9 **Half-close back vowel o.** Spanish o is pronounced with lips slightly rounded and the back of the tongue raised towards the soft palate. The sound is not as close as the ọ of French *peau, côte*. It is less open and shorter than *RP* ɔ in *bog* bɔg, *sop* sɔp, and it differs from the ɜw of *home* hɜwm, *noble* nɜwbl in that its tongue position is much less advanced and in that it contains no element of diphthongization. Examples: *toro* tóro, *sacó* sakó, *sorbete* sorβéte. See fig. 11.

NOTE

ǫ. A slightly more open variant of o is found in certain circumstances. The back of the tongue is lower, and the vowel can be classified as half-open. It is

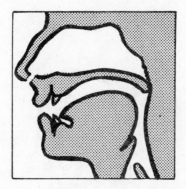

FIG. 11 o

not, however, as open as the sound written *o* in Frenche *note, pomme.*
Spanish ǫ is found:
1. Before x, as in *cojo* kǫ́xo, *escoger* eskǫxér, *alojero* alǫxéro.
2. Before and after r̄, as in *roca* r̄ǫ́ka, *porra* pǫ́ra, *rociada* r̄ǭθjáðǫ.
3. As the first element of a falling diphthong (7.10,7.12): *boina* bǫ́jna,
heroico erǫ́jko, *voy* bǫ́j.
4. In close syllables: *sordo* sǫ́r̄ðo, *sol* sǫ́l, *costa* kǫ́sta.

e

.10 **Half-close front vowel e.** Spanish e is pronounced with the lips spread and the
front of the tongue raised towards the hard palate. As with o, the sound is not
as close as the corresponding French vowel, in this case the ę of *pré, donner.*
It is more close than the vowel sound of *RP pen* pɛn, *death* dɛθ, *many*
mɛnɪ. It must also be distinguished from the ej diphthong of *RP make* mejk,
day dej, *weigh* wej: the Spanish vowel is more close than the first element of
the *RP* diphthong, and contains no element of diphthongization. Examples:
pera péra, *compré* kompré, *cabeza* kaβéθa. See fig. 12.

NOTE
ę. The allophone ę, a half-open vowel articulated with a tongue position
slightly lower than for Spanish close e, is similar to the vowel sound of *RP pen
death, many,* but slightly less open than the *e* of French *bel, même, perte.*
Spanish e is found in the same phonetic contexts as ǫ (6.9 n.): *teja* tę́xa,
remo r̄ę́mo, *perro* pę́r̄o, *peine* pę́jne, *deleite* delę́jte, *ley* lę́j, *papel* papę́l,
verdura bę̄rðúra, except that in a syllable closed by *m, n, s, d, z,* or *x +*
consonant the half-close vowel e is normal: *tiempo* tjémpo, *atento* aténto,
esta ésta, *huésped* wéspeð, *merezco* meréθko, *exponer* esponér, *respeto*
r̄espéto, *rentero* r̄entéro.

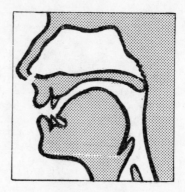

FIG. 12   e

6.11   Spanish has five vowel phonemes, /a/, /u/, /i/, /o/, /e/, which may distinguish between words which are otherwise identical sequences of sounds. Thus *paso, peso, piso, poso* and *puso* are distinguished one from the other only by the vowel phoneme which forms the syllabic nucleus. Each of the five vowel phonemes has a number of allophonic variants also capable of forming a syllabic nucleus. These are summarized in the following table.

PHONEME	ALLOPHONES
/a/	a in *caro* káro a̟ in *valle* báʎe a̠ in *caos* káos ā in *ambos* ámbos
/u/	u in *puro* púro u̞ in *lujo* lúxo ū in *umbral* ūmbrál
/i/	i in *pico* píko i̞ in *hijo* íxo ī in *niño* níɲo
/o/	o in *toro* tóro o̞ in *sol* sól õ in *once* ónθe
/e/	e in *pero* péro e̞ in *perro* pé̄ro ẽ in *enviar* ẽmbjár

Furthermore, each of these vowel phonemes suffers a slight relaxation in muscular tension when it occurs in an unstressed syllable.

6.12   The two phonemes /i/ and /u/ also have allophones j and w which are not capable of forming a syllabic nucleus (7.9 and n.). For the allophonic variant d͡j of the phoneme /i/, see 8.33–4.

6.13 As will be evident from 6.6–12, it is possible, in narrow phonetic transcriptions, to mark the small variations of timbre of each of the five vowel phonemes of Spanish according to the phonetic context of each and the position of the main stress accents in the rhythm group. These and finer distinctions are frequently essential to comparative and dialectal investigation, and may be found useful in some cases for practical language teaching. For the speaker whose mother tongue is English, however, the exercise of marking the finer distinctions in vowel quality in phonetic transcriptions brings little practical reward in terms of better pronunciation: it is in general more useful for him to be reminded of the uniformity of timbre of Spanish vowels in all positions than for his attention to be called to the slight variations in timbre, which, although in some cases (e.g. the distinction between e and ę, o and ǫ) perceptible to the Spanish ear, are never structurally significant. Accordingly, while in the detailed descriptions of the five vowel phonemes attention has been drawn in each case to the phonetic circumstances which produce positional variants, the simple allophonic transcription adopted throughout makes use only of the five vowel symbols **a, e, i, o, u.**

6.14 **FURTHER READING.** E. Alarcos (1948); (1965), II.2. J. B. Dalbor (1969), chs. 24–29, 32. P. Delattre (1966). D. Jones (1960), chs. 14 and 15. T. Navarro (1965), paras. 33–65. A. Quilis and J. A. Fernández (1964), ch. 5. G. L. Trager (1939), 217–18.

6.15 **EXERCISES ON CHAPTER 6**
1. Identify the close vowels in the following words: *hilo, puro, cara, mitin, infuso.*
2. Identify the front vowels in the following words: *junterilla, facultad, mentir, nitrocelulosa, humilde.*
3. Which two of the following words are most likely to be pronounced with a slightly nasalized vowel? *Santo, nombre, vencer, engarzar, cuenta.*
4. In which of the following words does the allophone ǫ appear? *Flojel, flota, terminó, romper, corro, estoy, boicotear, largo, roja, farol.*
5. In which of the following words does the allophone ę appear? *perico, excavar, reja, desde, leila, siempre, respigón, hablé, pereza, merezco.*

7 SPANISH SEMIVOWELS IN GREATER DETAIL. DIPHTHONGS AND TRIPHTHONGS. SYNALEPHA. THE CONJUNCTIONS 'y' AND 'u'

SEMIVOWELS

7.1 The Spanish semivowels are gliding sounds which are not capable of forming the nucleus of a syllable. A semivowel may take one of three forms:

(a) **Onglides.** In the articulation of a semivowel which occurs between consonant and vowel, as in *fuera* fwéra, *sueño* swéɲo, *fiel* fjél, *sierra* sjéra, the speech-organs start from the position of a fairly close vowel sound **u** or **i** and immediately move to a vowel sound of greater prominence. The timbre of the rapid glide thus produced is not uniform over the whole length of the sound: in an onglide the semivowel opens progressively towards the following vowel.

(b) **Offglides.** When a semivowel occurs between vowel and consonant, as in *pausa* páwsa, laurel lawrél, *baile* bájle, *naipe* nájpe, the reverse process takes place. Under these circumstances the speech-organs move rapidly from their position for the preceding vowel to take up their position for **u** or **i.** This gliding sound is also rapid, and uneven in timbre over its length; in an offglide the semivowel closes progressively.

(c) **Consonantal value.** Between vowels, or initial in a syllable, as in *playa* plája, *ahuesado* awesáðo, *póyo* pójo, *huelga* wélɣa, a semivowel remains fairly uniform over its length, and there may be a slight amount of audible friction.

7.2 In simple allophonic transcriptions, the phonetic symbols w and j are used to represent all semivowels, whether their function is that of an onglide, an offglide or a consonant, since the position of the semivowel in the syllable makes it quite clear which variety is indicated. The w of *bueno* bwéno occurs between consonant and vowel and is an onglide; the w of *causa* káwsa occurs between vowel and consonant and is an offglide; the w of *ahuecar* awekár is intervocalic and has consonantal value. Similarly, the j of *bien* bjén is an onglide, the j of *ley* léj is an offglide, and the j of *raya* rája has consonantal value.

NOTE
In more narrow allophonic transcripts the symbols w and j may be reserved for onglides — *bueno* bwéno, *bien* bjén; the symbols u̯ and i̯ may be adopted for offglides — *causa* káu̯sa, *peine* péi̯ne — and the symbols w̆ and j̆ for consonants — *hueco* w̆éko, *mayo* máj̆o (cf. T. Navarro, 1965, Quilis and Fernández, 1964, B. Malmberg, 1948, 117).

w	and	j

w LABIO-VELAR SEMIVOWEL. Written *u, hu*

.3 **In onglides.** Pronounced with voice and close lip-rounding, as for the vowel **u**, but with the back of the tongue initially raised higher towards the soft palate to narrow the air passage. The air passage is rapidly widened by increasing the gap between tongue and soft palate until the speech-organs begin to form the following vowel. Spanish w has closer lip-rounding and a greater degree of tension than the sound written *w* in English *twelve, swim, wait*, or that written *u* in English *suite, quite, equivalent*. The onglide is the sound of *u* when it occurs between a consonant and a vowel. Examples: *bueno* bwéno, *prueba* prwéβa, *vacuo* bákwo, *su hijo* swíxo.

.4 **In offglides.** The glide consists of a rapid transition between the vowel which precedes and the lip and tongue position for the vowel **u**. Again, Spanish w has closer lip-rounding and a greater degree of tension than its nearest English equivalent, the sound written *w* in English *cow, how, town*, or that written *u* in English *sound, out, bough*. The offglide is the sound of *u* when it occurs between a vowel and a consonant. Examples: *jaula* xáwla, *neutro* néwtro, *se usaba* sewsáβa.

.5 **As a consonant.** In the formation of consonantal w the aperture between tongue and velum may be slightly narrower than for the glide, and the lips more closely rounded. Consonantal w tends to be more even over its length than either the onglide or the offglide, but the sound is not sufficiently distinctive to justify the use of a separate phonetic symbol in simple allophonic transcriptions. Consonantal w is the usual pronunciation of *hu* or *u* between vowels or initial in a syllable. Examples: *ahuecar* awekár, *deshuesar* deşwesar, *este u otro* éste wótro, *mujeres u hombres* muxéreş wómbres, *soy huérfano* sój wérfano, *hueco* wéko, *huida* wíða, *las huertas* laş wértas.

NOTES
1. gw and ɣw. In popular speech, and dialectally both in Spain and Spanish America, the initial velar element of consonantal w tends to be further strengthened, and a fricative or plosive sound appears at the beginning of a syllable. This sound is a velar g, plosive or fricative according to the phonetic surroundings (8.12–13): *huerta* gwérta, *la huerta* la ɣwérta, *un hueco* uŋ gwéko, *ahuecar* aɣwekár.
2. In substandard speech it is the labial element of w which is strengthened, and bw or βw, according to phonetic context (8.4–5), replaces w: *hueco* bwéko, *ahuecar* aβwekár. This alternation bw/gw leads to confusion in other words, with gw or ɣw frequently replacing bw or βw in words such as *bueno* – pronounced gwéno – and *abuela* – pronounced aɣwéla.
3. The pronunciations w and gw, ɣw are alternative and equally acceptable pronunciations. Compare the alternatives *agua* áɣwa or áwa,

la guardia la ɣwárðja or la wárðja described in 8.13 n. 1. The conjunction *u* is not normally strengthened: *una u otra* úna wótra, *siete u ocho* sjéte wótʃo (7.23).

j UNROUNDED PALATAL SEMIVOWEL. Written *i, hi, y.*

7.6   **In onglides.** Pronounced with voice and with spread lips, as for the vowel **i**, but with the front of the tongue initially raised higher towards the hard palate to narrow the air passage. The gap between tongue and hard palate is rapidly widened until the speech-organs begins to form the following vowel. Spanish **j** is a more close and more tense sound than English *y* in *yellow, yard, beyond* or English *i* in *million, India.* The onglide is the sound of *i* when it occurs between a consonant and a vowel. Examples: *pie* pjé, *diario* djárjo, *lacio* láθjo, *mi acción* mjaɣθjón.

7.7   **In offglides.** The glide consists of a rapid transition between the vowel which precedes and the lip and tongue position for the vowel **i**. The Spanish offglide is a more close and a more tense sound than its nearest equivalent, which forms the second part of the diphthong written **i** in English *file* fajl, *rind* rajnd *smite* smajt or that written *y* in English *fly* flaj, *boy* bɔj, *employ* əmplɔj. The offglide is the sound of *i* or *y* where it occurs between a vowel and a consonant. Examples: *caigo* kájɣo, *estoico* estójko, *soy Juan* sój xwán. It is also the sound of *y* when it is final in a syllable before a pause. Examples: *ley* léj, *doy* dój, *hay* áj.

7.8   **As a consonant.** The speech-organs take up a position similar to that for the onglide **j**, but the aperture between tongue and palate is often narrower, so that air escapes with slight audible friction. The sound is more uniform over its length than that of the onglide or the offglide but, like consonantal **w**, may be denoted in simple allophonic IPA transcriptions by the same phonetic symbol, since the vocalic and the consonantal varieties have not been found to exist as separate phonemes in any language (IPA, *Principles,* 1949, 13). This is the usual sound of *y* and *hi* where they occur between vowels. Examples: *mayo* májo, *mi yerno* mi jérno, *la hierba* la jérβa, *delgado y alto* delɣáðo jálto, *canta y habla* kánta jáβla.

NOTES
1. Consonantal **j** is one of the most unstable sounds of Spanish. In some areas such as Galicia, where the sound may be very open and relaxed, its timbre approximates to that of the vowel **i**. In other areas, notably in the Argentine and in some parts of Andalusia and New Castile, there is a strong element of friction, and in the strong, syllable-initial position it is pronounced as ʒ or d͡ʒ without lip-rounding: *mayo* máʒo or mád͡ʒo, *mi yerno* mi ʒérno or mi d͡ʒérno. These are the extremes, and individual speakers may be heard to use these or almost any intermediate sound. In areas where *y* is pronounced as a fricative or affricate sound, the distinction between its articulation in the syllable-final and in the syllable-initial position is very marked indeed: *ley* léj but *leyes* lé-ʒes or lé-d͡ʒes.

2. In some phonetic contexts the sounds written *y, hi* are regularly pronounced as a palatal affricate consonant d͡ʒ (8.33).

,9   The speech-sounds i and j can be assigned to the same phoneme /i/ in Spanish, since they occur only as positional variants – *filo* **fílo**, *bien* **bjén**, *pláya* **plája**, *ley* **léj**, *leyes* **léjes**, *raíz* **raî̄θ**, *raicilla* **rajθíʎa**. Similarly, u and w occur only as positional variants, and can be assigned to the phoneme /u/ – *puro* **púro**, *bueno* **bwéno**, *causa* **káwsa**, *ahuecar* **awekár**, *usaron* **usáron**, *no usaron* **nówsáron**. One consequence of the assignment of i and j to the same phoneme /i/, and of u and w to the same phoneme /u/, is that it must be accepted that certain sounds form the syllabic nucleus (i.e. function as vowels) in some contexts, and in others appear on the syllabic margins (which is normal for consonants). The occurrence of a phoneme which comprises both vowel and consonant members is comparatively rare, but not without parallels in other languages. In *RP* 1 functions as a vowel in *bottle*, where it forms a syllable by itself, and as a consonant in *life;* D. Jones (1950, 85–7) draws attention to similar cases, including that of the Italian phoneme /i/, which has subsidiary members i and j, and A. Martinet (1964, 3.21) argues, for circumstances similar to those prevailing in Spanish, that 'there is no point in distinguishing two phonemes, one vocalic and one consonantal'.

Summary

PHONEME	SEMIVOWEL	ALLOPHONE		
/u/	w	*tuerto* twérto,	*cuarto*	kwárto
		pauta páwta,	*reunir*	ꝛewnír
		huella wéʎa,	*huir*	wír
/i/	j	*tieso* tjéso,	*viaje*	bjáxe
		reino ꝛéjno,	*baile*	bájle
		vaya bája	*puyazo*	pujáθo

NOTE
The manner of using a sound may in certain circumstances be taken into account in determining its phonemic status. As a result linguists have differed widely in their phonemic interpretation of the speech-sounds which are analysed in this book as allophones of the phonemes /i/ and /u/. The controversy has involved both the number of phonemes represented by these speech-sounds and the question of their phonemic status. T. Navarro (1918 and later editions) does not attempt a phonemic analysis; more recently, however, three scholars in particular have put forward contrasting views. Since all three use different phonetic systems, each of the following three schemata is presented with IPA symbols (with the additional symbol /y/ to represent a palatal consonant phoneme), in order to facilitate comparison.

1. **G. L. Trager** (1939). Trager's scheme, based upon the data presented by T. Navarro (1918), is:

PHONEME	ALLOPHONES
/i/	j, i̯
/u/	w, u̯
/ʒ/	j, d͡ʒ

Trager does not mention consonantal w.

2. **J. D. Bowen and R. P. Stockwell (1955)**

PHONEME	ALLOPHONES
/i/	
/u/	
/y/	j, d͡j, i̞
/w/	w, gw, u̞

Bowen and Stockwell differ from earlier scholars by attributing j, d͡j and i̞
to the consonantal phoneme /y/, and arguing for the existence of a
consonantal phoneme /w/, to which they attribute the allophones w, gw and u̞.
Sol Saporta (1956) appears to accept Bowen and Stockwell's four phonemes,
but argues that the allocation of j and i̞, w and u̞ to consonantal phonemes
creates more problems than it solves. Bowen and Stockwell (1956) defend
their position against Saporta.

3. **E. Alarcos (1965)**

PHONEME	ALLOPHONES
/i/	j, i̞
/u/	w, u̞
/y/	j, d͡j
/g/ + /u/	w, gw, ɣw

Basing himself on the premise that there is a difference in kind between
vowels and consonants, Alarcos argues (with Trager and against Bowen and
Stockwell) for three phonemes rather than four. Unlike Trager, he deals with
the problem of consonantal w, gw, ɣw, which he analyses as allophones of the
combination of phonemes /g/ + /u/.

DIPHTHONGS

7.10   The diphthongs of Spanish are combinations of vowels and glides which
       together constitute one syllable (5.16–17). A diphthong may be formed in
       one of two ways:

(a) A vowel is preceded by an onglide. In this case, since the vowel is the more
prominent of the two elements, there is a continuous increase in perceptibility
over the length of the combination, which is described as a rising diphthong.
Examples: wa in *cuanto* kwánto, je in *siete* sjéte.

(b) A vowel is followed by an offglide, when there is a continuous fall in
perceptibility over the length of the combination, which is described as a
falling diphthong. Examples: aw in *causa* káwsa, ej in *treinta* tréjnta.
In both types the more prominent of the two sounds, the vowel, forms the
nucleus of the syllable and bears the main stress in that syllable.

11 **Rising diphthongs.** In diphthongs which consist of semivowel plus vowel, the speech-organs glide from a relatively close position to a relatively open one. The syllabic nucleus is always the second element, the vowel. Spanish has eight rising diphthongs:

wa	*agua* á-ɣwa	*puntual* pun-twál
	suave swáβe	*aduana* a-ðwá-na
we	*fuera* fwé-ra	*puente* pwén-te
	nuez nwéθ	*luego* lwé-ɣo
wi	*muy* mwí	*ruido* r̄wí-ðo
	suiza swí-θa	*pituita* pi-twí-ta
wo	*antiguo* an-tí-ɣwo	*cuota* kwó-ta
	arduo ár-ðwo	*duodenal* dwo-ðe-nál
ja	*hacia* á-θja	*arriar* a-r̄já̇r
	diálogo djá-lo-ɣo	*viaje* bjá-xe
je	*pie* pjé	*miedo* mjé-ðo
	tienta tjén-ta	*piélago* pjé-la-ɣo
jo	*vio* bjó	*radio* r̄á-ðjo
	idiota i-ðjó-ta	*comercio* ko-mér-θjo
ju	*ciudad* θju-ðáð	*piular* pju-lár
	diurno djúr-no	*viuda* bjú-ða

NOTES
1. Unlike English, Spanish does not generally admit the combinations **wu, ji**: cf. English *swoon* swuwn, *woo* wuw, *yield* jïjld, *yeast* jïjst. The only exceptions to this, apart from a few loan words, are rare diminutives of the type *mayico* majîko, *rayita* r̄ajíta.
2. For the onglide in a rising diphthong, the majority of Spanish writers, including T. Navarro (1965), E. Alarcos (1950) and Quilis and Fernández (1964), use the term **semiconsonante**.

.12 **Falling diphthongs.** In diphthongs which consist of vowel plus semivowel the speech-organs glide from a relatively open position to a relatively close one. The syllabic nucleus is always the first element — the vowel. Eight falling diphthongs are possible in Spanish.

aw	*auto* áw-to	*raudo* r̄áw-ðo
	caudal kaw-ðál	*la uñeta* law-ɲé-ta
ew	*neutro* néw-tro	*deuda* déw-ða
	feudal few-ðál	*se unió* sew-njó
iw	*vi humazo* bíw-má-θo	*colibrí uruguayo* ko-li-βríw-ru-ɣwá-jo
	salí huyendo sa-líw-jén-do	*jabalí unicolor* xa-βa-líw-ni-ko-lór
ow	*no usó nada* nów-só-ná-ða	*lo humilló* low-mi-ʎó
	sólo usted só-lows-té	*encargo urgente* eŋ-kár-ɣowr-xén-te

aj	*fraile* fráj-le	*paisaje* paj-sá-xe	
	vainilla baj-ní-ʎa	*Juana y Juan* xwá-naj-xwán	
ej	*ley* léj	*treinta* tréjn-ta	
	aceite a-θéj-te	*de hijuelos* dej-xwé-los	
oj	*doy* dój	*boina* bój-na	
	heroico e-rój-ko	*lo influye* lojŋ-flú-je	
uj	*vermú italiano* ber-múj-ta-ljá-no	*el Perú imperial* el-pe-rújm-pe-rjál	
	cucú inaudible ku-kúj-naw-ði-βle	*ñandú imponente* ɲan-dújm-po-nén-te	

NOTES
1. The combination iw is extremely uncommon. It occurs in the Catalan place-name *San Feliu* saṃ-fe-líw but otherwise only in the rare cases when a final stressed -í of one word precedes initial u- of another word in a rhythm group (see 'Synalepha', 7.15).
2. Apart from unusual forms like *bou* bów 'fishing with a net dragged by two boats' and the proper name *Bousoño* bow-só-ɲə the combination ow occurs only when final -o of one word precedes initial u- of another word in a rhythm group (See 'Synalepha', 7.15).
3. The offglide in a falling diphthong, because of its short duration and its relative lack of prominence, is sometimes described as a **consonantal vowel**. T. Navarro (1965), E. Alarcos (1950) and Quilis and Fernández (1964) use the term **semivocal**.

7.13   Although the term 'diphthong' is a convenient one for descriptive purposes, the combinations of sounds which are treated as monosyllabic in Spanish are not diphthongs in the strict sense of the term. D. Jones (1960), para. 219, defines a diphthong as 'an independent vowel-glide not containing within itself either a "peak" or "trough" of prominence'. The Spanish diphthongs are vowel-glides in that each contains either an onglide or an offglide. They contain no peak or trough of prominence in that one end of the diphthong is always more prominent than the other, so that there is a continuous increase or decrease in prominence. But they are not 'independent', since under certain circumstances the two parts of the diphthong may be distributed over two syllables, when the offglide becomes consonantal: *rey* r̄éj, but *reyes* r̄é-jes; hoy ój, but *oy es tarde* ó-jés-tár-ðe. Equally, the diphthong may come into being as a result of *synalepha* (7.15–21), when two normally independent vowel sounds, adjacent in a rhythm group, are combined to form one syllable in the form of a falling diphthong: *compré una casa* kom-préw-na-ká-sa, *las cinco y media* las-θíŋ-koj-mé-ðja. Spanish diphthongs are not single phonemes but two independent phonemes which are combined to form one syllable;[1] here they differ in kind from RP diphthongs like the ej of *plain* plejn, the ɜw of *home* hɜwm, the aj of *time* tajm, the aw of *loud* lawd.

----

[1] Cf. Trubetzkoy (1935; trans. Murray 1968), rule V: 'Only a sound group the constituent parts of which, in the language concerned, are never spread over two syllables, can be regarded as a realization of one single phoneme.'

which are indivisible and monophonemic. For a more detailed treatment of the
Spanish diphthongs see E. Alarcos (1965), para. 96, from which the Spanish
examples are taken. For the English diphthongs see D. Jones (1960), paras.
219–33, 378–466.

TRIPHTHONGS

14 The triphthongs of Spanish consist of the combination onglide + vowel +
offglide. The syllabic nucleus is always the central sound, the vowel.
Examples:

situáis si-twájs	*buey* bwéj
miau mjáw	*guau* gwáw

Spanish triphthongs are combinations of three phonemes which together
constitute one syllable. Within a word, Spanish triphthongs rise to and fall
from a peak of prominence which is always the central vowel. Triphthongs and
larger groups of vowels formed in synalepha may rise or fall in prominence, or
may have a central peak of prominence (7.18).

SYNALEPHA

15 In Spanish two successive vowels which are normally in hiatus within a single
word may be run together, in syneresis, to form a single syllable (5.15–16):
peonada pe-o-ná-ða or peo-ná-ða, *aeropuerto* a-e-ro-pwér-to or ae-ro-pwér-to.
A similar type of process occurs, with greater frequency, when two or more
vowels of different words which come into contact in a rhythm group are
combined to form a single syllable: *me ocurre* me-o-kú-r̄e or meo-kú-r̄e, *para
él* pa-ra-él or pa-raél. This process, whereby the final vowel or vowels of one
word may be combined with the initial vowel or vowels of the following word
in a rhythm group to form a single syllable, is known as **synalepha**. Spanish has
no glottal stop ʔ (3.17 n.1): in a group like *mira atrás*, where the native English
speaker is capable of separating the final *a* of *mira* from the initial *a* of *atrás* by
bringing his vocal cords together and completely closing the glottis for an
instant between the two vowels – **mira ʔ atrás** – the Spanish speaker does not
do so. In Spanish the group is pronounced with the vocal cords vibrating continuously over the whole length of the central vowel. In slow, careful speech
this may be articulated as a comparatively long vowel, spread over two syllables –
mí-ra-a-trás: more commonly the combination is reduced to a single vowel of
normal length – **mí-ra-trás**.

16 Two like vowels which come together in a rhythm group are pronounced in
the same syllable: *para hacerlo* pa-ra-θér-lo, *le echa fuera* le-tʃa-fwé-ra, *casi
igual* ká-si-ɣwál, *todo oficio* tó-ðo-fí-θjo.

17 Two unlike vowels which come together in a rhythm group combine to form
a single syllable: *se puede hacer* se-pwé-ðea-θér, *un oído experto* ú-no-í-ðoes-
pér-to, *una holandesa* ú-nao-lan-dé-sa, *se allana el pais* sea-ʎá-nael-pa-ís. When
one of the vowels is *u* or *i*, it is pronounced, according to its position in the

syllable, as an onglide or offglide: *su hermano* swer-má-no, *la undécima* lawn-dé-θi-ma, *mi oficio* mjo-fí-θjo, *esta idea* és-taj-ðé-a.
Exceptionally, hiatus (5.16) may be preferred when the words involved are strongly emphasized in the rhythm group: *no hay nada* nó-áj-ná-ða, *su hijo y el tuyo* sú-í-xo-jel-tú-jo, *la 'r' y la 'rr' son fonemas* la-é-re-i-la-é-r̄e-sóm̩-fo-né-mas. Hiatus may also occur, especially in verse, when the contiguous vowels come at the end of a rhythm group: *ella compró una* é-ʎa-kom-pró-ú-na, *no sabía que iba* nó-sa-βí-a-ke-í-βa, *ampara el sueño* am-pá-ra-el-swé-ɲo, *de hora ufana* de-ó-ra-ú-fá-na.

7.18   When more than two unlike vowels come together, they may be combined to form a single syllable provided that the syllable contains a continuous rise or a continuous fall in prominence, or a peak of prominence.
(a) **Continuous rise in prominence.** Examples:

> *uoa:*   *su mutuo amor* su-mú-twoa-mór
> *iea:*   *no está nadie aquí* nóes-tá-ná-ðjea-kí
> *ioa:*   *un genio astuto* úŋ-xé-njoas-tú-to

(b) **Continuous fall in prominence:** Examples:

> *aoi:*   *para oidores* pa-raoj-ðó-res
> *aeu:*   *hablaba Eugenia* a-βlá-βaew-xé-nja
> *aei:*   *sagrada e inmortal* sa-ɣrá-ðaej^m-mor-tál

(c) **Peak of prominence.** Examples:

> *ueu:*   *fue una chica* fwéw-na-t͡ʃí-ka
> *uoi:*   *su antiguo instituto* swan-tí-ɣwojns-ti-tú-to
> *eai:*   *línea indecisa* lí-neajn-de-θí-sa
> *iou:*   *necio ultraje* né-θjowl-trá-xe
> *oai:*   *no hay nada* noáj-ná-ða
> *ioaeu:* *envidio a Eusebio* em-bí-ðjoaew-sé-βjo

7.19   Where a combination of vowels contains a trough of prominence, the vowels are spread over two syllables. Examples:

> *aui:*   *la huida* la-wí-ða
> *aie:*   *mucha hierba* mú-t͡ʃa-jér-βa
> *aoa:*   *roja o amarilla* r̄ó-xa-oa-ma-rí-ʎa
> *eie:*   *calle y escuche* ká-ʎe-jes-kú-t͡ʃe
> *eue:*   *parece huérfano* pa-ré-θe-wér-fa-no
> *oie:*   *todo hierro* tó-ðo-jé-r̄o
> *ouo:*   *uno u otro* ú-no-wó-tro

The trough of prominence is created when a less perceptible vowel occurs between two more perceptible vowels. Usually, but not always, the less perceptible vowel begins the second syllable, especially when the conjunctions *y, o, u* are involved: *canta y habla* kán-ta-já-βla, *siete u ocho* sjé-te-wo-t͡ʃo, *canta o habla* kán-ta-oá-βla. In some cases, however, it may be grouped with either the first or the second syllable: *voy a ver* bój-a-βér or bó-ja-βér, *ya he acabado* d͡jáe-a-ka-βá-ðo or d͡já-ea-ka-βá-do, *la huida* law-í-ða or la-wí-ða.

20 A group of vowels which contains *a, e* or *o* with stressed *i* or *u* is not normally reduced to a single syllable:

aoí	*para oírlo* pa-rao-ír-lo
íae:	*recibía en su casa* r̄e-θi-β í-aen-su-ká-sa
úao:	*continúa hojeando* kon-ti-nú-ao-xe-án-do

21 The nucleus of a syllable is always its more or most open vowel. Consequently, when the process of synalepha brings unlike vowels together to form a single accented syllable, the main stress in that syllable tends to fall upon the more or most perceptible of the vowels. As a result, the stressed vowel in a group brought together in synalepha may be a vowel which is not normally stressed when the word to which it belongs is pronounced in isolation. For example, *hizo*, pronounced in isolation, bears a natural stress on its first syllable: í-θo. In the group *lo hizo*, the final *o* of *lo* and the initial *í* of *hízo* may be combined in synalepha to form the diphthong oj (7.17). In this case the stress shifts from the i of *hizo* to the o of *lo*, the more open of the two elements of the diphthong: *lo hizo* lój-θo. Similarly the natural stress accent on the u of *unen* will shift to the e of *se* when the group *se unen* is pronounced with synalepha: séw-nen. The vowel *a*, especially the preposition *a*, has a particularly strong tendency to attract the accent: *unos a otros* ú-no-sáo-tros, *junto a ellos* xún-toáe-ʎos.

Further examples:

> *de una vez* déw-na-β éθ
> *venció a un enemigo* ben-θjoáw-ne-ne-mí-ɣo
> *revela a otros* r̄e-β é-láo-tros
> *ya he acabado* d͡já-eá-ka-β á-ðo
> *encontró a su marido* eŋ-kon-troá-su-ma-ri-ðo
> *su madre iba* su-má-ðréj-β a
> *pero ahora no* pe-roáo-ra-nó
> *vale para uno* bá-le-pa-ráw-no

NOTE
When *e* and *o* come together in a stressed syllable as a result of synalepha, the accent may fall on either: éo, óe, or eó, oé, with a slight preference for the rising diphthongs eó and oé:

éo:	*no sé organizar* nó-séor-ɣa-ni-θár
óe:	*rompió en aplausos* r̄om-pjóe-na-pláw-sos
eó:	*compré hongos* kom-preóŋ-gos
oé:	*lo comió ella* lo-ko-mjoé-ʎa

THE CONJUNCTION 'y'

7.22   The pronunciation of the conjunction *y* in the rhythm group depends upon
        its phonetic context.

        (a) **Between consonants,** it is pronounced as a vowel: *ir y venir* í-ri-β e-nír,
        Juan y Pepe xwá-ni-pé-pe, *hiel y vinagre* d͡je-li-βi-ná-ɣre.

        (b) **Initial in a rhythm group** it is pronounced i before a consonant, and j
        before a vowel: *y se acabó* i-sea-ka-βó, *y ¿ qué hicieron?* i-kéj-θjé-ron,
        y-así continuaba ja-sí-kon-ti-nwá-βa, *y uno más* jú-no-más.

        (c) **Elsewhere** it is pronounced j. Between consonant and vowel, or between
        vowel and consonant, this j is a glide which is grouped syllabically with the near-
        est vowel: *toman y echan* tó-ma-ɲjé-t͡ʃan *feliz y alegre* fe-lí-θja-lé-ɣre, *blanco y*
        negro blán-koj-né-ɣro, *alegre y feliz* a-lé-ɣrej-fe-líθ, *tú y yo* túj-jó,
        carne y hueso kár-nej-wé-so. Between vowels, j functions as a consonant (7.8),
        and is grouped syllabically with the following vowel: *grande y alto*
        grán-de-jál-to, *diciembre y enero* di-θjém-bre-je-né-ro, *canta y habla*
        kán-ta-já-βla.

THE CONJUNCTION 'u'

7.23   This occurs only before words beginning with *(h)o,* where it is pronounced as
        consonantal w (7.5) and grouped syllabically with the following vowel:
        una u otra ú-na-wó-tra, *siete u ocho* sjé-te-wó-t͡ʃo, *mujeres u hombres*
        mu-xé-reş-wóm-bres, *amor u odio* a-mór-wó-ðjo.

7.24   **FURTHER READING.** E. Alarcos (1965), paras. 96–100. J. D. Bowen and
        R. P. Stockwell (1955), 236–40; (1956), 290–92. J. B. Dalbor (1969),
        chs. 28–30, 32. A. M. Espinosa (1924), 299–309. International Phonetic
        Association, *Principles* (1949). D. Jones (1950), chs. 14–16; (1960), chs. 12,
        15, 22. D. Jones and I. Dahl (1944). A. Martinet (1964), ch. 3. T. Navarro
        (1965), paras. 48–50, 64–9. K. L. Pike (1947a), 151–9. A. Quilis and
        J. A. Fernández (1964), chs. 6 and 14. S. Saporta (1956), 287–90.
        G. L. Trager (1939), 217, 220.

7.25   **EXERCISES ON CHAPTER 7.**
        1. Transcribe phonetically (in each word the phonetic symbols for the
        consonants correspond to the letters used in normal Spanish orthography):
        fuera, serio, traía, faisán, peine, mutuo, limpiáis, fiambre, neumonía, pausa,
        soy, tieso, suite, tuatúa, alías.
        2. Which of the following words contain a rising diphthong? *Cualidad, seudo,*
        servicio, requiere, deleitar, acentúa, llegué, estoicismo, sueco, envían,
        cuidado, pausa, viuda, chirriar, paisano.
        3. Divide these rhythm groups into syllables, and transcribe phonetically any
        diphthong which may be created through synalepha: *cada hoguera;*
        ¿ de qué sirve el rey? cuando el aire es sútil; se hallan dos tumbas; empieza a

hablar; hizo una manea; lo unificó entonces; burbujeó el agua; antes no acontecía y ahora sí; la idea de iniciarlo.

4. Divide these rhythm groups into syllables, and transcribe phonetically any diphthong or triphthong which may be created through synalepha: *ya le trae una camarera; corría hacia el cordel; desfallecía en arrobo inefable; de habla eufónica; en perpetua embriaguez; vino a enterarse; los había instruído una y otra vez; el indio explotado y oprimido; voy en seguida; el prejuicio europeo.*

5. Read the following phonetic transcripts aloud, and write each one out in normal Spanish orthography: **dés-te-mo-mén-to; ma-té-rjan-te-rjór; ál-toj-trís-te; laes-pó-sa-je-les-pó-so; pen-sár-wo-pi-nár; ó-ra-sjó-ras; per-mí-teáo-tros; pró-sa-li-te-rá-rjaew-ro-pé-a; nó-tjé-ne-jél; swin-tér-pre-te.**

8 PLOSIVE, FRICATIVE AND AFFRICATE CONSONANTS IN GREATER DETAIL

8.1 In the formation of plosive consonants like the *b* of *bata* or the *d* of *dueño* the breath is completely stopped at some point in the mouth, whether by the lips or by the tongue, and then released with a sharp explosion. For fricative consonants like the *f* of *faja* or the *s* of *sueño* air is forced through a narrow opening in the mouth, where it causes audible friction of various kinds. Affricate consonants like the *ch* of *chico* are formed as plosive consonants, but with slow separation of the articulating organs, so that a fricative sound is audible as the separation takes place.

8.2 In the articulation of the English voiced plosive consonants **b** as in *boy*, **d** as in *den*, **g** as in *gun*, the vocal cords begin to vibrate at the same time as the speech-organs separate to make the explosion. In Spanish the vocal cords begin to vibrate a fraction of a second **before** the speech-organs separate. As a result, if Spanish plosives are pronounced in an English way, there is a danger that the Spanish hearer, aware of less voice than he expects, will interpret what he hears as the voiceless equivalents **p, t, k**, hearing *peso* for *beso*, *tomar* for *domar*, *coma* for *goma*, and so on. It is essential for any learner of Spanish whose mother tongue is English to practise early voicing of the Spanish voiced plosives, making sure that he articulates them with the vocal cords vibrating audibly while the air passage is still blocked, and before the moment of explosion.

p	b	β

8.3 **p. Voiceless bilabial plosive.** Written *p.* The air passage is completely blocked by closing the lips and raising the soft palate while the rest of the mouth takes up its position for the following vowel or consonant. When the lips are opened, the trapped air suddenly escapes with an explosive sound. The vocal cords do not vibrate. Examples: *pata* **páta**, *capa* **kápa**, *playa* **plája**, *cumple* **kúmple**. See fig. 13.

NOTES
1. Spanish **p** is pronounced with a sharp, crisp explosion of breath. In this respect, it differs markedly from the **p** of *RP*, which, especially when it is followed by a stressed vowel, is accompanied by an audible puff of breath most commonly represented phonetically by ^{h}: *park* **p^{h}ɑk**, *pool* **p^{h}uwl**, *pardon* **p^{h}ɑdn**. Spanish **p** is never followed by this aspiration.
2. For implosive **p**, see 8.16, 8.19.

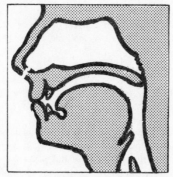

FIG. 13   p, b

b. Voiced bilabial plosive. written *b* or *v*. The plosive b of Spanish is formed with the speech-organs as for p, but with the vocal cords vibrating. It is a weaker consonant than p, in that breath is pushed out by the lungs with slightly less force. Spanish b is found at the beginning of a rhythm group, and after the nasal m, written *m* or *n* (9.7): *basta* **básta**, *vale* **bále**, *ambos* **ámbos** *enviar* **embjár**, *un buen viaje* **úm bwém bjáxe.**

NOTE
When b appears at the beginning of a rhythm group the vocal cords begin to vibrate fractionally before the lips separate (8.2). The articulation of Spanish b should present few problems. It is the same sound as in English *bat, bull, blood* etc., and its main variants occur in the same phonetic contexts as in English. It occurs, however, much less frequently in Spanish than in English — in normal unemphatic speech only in the two positions mentioned above.

β. **Voiced bilabial fricative.** Written *b* or *v*. Spanish fricative β is formed with the speech-organs as for b, but with no complete stoppage of breath at the lips. The lips are held slightly apart, and breath is allowed to escape

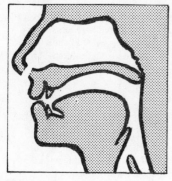

FIG. 14   β

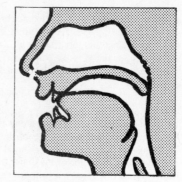

FIG. 15   t, d

continuously, with audible friction. Fricative β is the sound of *b* and *v* in all positions except at the beginning of a rhythm group or after a nasal: *ave* áβe, *cabra* káβra, *alba* álβa, *no vale* nó βále, *el bolo* el βólo, *para vender* para βendér. See fig. 14.

NOTES
1. The fricative sound β does not exist in English.
2. For the pronunciation of *p* and *b* in an implosive position, see 8.16, 8.19.

8.6   The phonemes /p/ and /b/ distinguish between minimal pairs such as *pata* and *bata*, *paso* and *vaso*, *cupo* and *cubo*, *rapo* and *rabo*. The speech sounds b and β are allophonic variants of the phoneme /b/ and occur in complementary distribution.

8.7   **t. Voiceless dental plosive.** Written *t*. The air passage is completely blocked by raising the soft palate and raising the tip of the tongue to touch the inside of the upper front teeth. Air is trapped briefly, and when the tongue is removed from the teeth the air escapes with an explosive sound. The vocal cords do not vibrate. Examples: *tomo* tómo, *traje* tráxe, *cinta* θínta, *puerta* pwérta. See fig. 15.

NOTES
1. Spanish t differs in two respects from the *t* sound of *RP*. In *RP* t is a consonant articulated with the tip of the tongue against the alveoles. Spanish t is a **dental** sound, articulated with the tongue pushed well forward, clear of the gums, and touching the teeth. Moreover, *RP* t is aspirated in the same way as p (when followed by a vowel in a stressed syllable): *tap* t^{h}æp, *take* t^{h}ejk, *tool* t^{h}uwl. Spanish t is sharply exploded, with no trace of aspiration.
2. For the pronunciation of implosive t see 8.18, 8.19.

8.8   **d. Voiced dental plosive.** Written *d*. Plosive d is formed with the speech-organs as for t, but with the vocal cords vibrating. It is articulated with less force than its voiceless counterpart. The plosive sound occurs when d is initial in a rhythm group, and after the consonants n or l: *dan* dán, *dueña* dwéɲa, *caldo* káldo, *andan* ándan, *son decanos* són dekános, *píldora,* píldora, *el dato* el dáto.

NOTES
1. When d is initial in a rhythm group the vocal cords begin to vibrate fractionally before the tip of the tongue is removed from the teeth (8.2).
2. Spanish d, like Spanish t, is a **dental** sound, articulated with the tip of the tongue against the inside of the upper front teeth, and contrasting with the English alveolar d of *dash, down, hiding*. Since the d sounds of both languages are voiced neither is liable to be followed by an aspiration.

.9 ð. **Voiced (inter)dental fricative.** Written *d*. The fricative sound is formed with the tip of the tongue pushed slightly further forward than for **d**, so that it lightly touches the bottom edge of the upper front teeth. The outward flow of air is constricted but not completely stopped, and the vocal cords vibrate. The fricative sound is the sound of *d* in all positions except at the beginning of a rhythm group and after the consonants *n* or *l*: *modo* **móðo**, *no dan* **nó ðán**, *una dueña* **úna ðwéɲa**, *piedra* **pjéðra**, *admirable* **aðmiráβle**. See fig. 16.

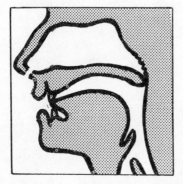

FIG. 16 ð

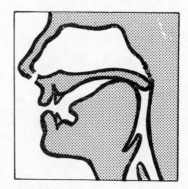

FIG. 17 k, g

NOTES

1. In the ending *-ado*, fricative ð is generally articulated with very little force, and in rapid speech may be omitted altogether: *tomado* or **tomá**ᵟ**o** or **tomáo**, *soldado* **soldá**ᵟ**o** or **soldáo**. In substandard speech there is a tendency for the final vowel to be closed still further, and realized as the offglide w: **tomáw, soldáw**.

2. When *d* is final in a rhythm group it is also very weak and partially devoiced. The tongue takes up its position for ð, but the vocal cords cease to vibrate almost simultaneously and the frication is so shortlived as to be almost imperceptible: *huésped* **wéspeð̥**, *bondad* **bondáð̥**, *traed* **traéð̥**. This final ð̥ differs from θ (8.23) only in that it is uttered with much weaker breath force, and in Madrid, even among educated speakers, full devoicing of final ð may take place: **wéspeθ, bondáθ, traéθ** etc. There is also a tendency for final **d** to be omitted altogether, especially in the words *Madrid* **maðrí**, *usted* **usté**.

3. For the pronunciation of implosive *d* see 8.18, 8.19.

4. Spanish ð is very like the sound of *th* in English *this* **ðıs**, *then* **ðen**, *bathe* **bejð**. Although most English speakers pronounce *th* as a dental in these words, an interdental pronunciation is not uncommon.

5. For the interdental fricative θ̬, written *z* in *diezmo, juzgar*, etc., see 8.24.

.10 The phonemes /t/ and /d/ distinguish between minimal pairs such as *tomar* and *domar, tía* and *día, suelto* and *sueldo, roto* and *rodo*. d and ð, which occur in complementary distribution, are allophones of the phoneme /d/.

NOTE
In English, /d/ and /ð/ are contrasting phonemes which distinguish between
pairs such as *day* dej and *they* ðej *seed* sijd and *seethe* sijð, *den* dɛn and
then ðɛn.

8.11   **k. Voiceless velar plosive.** Written *c, qu, k.* The air passage is completely
blocked by raising the back of the tongue to touch the front part of the soft
palate. When the tongue is lowered sharply to break contact with the
palate, compressed air escapes suddenly to produce an explosive sound:
Examples: *caro* káro, *requiere* ⁻rekjére, *kilo* kílo, *cinco* θíŋko. See fig. 17.

NOTES
1. The precise point at which the tongue touches the palate varies considerably
according to the nature of the vowel which follows k. Before the back vowels
u, o, and before the central vowel a, the sound is fully velar: *cubo* kúβo,
cosa kósa, *cava* káβa; before the front vowels e and i the tongue position is
slightly further forward and contact is made with the back part of the hard
palate: *quepa* képa, *quinto* kĭnto, *kilómetro* kilómetro. In phonetic
transcripts the symbol k is generally used for all varieties, since the point of
articulation is wholly governed by the following vowel and has no structural
significance; the special symbol k̒ is available, however, to represent the more
advanced varieties where there is a need to distinguish these, as for example in
tracing the historical development of Latin K before a palatal vowel (11.18).
2. English k, like English p and t, is sometimes followed by a slight aspiration:
cool k^{h}uwl, *cold* k^{h}ɜwld, *key* k^{h}ij. Spanish k has no element of aspiration.
3. In a final position, *k* is a very relaxed sound and is generally articulated as
a weak voiced ɣ or even lost entirely: *frac* fráɣ or frá, *coñac* koɲáɣ or koɲá.

8.12   **g. Voiced velar plosive.** Written *g, gu.* Articulated in the same way as k, except
that the vocal cords vibrate. Spanish g occurs at the beginning of a rhythm
group and after *n*: *gata* gáta, *guerra* gé⁻ra, *un gato* úŋ gáto, *ganga* gáŋga,
distinguir distiŋgír.

NOTE
Except that the vocal cords begin to vibrate fractionally before the tongue
breaks contact with the palate (8.2), Spanish g is articulated in the same way
as English g in *gate, golf, egg* etc. Its precise point of articulation, like that of
k, varies according to the nature of the following vowel, as does the degree of
lip-rounding involved in its articulation: e.g. a strongly lip-rounded g appears
before the w of *guardia* gwárðja, *gusano* gusáno. More forward varieties may
be represented by the symbol ǵ when there is a need to distinguish these, as in
tracing the historical development of Latin G before a front vowel (11.18).

8.13 ɣ, **Voiced velar fricative.** Written *g, gu, (x)*. Articulated with the back of the tongue raised towards the soft palate, so as to constrict but not entirely stop the outward flow of air. The vocal cords vibrate. Fricative ɣ is the sound of *g* before *a, o, u*, and of *gu* before *e, i* in all positions except at the beginning of a rhythm group and after *n: la gata* la ɣáta, *vagar* baɣár, *alargué*, alarɣé, *agrio* áɣrjo, *signo* síɣno. The graph *x* represents ɣs in *exaltar* eɣsaltár, *examen* eɣsámen (8.17). See fig. 18.

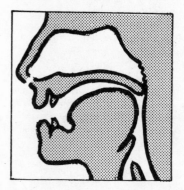

FIG. 18 ɣ

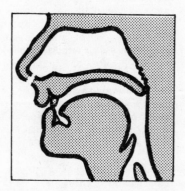

FIG. 19 f

NOTES
1. In rapid speech, ɣ between vowels is pronounced with very little breath force, and before the velars w and u tends to disappear completely: *agua* áᵞwa or áwa, *la guardia* la ᵞwárðja or la wárðja, *aguja* aᵞúxa or aúxa, *agujerear* aᵞuxereár or awxereár.
2. For the pronunciation of implosive *k, g,* see 8.15, 8.17, 8.19.
3. The fricative sound ɣ does not exist in English.

8.14 The phonemes /k/ and /g/ serve to distinguish between *casa* and *gasa, col* and *gol, toca* and *toga, vaco* and *vago;* g and ɣ are allophones of the phoneme /g/ which occur in complementary distribution.

IMPLOSION

8.15 In some phonetic circumstances it becomes extremely difficult to articulate plosive consonants in the normal way. The difficulties arise when a plosive consonant closes a syllable and is immediately followed by another plosive. Thus in normal pronunciation of English *apt, sipped,* only the stop part of p is articulated; the lips close, but the speech-organs immediately take up their position for the following t and the p has no explosion. Similarly, in *select, effect,* the tongue does not leave the roof of the mouth in passing from k to t; only the stop part of k is pronounced, and there is no explosion of breath. In phonetic contexts where a following consonant prevents a stop from being fully articulated, the stop is said to be **implosive**. In Spanish, the most common effect of implosion, especially in conversation, is that the voiceless stops p, t, k are pronounced as the voiced fricatives β, ð, ɣ respectively.

8.16   **Implosive p.** When p closes a syllable it is one of the least perceptible of sounds, and is regularly omitted in some words (e.g. *séptimo* **sétimo**, *autopsia* **awtósja**, *septiembre* **setjémbre;** in rapid or popular speech it is commonly omitted from any **pt** group: *concepto* **konθéto**, *adepto* **aðéto** etc. Before another consonant, the voiced/voiceless opposition between p and b is obscured, as is the plosive/fricative contrast between b and β; *p* may be articulated as a voiced fricative in *apto* **áβto**, *adoptar* **aðoβtár**, *suscripción* **suskriβθjón**, *inepcia* **inéβθja**, *cápsula* **káβsula**, *eclipse* **eklíβse**.

8.17   **Implosive k.** When k closes a syllable the velar is pronounced as a weak voiced fricative in *aspecto* **aspéɣto**, *actor* **aɣtór**, *dicción* **diɣθjón**, *occidente* **oɣθiðénte**, *técnica* **téɣnika**, *anécdota* **anéɣðota**. The graph *x* represents ks in normal Spanish orthography. Where *x* occurs between vowels it is generally pronounced ɣs: *examen* **eɣsámen**, *éxito* **éɣsito**; when *x* precedes a consonant only the s remains: *excepto* **esθéβto**, *expectación* **espeɣtaθjón**.

8.18   **Implosive t.** When t closes a syllable the dental is pronounced as the weak voiced fricative ð: *atlas* **áðlas**, *ritmo* **r̄iðmo**, *atmosférico* **aðmosfériko**, *etnólogo* **eðnóloɣo**.

8.19   A feature of slow or emphatic pronunciation is the articulation of *p, k* and *t* as voiceless sounds in an implosive position: **ápto, eklípse, dikθjón, éksito, r̄itmo, etnóloɣo**, etc. When *p, k* and *t* are pronounced as voiceless implosive stops there is a strong tendency for *b, g* and *d* also to be devoiced where they close a syllable: *obtener* **optenér**, *absurdo* **apsúrdo**, *adscrito* **atskríto**, *adquiere* **atkjére**, *signo* **síkno**, *regnícola* **r̄ekníkola**.

8.20   In an implosive position, the oppositions *p/b, k/g, t/d* are neutralized and non-distinctive (1.10–11). In conversation, *p* and *b* are generally pronounced as the voiced fricative β, *k* and *g* as the voiced fricative ɣ, and *t* and *d* as the voiced fricative ð; in slower or more formal speech they tend to be articulated as the voiceless sounds p, k and t. The contrasts between voiced and voiceless sounds, and between plosive and fricative sounds (which are distinctive in other phonetic contexts) become irrelevant when the phonemes /p/, /b/, /k/, /g/, /t/, /d/ occur at the end of a syllable. Voice, or lack of voice, is here an automatic consequence of the speech habits of the individual speaker.

f

8.21   **f. Voiceless labiodental fricative.** Written *f*. Formed by pressing the lower lip against the upper teeth and forcing air to escape continuously partly between the upper teeth but principally through the gap between lip and teeth. The positions of tongue and lips as a consonant is articulated are approximately those of adjacent vowels. The vocal cords do not vibrate. Examples: *fama* **fáma,** *fuera* **fwéra,** *rufián* **r̄ufján,** *sufre* **súfre.** See fig. 19.

NOTE.
Castilian has no voiced labiodental corresponding to the sound written *v* in English *vest, vicar, glove.* The sound represented by *v* in Spanish orthography is pronounced b or β according to its phonetic context: *viene* **bjéne,** *no viene* **nó βjéne** (8.4–5).

8.22 The phoneme /f/ has no allophonic variants. It contrasts principally with /b/, /p/, /θ/ and /s/ and serves to distinguish minimal pairs such as *feo/veo, fresa/presa, afeite/aceite, café/casé.*

θ   and   θ̬

8.23 θ. **Voiceless interdental fricative.** Written *c,* before *e* and *i,* and written *z* else-where. The tip of the tongue protrudes slightly between the teeth, resting gently against the upper teeth to leave a narrow air passage. The tongue is flat and the vocal cords do not vibrate. This is the sound of *c* before *e* and *i,* and of *z* before vowels and voiceless consonants: *cepo* **θépo,** *razón* **r̄aθón,** *placer* **plaθér,** *luz* **lúθ,** *conozco* **konóθko.** See fig. 20.

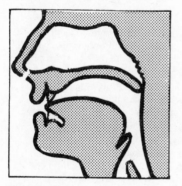
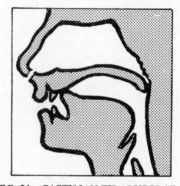

FIG. 20 θ, θ̬   **FIG. 21** CASTILIAN TIP-ALVEOLAR s, ʂ

NOTES
1. **Seseo.** In many parts of the Spanish-speaking world, principally in Andalusia and Latin America, the interdental fricative sound of Castilian is replaced by /s/ in all positions: *cepo* **sépo,** *razón* **r̄asón** etc. This phenomenon, known as **seseo,** is generally treated as an acceptable variant pronunciation. For the historical origins of *seseo,* see 18.8 n.
2. Castilian θ is very similar to the sound written *th* in English *thin* **θɪn,** *author* **ɒθə,** *breath* **brɛθ.** It differs only in that the tip of the tongue protrudes

slightly more forward (between, rather than behind, the teeth) in Castilian Spanish, and in that the Spanish sound is articulated with slightly more breath force than the corresponding English fricative.

8.24   θ̪. **Voiced interdental fricative.** Written *z*. The speech-organs take up the same positions as for θ, and the vocal cords vibrate. This is the sound of *z* before a voiced consonant: *diezmo* djéθ̪mo, *juzgar* xuθ̪γár, *la luz del día* la lúθ̪ ðel día, *en vez de comprar* em béθ̪ ðe komprár.

NOTE
For the voiced fricative ð, written *d* in *modo, piedra*, etc., see 8.9.

8.25   /θ/ is a phoneme of Spanish, contrasting principally with /s/, /x/, /b/, /t/ to distinguish pairs such as *caza* and *casa, caza* and *caja, caza* and *cava, caza* and *cata*. θ and θ̪ are allophones of the phoneme /θ/, in complementary distribution.

NOTE
In areas of **seseo** (8.23 n. 1) and **ceceo** (8.26 n. 4) the contrastive effect of the /s/−/θ/ phonemic opposition is lost, so that *casa* and *caza, siega* and *ciega, coser* and *cocer* become **homophones**.

s   and   s̪

8.26   s. **Voiceless alveolar fricative.** Written *s, x*. In the formation of Castilian s the tip of the tongue reaches upwards to make contact with the alveoles, close to the hard palate, leaving a small and slightly rounded aperture between tongue and alveoles in the centre of the mouth. Air is forced through this rounded aperture to produce audible friction. The front part of the tongue is slightly concave. The vocal cords do not vibrate. This is the sound of Castilian *s* in all positions except before a voiced consonant, and of *x* before a consonant: *sala* sála, *silo* sílo, *escala* eskála, *piso* píso, *excavar* eskaβár, *expedido* espeðíðo, *textual* testwál. The sibilant may be fully defined as a **voiceless tip-alveolar fricative**. The alternative terms **retroflex, apical** and **cacuminal** are also used by linguists to describe Castilian **s**. See fig. 21.

Over extensive areas of Andalusia and Spanish America, s is pronounced very weakly or not at all when final in a syllable or word. Commonly, the sound is reduced to a simple aspiration: *las casas* la[h] kása[h], *estos* é[h]to[h], *después* de[h]pwé[h]. Equally commonly, the sound disappears completely: *las casas* la kása, *estos* éto, *después* depwé. For the consequential effect on preceding vowel sounds, see 18.10c.

NOTES
1. Castilian s differs from English s in a number of respects. In the articulation of the most common type of English s it is the **blade** (or tip and blade) of the

tongue which makes contact with the alveoles, while at the same time the front of the tongue is partly raised towards the hard palate. The front part of the tongue is thus slightly convex (fig. 22). English s may be fully defined as a **voiceless blade-alveolar fricative**. The term **predorsal** is also used for English **s**.

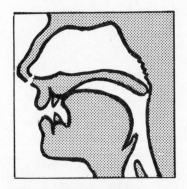
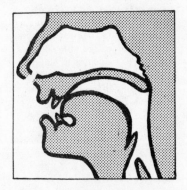

FIG. 22 ENGLISH BLADE-   FIG. 23   SPANISH CORONAL s, ş
        AVEOLAR s, z

2. Before a voiceless dental **t** or interdental θ the tip of the tongue moves slightly forward in anticipation of the next sound, but the characteristic slightly rounded aperture remains (Quilis, 1966): *bastar* **bastár,** *estoy* **estój,** *escena* **esθéna,** *excelso* **esθélso.**

3. While the retroflex *s* is characteristic of Castilian Spanish, other types of *s* are to be found in the Spanish-speaking world. A **blade-dental s**, slightly more forward than the English sound, is found in parts of Andalusia and over much of South America, as is a **coronal** variety of the latter in which the tongue lies nearly flat in the mouth, with the blade touching the lower edge of the upper front teeth and the tip touching the back of the lower front teeth (fig. 23).

4. **Ceceo.** In large areas of southern Andalusia the sounds written *s, z* and *c* (before *e* and *i*) are all pronounced in the same way, as a dental or interdental sound of the θ type. This pronunciation is known as **ceceo**. Tongue-position varies somewhat from area to area, but the characteristic feature of ceceo is that frication is made with the tongue flat, and not rounded as for Castilian **tip-alveolar s.** Ceceo is generally considered much less acceptable among educated speakers than **seseo.** For the historical origins of *ceceo,* see 18.8 n.

8.27   **ş. Voiced alveolar fricative.** Written *s*. The vocal cords vibrate, and air pressure is weak, but otherwise the speech-organs are as for tip-aveolar **s.** Voiced ş occurs only immediately before a voiced consonant: *esbelto* **eşβélto,** *musgo* **múşɣo,** *los modos* **loş móδos,** *mis niños* **miş níɲos,** *los brazos* **loş βráθos.**

NOTES
1. Before the voiced dental *d*, the tip of the tongue is attracted slightly further forward in anticipation of the following sound but, as with the combinations s̩t and s̩θ (8.26 n. 2), the two sounds are not sufficiently distinctive to justify a separate phonetic symbol: *desde* dés̩ðe, *las dueñas* las̩ ðwéɲas, *los dedos* los̩ déðos.
2. In the group -*sr*-, the sibilant is extremely weak. It may be articulated as a fricative ř, and in conversation tends to disappear entirely: *Israel* iřraél or íraél, *los ríos* lor̄ ríos or lo ríos, *dos reales* dóř reáles or dó reáles. In the popular pronunciation of Madrid it is common for *s* to be articulated as a fricative ř before any voiced consonant: *desde* déřðe, *esbelto* eřβélto etc.
3. Spanish s̩ differs from English z in *zeal, razor, trees* not only with respect to tongue position but also in that it is articulated with weaker breath force.

8.28   The phoneme /s/ contrasts principally with /θ/, /f/, /x/ and /t͡ʃ/ to distinguish minimal pairs such as *masa* and *maza, suerte* and *fuerte, puso* and *pujo, cansa* and *cancha*. s and s̩ are allophones of the phoneme /s/, in complementary distribution.

8.29   **x. Voiceless velar fricative.** Written *j, g*. The back of the tongue is raised high against the soft palate so as to constrict but not quite stop the outward flow of air. Air is forced continuously through the narrow gap with a harsh, rasping sound. In energetic pronunciation the sound may become a vibrant. The vocal cords do not vibrate. This is the sound of *j* in all positions, and of *g* before *e* and *i*: *ajo* áxo, *joroba* xoróβa, *gente* xénte, *mujer* muxér. See fig. 24.

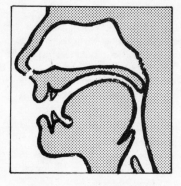
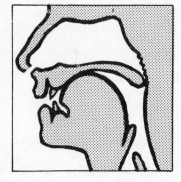

FIG. 24 x   FIG. 25 t͡ʃ

NOTES

1. In a final position x is relaxed, and may in some words be omitted altogether: *boj* bó^x, *troj* tró^x, *reloj* r̄eló.

2. In all other positions, x is pronounced with strong breath force (fortis). The x of *ajo* áxo contrasts with the ɣ of *hago* áɣo in that it is voiceless, articulated with greater energy and pronounced slightly further back in the mouth.

3. Castilian x is very similar to the sound written *ch* in Scottish *loch*, Welsh *bach*. In much of South and Central America, however, the velar has become very relaxed and pharyngeal, and has much in common with English **h**: *ajo* áho, *joroba* horóβa, *gente* hénte etc. (Canfield, 1962, 81–82 and Map III).

30   The phoneme /x/ contracts principally with /k/, /g/, /f/, /θ/ and /s/ to distinguish pairs such as *roja* and *roca*, *lejos* and *legos*, *juego* and *fuego*, *baja* and *baza*, *caja* and *casa*. In the popular speech of areas such as eastern León where initial f is pronounced as x (R. Menéndez Pidal, 1961, 61–4) the contrastive function of the opposition between x and f is lost.

31   **t͡ʃ. Voiceless palatal affricate.** Written *ch*. The air passage is first completely blocked by raising the front of the tongue to make firm contact with the forward part of the hard palate and the alveoles; then the tongue is gradually removed in such a way that the effect of a fricative ʃ is heard before the next sound is reached. The vocal cords do not vibrate. Examples: *chino* t͡ʃíno, *tachar* tát͡ʃár, *muchacho* mut͡ʃát͡ʃo, *leche* lét͡ʃe. See fig. 25.

NOTES

1. Spanish t͡ʃ is rather more palatal in nature than the sound written *ch* in English *cheap* t͡ʃijp, *rich* rit͡ʃ, *watch* wɔt͡ʃ, and in its articulation a larger area of the tongue is pressed against the palate.

2. The digraph t͡ʃ does not imply that the Spanish affricate is a combination of the two phonemes /t/ and /ʃ/. The digraph is, however, a convenient method of representing the voiceless affricate of Modern Spanish and at the same contrasting it with its voiced equivalent, the d͡ʒ sound of Old Spanish (16.5). An alternative symbol for the voiceless palatal affricate of Modern Spanish, also recommended by the IPA, is c.

32   /t͡ʃ/ is the only affricate phoneme of Spanish. As such, it contrasts with all non-affricate phonemes, principally with /i/ and /s/: *ocho/hoyo*, *macho/mayo*, *pecho/peso*, *bicho/viso*.

33   **d͡ʒ. Voiced (pre)palatal affricate.** Written *y, hi*. Formed with the speech-organs approximately as for t͡ʃ, except that the vocal cords vibrate and that as the

tongue is removed from the palate the effect is closer to j than to ʒ. This is
the usual sound of *y* and *hi* at the beginning of a rhythm group and after a
consonant: *yerno* d͡jérno, *hielo* d͡jélo, *inyectar* iɲd͡jeɣtár, *el yugo* eʎ d͡júɣo,
deshielo dezd͡jélo, *abyecto* aβd͡jéɣto, *estas hierbas* éstaṣ d͡jérβas.

NOTES
1. At the beginning of a rhythm group the pronunciation j is also common:
hierba d͡jérβa or jérβa, *hierro* d͡jéro or jéro. In emphatic pronunciation, d͡j
may be strengthened to d͡ʒ at the beginning of a rhythm group: *yo* d͡ʒó,
ya d͡ʒá.
2. As with t͡ʃ, the digraph d͡j does not imply that the voiced palatal affricate
is a combination of the phonemes /d/ and /i/. In this case, the digraph serves
the useful purpose of calling attention to the difference between the
prepalatal affricate of Castilian Spanish and **central palatal** affricate d͡ʒ found
in English *June, jewel, page, religion*. In English the nearest, but by no means
equivalent, sound to the voiced palatal affricate of Spanish is the less tense
combination consonant + onglide in words such as *dune* d͡juwn (cf. *June*
d͡ʒuwn) and *dual* d͡juəl (cf. *jewel* d͡ʒuəl).
3. There is no voiceless palatal affricate sound in Spanish which corresponds
exactly to d͡j. The voiced equivalent of t͡ʃ is d͡ʒ.
4. For the pronunciation of the conjunction *y* at the beginning of a rhythm
group see 7.22.

8.34   j and d͡j are positional variants of the phoneme /i/, which occur only in
complementary distribution: d͡j is normal for the graphs *y, hi* at the
beginning of a rhythm group and after *n* or *l*, whereas j is normal for these
graphs elsewhere. There is also a considerable amount of free variation
among the consonantal allophones of /i/. In certain circumstances the
phoneme may be realized in the same phonetic context as j or d͡j (8.33 n.1),
and ʒ and d͡ʒ are further possible realizations (7.8–9 and 8.33 n. l). Since the
palatal sounds i, j, d͡j occur only in complementary distribution – *filo* fílo,
bien bjén, *ley* léj, *playa* plája, *yerno* d͡jérno – or else in free variation, it is
logical to group all three, and their variants, within the same phoneme
(7.9 and n.).

8.35   Among plosive, fricative and affricate consonants, Spanish has eleven
consonant phonemes, /p/, /b/, /t/, /d/, /k/, /g/, /f/, /θ/, /s/, /x/, /t͡ʃ/, which
may distinguish between words which are otherwise identical sequences of
sounds. The affricate d͡j is an allophonic variant of the vowel phoneme /i/
(8.33–4). The pattern is summarized in the following table:

PHONEME	ALLOPHONES
/p/	p in *pata* páta
/b/	b in *basta* básta
	β in *haba* áβa

/t/	t	in *tomo* tómo
/d/	d	in *dato* dáto
	ð	in *prado* práðo
/k/	k	in *corto* kórto
/g/	g	in *gafas* gáfas
	ɣ	in *higo* íɣo
/f/	f	in *folio* fóljo
/θ/	θ	in *cita* θíta
	θ̬	in *bizma* bíθ̬ma
/s/	s	in *sastre* sástre
	s̬	in *plasma* plás̬ma
/x/	x	in *dejo* déxo
/t͡ʃ/	t͡ʃ	in *chopo* t͡ʃópo
(/i/)	d͡ʒ	in *yute* d͡ʒúte

6 FURTHER READING. E. Alarcos (1965), II.3. A. Alonso (1951b), 111–200.
J. B. Dalbor (1969), chs. 8–17. D. Jones (1958), paras. 220–70, 322–74;
(1960), chs. 17, 18, 21. R. Lapesa (1957–8), I, 67–94. B. Malmberg (1948),
104–5. T. Navarro (1965), paras. 71–84, 88–109, 118–21, 125–32.
A. Quilis (1966), 335–43. A. Quilis and J. A. Fernández (1964), chs. 7–9.
G. L. Trager (1939), 218–19, 221–2. A. Zamora Vicente (1960), 236–44.

7 EXERCISES ON CHAPTER 8[1]
1. Transcribe phonetically: *vagido, todavía, vacuidad, pavito, godesco,
tumbaga, sueldo, hablado, guisado, existo.*
2. Transcribe phonetically: *ceguedad, sus dedos, portazgo, vaciada, hojita,
desdibujado, chiquito, hierático, geodesta, pazguato.*
3. Transcribe phonetically: *aptitud, mixto, exacta, atlético, istmo, occipucio,
sáxeo, dictado, silepsis, capciosidad.*
4. Transcribe phonetically: *sociedad, yugoeslavo, ahijado, siesavo, mayorazgo,
hierbabuena, payasada, suicidio, bailable, diez hienas.*
5. Read the following transcripts aloud, and write each one out in normal
Spanish orthography: d͡ʒá-sé-ke-si-ɣe-kre-jén-do-lo; lo-xúθ-ɣojm-po-si-βle;
tó-ðoes-tá-βa-tra-βá-ðoj-ðis-pwés-to; sjé-sú-nes-θe-lén-te-su-xé-to;
es-pú-seáw-na-mí-ɣo-mí-oel-pro-jéɣ-to; laes-kri-tú-ra-θjen-tí-fi-ka;
leá-θe-ði-βu-xár-pa-xa-rí-tas; sjén-tes-twi-ma-xi-na-θjón-sa-tis-fé-t͡ʃa; pa-ré-θejm-
po-sí-βle-ke-sé-a-jé-ðra; bá-sus̬-βrá-θo-si-ses-tré-t͡ʃa-ni-se-man-tjé-ne-nen-si-lén-
θjo.

---

[1] Where the letters *r, l, m, n* occur in the exercises on Chapter 8 they should
be transcribed by the symbols **r, l, m, n** respectively.

9 VIBRANTS, LATERALS AND NASALS IN GREATER DETAIL

9.1   **r. Voiced alveolar vibrant (flapped).** Written *r*. The tip of the tongue is raised to tap once against the teeth ridge as the vocal cords vibrate. Air is completely stopped for a moment, but the breath force is weak. This is the sound of *r* except where it is initial in a word or preceded by *l, n* or *s: puro* **púro,** *arte* **árte,** *pronto* **prónto,** *atrás* **atrás.** See fig. 26.

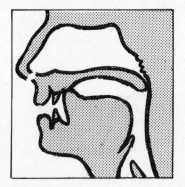
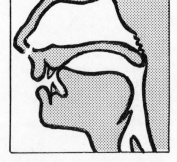

FIG. 26   r, r̄   FIG. 27   l

NOTES
1. Many English speakers use a flapped *r* in an intervocalic position, as in *parade, serious, your own.* The most common variety of English *r* is, however, a fricative sound in which the tip of the tongue is brought close to, but not quite touching, the teeth ridge: this is the usual sound of *r* in *RP* when a vowel sound follows, as in *red, write, arrest.* Some Spanish speakers also use a fricative *r*, which can be transcribed ř, in place of flapped **r**, especially in the intervocalic and final positions: *para* **pářa,** *toro* **tóřo,** *color* **kolóř,** *vivir* **biβíř.** See also 8.27 n. 2 and 9.2 n. 1.
2. The *IPA* symbol for flapped *r*, which may be necessary for comparative work in English and Spanish, is ɾ.

9.2   **r̄. Voiced alveolar vibrant (rolled).** Written *rr, r.* Rolled lingual r̄ is formed by a rapid succession of taps made by the tip of the tongue against the teeth ridge. The movements of the tongue are not muscular; the tip of the tongue is held close to the alveoles and made to vibrate by the force of the air-stream. This is the sound *rr*, and of *r* when initial in a word or interior in a word and preceded by *l*, *n* or *s: sierra* sjér̄a, *carro* kár̄o, *torre redondo* tór̄e r̄eðóndo, *alrededor* alr̄eðeðór, *honra* ónr̄a, *Israel* ir̄aél.

NOTES

1. A fricative version of this sound (generally transcribed ř) is to be found in some areas of Central and South America, including Guatemala, Costa Rica, Ecuador, Bolivia, Bogotá, Chile, Paraguay and Argentina. The multiple fricative may be voiced or voiceless, and is articulated in a manner very similar to that of the tip-alveolar s of Castile (8.26). As a result, the pronunciation of Guatemalan *ropa* has much in common with that of Castilian *sopa* (Canfield, 1962, 88–9 and Map VII).

2. The initial *r* of a word is always pronounced r̄ irrespective of the position of the word in a rhythm group. Thus *rojo* r̄óxo, *verde o rojo* bérðe o r̄óxo; *rosada* r̄osáða, *pantalla rosada* pantáʎa r̄osáða. Its treatment is consequently very different from that of the phonemes /b/, /d/, and /g/, pronounced as plosives when initial in a rhythm group – *bueno* bwéno (8.4), *donde* dónde (8.8), *gala* gála (8.12) – but as fricatives in an intervocalic position: *lo bueno* lo βwéno (8.5), *adonde* aðónde (8.9), *la gala* la ɣála (8.13).

.3 The phonemes /r/ and /r̄/ contrast in an intervocalic position, where they distinguish between minimal pairs such as *pera* and *perra, caro* and *carro, cero* and *cerro, ahora* and *ahorra*. In all other phonetic contexts the distinction between /r/ and /r̄/ is neutralized (1.10–11), and the graph *r* is realized as r̄, r or ř, according to the nature of the surrounding sounds.

.4

l. **Voiced alveolar lateral.** Written *l*. The tip of the tongue touches the teeth ridge so that there is a stoppage in the centre of the mouth. A passage is left on one or both sides of the tongue and air is allowed to escape along either one side or both sides with slight friction. The tongue is held fairly flat in the mouth and the sound is voiced. Examples: *león* león, *palo* pálo, *habla* áβla, *alrededor* alr̄eðeðór. See fig. 27. This partial stoppage, which is quite unlike the stoppage made for other consonants, gives l a very special vowel-like character. It could be described as a lateralized vowel, since any vowel can be lateralized by raising the tip of the tongue to touch the teeth-ridge while the vowel is being articulated. The differences in quality between a lateralized *i* and a lateralized *u* will be obvious even to a casual ear, and in fact the *l* sound has as many varieties as there are vowels. For practical purposes phoneticians normally distinguish only two types: those lateralized articulations which have the resonance of front vowels are called **clear** *l* sounds and are transcribed l; those lateralized articulations which have the resonance of back vowels are called **dark** *l* sounds and are transcribed ł. In *RP*, clear *l* occurs before vowels, as in *lick, employ, jelly, floor,* and dark *l* before consonants and in a final position, as in *field, pulpit, double, curl.* In certain English-speaking areas (parts of Scotland, for example), dark ł is used in all positions: in others (parts of Ireland, for example), clear l is used in all positions. Although in the Iberian peninsula dark ł may be heard in Çatalan areas, Castilian Spanish contains only clear l sounds, all the others having lost their lateral contact in the course of the evolution of the language, and become pure vowels.

NOTES

Although in Modern Spanish all *l* sounds are fairly uniform in resonance they are very easily attracted, by a process of contextual assimilation (2.11), towards the point of articulation of a following consonant:

1. ḷ. Before a dental consonant the tip of the tongue, anticipating the following sound, makes contact with the upper teeth instead of the alveoles. The result is a **voiced dental lateral,** which can be represented in narrow transcriptions by the symbol ḷ: *alto* álto, *sueldo* swéḷdo, *el toro* eḷ tóro, *el dueño* eḷ dwéno.

2. ḷ. Before an interdental consonant the tip of the tongue is similarly attracted towards the point of articulation of the following sound, and the *l* is pronounced as a **voiced interdental lateral:** *alzar* aḷθár, *calzado* kaḷθáðo, *el cielo* eḷ θjélo.

3. For the palatalized *l* of *colcha, el yate* etc. See 9.5.

9.5   ʎ. **Voiced palatal lateral.** Written *ll, l.* The tip of the tongue is held low, touching the lower teeth. The front of the tongue is raised to make extensive contact with the hard palate and air is allowed to escape at one or both sides of the tongue. The vocal cords vibrate. This is the pronunciation of *ll,* and of *l* where is precedes a palatal consonant. Examples: *calle* káʎe, *silla* síʎa, *colcha* kóʎt͡ʃa, *el llano* eʎ ʎáno. See fig. 28.

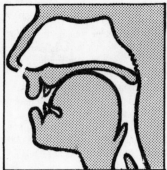

FIG. 28   ʎ   FIG. 29   m

NOTES

1. English has no ʎ sound. The nearest equivalent is the combination lj which appears in *million, familiar* etc., but which is phonetically quite distinct from

Spanish ʎ. The palatal lateral of Spanish is articulated as one sound, not two; it requires a much more extensive contact between tongue and palate than for the combination lj, and whereas closure is made at the palate for ʎ, it is made principally at the alveoles for lj. The pairs *hallado* aʎáðo and *aliado* aljáðo, *lleve* ʎéβe and *lieve* ljéβe are not likely to be confused in Spanish.

2. Yeísmo. In most of the southern half of Spain, in the Spanish of Madrid and in Latin America, /ʎ/ is replaced by the phoneme /i/. In these areas all the consonantal allophonic variants of /i/ appear: *calle* may be pronounced káje, kádje, káȝe, kádȝe etc. The substitution of /i/ for /ʎ/ is known as yeísmo, and in areas where yeismo is the norm the phonemic distinction between /i/ and /ʎ/ is obscured: *halla* and *haya* are both pronounced /áia/, *pollo* and *poyo* are both pronounced /póio/.

The phonemes /l/ and /ʎ/ distinguish in initial and intervocalic positions between minimal pairs such *vale* and *valle*, *loro* and *lloro*, *calar* and *callar*, *velo* and *bello*. The phoneme /l/ has allophones l, ḻ and ļ which occur in complementary distribution. The phoneme /ʎ/ has no allophones in Castilian Spanish; in some areas of the Peninsula and Latin America it is replaced by the phoneme /i/. In syllables closed by a lateral the distinction between /l/ and /ʎ/ is neutralized (1.10–11), and the phonetic realization of the lateral may be l, ḻ, ļ or ʎ, according to the phonetic context: *salvo* sálβo, *salto* sáḻto, *ensalce* ensálθe, *colchón* koʎʧón.

m

m. Voiced bilabial nasal. Written *m, n*. The speech-organs take up their positions as for b, but the soft palate is lowered and air allowed to escape only through the nose. Examples: *madre* máðre, *toma* tóma, *ambos* ámbos, *empieza* empjéθa. When in a rhythm group *n* precedes *p, b* or *v*, the nasal is pronounced as a bilabial and the consonant as a plosive: *un pie* um pjé, *bien poblado* bjém poβláðo, *un bastón* um bastón, *son buenos* sóm bwénos, *enviar* embjár, *con valor* kom balór. When in a rhythm group *n* precedes *m*, the first nasal may be articulated as an alveolar in carefully enunciated speech: *con mucho* kon múʧo; in more rapid speech it becomes a weak bilabial: *con mucho* koᵐ múʧo, *inmediato* iᵐmeðjáto, *son mujeres* sóᵐ muxéres, *un militar* úᵐ militár. See fig. 29.

The nasal phoneme /m/ contrasts principally with /b/, /p/, /n/ and /ɲ/ to distinguish pairs such as *muela* and *vuela*, *cama* and *cava*, *mozo* and *pozo*, *cama* and *capa*, *mata* and *nata*, *cama* and *cana*, *amo* and *año*, *cama* and *caña*.

n   m̩   ŋ   ɲ

n. Voiced alveolar nasal. Written *n, m*. The passage of air through the mouth is blocked by raising the tip of the tongue to touch the teeth-ridge; the soft

palate is lowered and air allowed to escape through the nose only. The vocal
cords vibrate. This is the sound of *n* when it is initial or final in a syllable,
when it is intervocalic, and when it is followed by an alveolar consonant.
Examples: *nana* **nána,** *son* **són,** *carne* **kárne,** *ensayo* **ensájo,** *enlace* **enláθe.** It is
also the sound of final *m*: *álbum* **álbun,** *ultimátum* **ultimátun,** *referendum*
‾referéndun. See fig. 30.

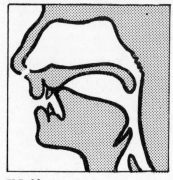

FIG. 30   n

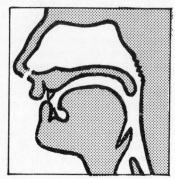

FIG. 31   m̩

NOTES.
Like *l*, the nasal is easily attracted in contextual assimilation (2.11) towards
the point of articulation of a following consonant.
1.   n̪. Before a dental consonant the tip of the tongue makes contact with the
teeth in anticipation of the following dental sound. The result is a **voiced
dental nasal,** which can be represented in narrow transcriptions by the symbol
n̪: *antes* **ántes,** *conde* **kónde,** *con tu permiso* **kon̪ tu permiso.**
2.   n̟. Before an interdental consonant, the tip of the tongue is also attracted
forward and protrudes slightly between the teeth. The **voiced interdental
nasal** which results can be represented in narrow transcriptions by the symbol
n̟: *once* **ón̟θe,** *conciencia* **kon̟θjén̟θja,** *sincero* **sin̟θéro.**
3.   For the palatalized *n* of *planchar, Sancho* etc. See 9.12.

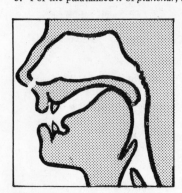

FIG. 32   ŋ

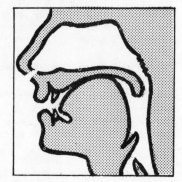

FIG. 33   ɲ

10   ɱ. When *n* precedes the labiodental consonant **f**, teeth and lips take up their positions in readiness for the following consonant; the soft palate is lowered and air is allowed to escape through the nose to produce the **voiced labiodental nasal** ɱ: *confuso* **koɱfúso**, *sin fuerza* **siɱ fwérθa**, *confiar* **koɱfjár**. Some English speakers use this sound in similar phonetic contexts: *triumph, comfort, in front* etc. See fig. 31.

11   ŋ. When *n* precedes a velar consonant, the back of the tongue is raised to block the passage of air; the result is the **voiced velar nasal** ŋ: *cinco* **θíŋko**, *ninguno* **niŋgúno**, *ángel* **áŋxel**, *un clérigo* **úŋ klériɣo**. See fig. 32.

NOTES
1. When *n* is followed by consonantal **w** there is very little friction and the nasal consonant may disappear entirely after nasalizing the preceding vowel: *un hueco* **ũ wéko**, *con huevos* **kõ wéβos**. When the velar nasal is pronounced, there is a strong tendency for the allophone **gw** to represent the graph *w*: *un hueco* **úŋ gwéko** (7.5 n.1).
2. Some speakers, both in Spain (particularly in the North) and in Spanish America, employ a velar nasal when *n* occurs in a final position: *bien* **bjéŋ**, *ratón* **ratóŋ**, *nailón* **nailóŋ** In Spanish America this pronunciation is fairly widespread, even among educated speakers.

12   ɲ. **Voiced palatal nasal.** The tip of the tongue is held low, touching the bottom teeth, and the blade and front of the tongue make extensive contact with the alveoles and hard palate to prevent air from escaping through the mouth. The soft palate is lowered and air allowed to escape only through the nose. This is the pronunciation of *ñ*, and of *n* where it precedes a palatal consonant. The vocal cords vibrate. Examples: *señor* **seɲór**, *ñandú* **ɲandú**, *leña* **léɲa**, *rebaño* **reβáɲo**, *planchar* **plaɲʧár**, *Sancho* **sáɲʧo**, *inyectar* **iɲdjeɣtár**, *sin llegar* **siɲ ʎeɣár**. See fig. 33.

NOTE
English has no ɲ sound. The nearest equivalent is the combination **nj** which appears in *onion, simultaneous* etc., but which differs from Spanish ɲ in much the same way as English **lj** differs from Spanish ʎ (9.5 n. 1). Spanish ɲ is one sound, not two; the area of contact between tongue and palate is much greater than for **nj** and the tip of the tongue, which touches the alveoles for **nj**, touches the lower teeth for ɲ. The pairs *huraño* **uráɲo** and *uranio* **uránjo**, *de moño* **de móɲo** and *demonio* **demónjo** are not easily confused.

13   In an intervocalic position the phonemes /n/ and /ɲ/ distinguish between minimal pairs such as *mono* and *moño*, *sonar* and *soñar*, *una* and *uña*. The phoneme /n/ has allophones n, ṇ, ṇ, ɱ and ŋ, all of which occur in complementary distribution. The phoneme /ɲ/ has no allophones. In syllables closed by a nasal the distinction between /m/, /n/ and /ɲ/ is neutralized (1. 10–11), and the phonetic realization of the nasal may be **m, n, ṇ, ṇ, ɱ, ŋ** or ɲ, according to context: *ambos* **ámbos**, *enviar* **embjár**, *tenso* **tenso**, *antes* **áṇtes**, *once* **óṇθe**, *confuso* **koɱfúso**, *vengo* **béŋgo**, *planchado* plaɲt͡ʃaðo. Neutralization also occurs at the end of a rhythm group, but in this context, since the phonemes /m/ and /ɲ/ never occur in an absolutely final position, the phonetic realization (although some speakers use ŋ, 9.11 n. 2), is generally n: *son* són, *quien* kjén, *álbum* álβun, *referendum* r̄eferéndun. 'Lo que vale fonológicamente en la nasal final de sîlaba es tan sólo la resonancia nasal del soplo sonoro; eso es lo necesario y a la vez lo suficiente' (A. Alonso, 1945, 95).

NOTE.
Whereas in Spanish ŋ is an allophone of /n/ which occurs only before velar consonants, so that n and ŋ are in complementary distribution, in English /n/ and /ŋ/ are separate phonemes, contrasting in minimal pairs such as *sinner* sɪnə and *singer* sɪŋə, *son* sʌn and *sung* sʌŋ, *run* rʌn and *rung* rʌŋ.

9.14   Spanish has two vibrant phonemes /r/ and /r̄/, two lateral phonemes /l/ and /ʎ/, and three nasal phonemes /m/, /n/ and /ɲ/. Of these, only /r/, /l/ and /n/ have allophonic variants. Those allophones of /r/, /l/ and /n/ marked with an asterisk are discussed in footnotes to 9.1, 9.4 and 9.9, but are not employed in the simple allophonic transcriptions used throughout this book. This is summarized in the following table:

PHONEME	ALLOPHONES
/r/	r in *toro* tóro
	*ř in *cantar* kantář
/r̄/	r̄ in *terreno* ter̄éno
/l/	l in *lomo* lómo
	*l̯ in *caldo* kál̯do
	*l̪ in *calza* kál̪θa
/ʎ/	ʎ in *pillo* píʎo
/m/	m in *mote* móte
/n/	n in *nena* néna
	*n̪ in *ente* én̪te
	*n̟ in *encía* en̟θía
	m̩ in *infinito* im̩finíto
	ŋ in *ronco* r̄óŋko
/ɲ/	ɲ in *peña* péɲa

9.15   **FURTHER READING.** E. Alarcos (1950), chs. 3 and 4. A. Alonso (1945), 91–101; (1961), 159–267. C. Blaylock (1968), 392–409. D. Catalán (1954), 1–44. J. B. Dalbor (1969), chs. 18–22. J. Corominas (1953), 81–7. A. Galmés (1957), 273–307. S. Gili Gaya (1921), 271–280. V. Honsa (1965), 275–83. D. Jones (1958), paras. 271–321; (1960, chs. 19, 20, 21. T. Navarro (1965), paras. 85–7, 95, 96, 103, 104, 110–17, 122–4, 130. A. Quilis and J. A. Fernández (1964), chs. 10 and 11. G. L. Trager (1939), 218–19, 221–2. A. Zamora Vicente (1960), 244–7.

9.16

EXERCISES ON CHAPTER 9.

1. Transcribe phonetically: *rallo, lloviznar, colchón, ametralladora, ramillete, israelita, el yate, lo rebaja, las reglas, para recorrer.*

2. Transcribe phonetically: *comprar, enfermo, yanqui, tándem, avalancha, inyección, niñería, un macho, sin fama, con llamas.*

3. Read the following phonetic transcript aloud, and write it out in normal Spanish orthography: lo-kwal-βjé-nea-siɣ-ni-fi-kár-ke-los-kraw-sís-tas / ko-mo-lo-si-ðe-ó-kra-taş-ðe-tó-ðaş-la-sé-po-kas/ só-ni-ná-βi-le-sis-to-rja-ðó-res// nóes-ke-ðé-ʎoˢ-se-pwě-ða-ðe-θír/ kejn-ter-pré-tan-lajs-tó-rja-su-mó-ðo/és-toés/ iṇ-djeɣ-tán-do-la-ðe-pre-xwí-θjos/ de-pa-sjó-nes/ de-ðe-síɣ-njos-per-so-ná-les// é-so-se-rí-a-lo-na-tu-rá-li-to-le-rá-βle// lo-ke-pá-sa/ és-ke-nó-lajn-ter-pré-ta-nal-mó-ðo-ðe-ná-ðje//

4. Transcribe the following phrases into phonetic script: *no vio más que un grupo de jóvenes; fuera de sus cauces rotos; y empieza ahora un verdadero horror; conozco mi enfermedad; aunque el individuo haya muerto como tal; para un joven dando el brazo a una muchacha; hay quien pone al silencio un ademán soñador; todos fuman y los más meditan; unas piden para los viejos, otras para los incurables; quieren participar de su fuerza sagrada e inmortal.*

5. Write a phonetic transcription of the following passage: *Veo un territorio montañés y risueño, bien poblado y cultivado en forma de bancales, lleno de alquerías blancas que adornan con su candidez la reciente verdura de la primavera. Pronto se allana el país y se hace más fecundo y rico. Entramos en la tierra de Barros, célebre por su fertilidad.*

APPENDIX

PHONETIC TEXTS

1. so-ní-ðo-si-fo-né-mas

kwan-do-ðóˢ-so-ní-ðos-pwé-ðe-nal-ter-ná-ren-la-míṣ-ma-pa-lá-βra / sim-pro-
ðu-θí-re-féɣ-to-per-θeβ-tí-βlen-la-siɣ-ni-fi-ka-θjóŋ-koŋ-ke-tál-pa-lá-βráes-ko-no-
θí-ða / loˢ-so-ní-ðo-sin-di-ká-ðoṣ-nó-són-si-no-mo-ði-fi-ka-θjó-neṣ-ðéwᵐ-mis-mo-
fo-né-ma // eŋ-kám-bjo / kwan-do-ðóˢ-so-ní-ðos-nó-pwé-ðen-suṣ-ti-twír-se-mú-
twa-mén-te / si-na-feɣ-tá-rel-sen-tí-ðo-ðel-βo-ká-βloeŋ-ke-seá-ʎan / loˢ-so-ní-
ðo-sin-di-ká-ðoˢ-sóm̦-fo-né-mas-ðis-tín-tos // és / pwés / bá-se-sen-θjál-pa-ra-la-
ði-fe-ren-θja-θjó-nen-tre-so-ní-ðo-si-fo-né-mas / e-le-féɣ-to-ke-los-kám-bjos-fo-
né-ti-ko-se-xér-θen-so-βrel-βa-lór-se-mán-ti-ko-ðe-las-pa-lá-βras // las-mo-ði-fi-
ka-θjó-nes-ðear-ti-ku-la-θjó-ni-so-no-ri-ðáð-ke-la-é-ne / po-re-xém-plo̯ / es-pe-ri-
mén-taeŋ-kom̦-fú-so / en-θí-ma / i-θíŋ-ko / són-so-ní-ðos-déwᵐ-míṣ-mo-fo-né-
ma // la-í-ðe-má-jo / kom-pro-nun-θja-θjón-swá-βe / a-fri-ká-ðao-r̄ej̆-lán-te /
kons-ti-tú-jej-ɣwál-mén-téw-na-só-law-ni-ðáð-fo-no-ló-xi-ka // la-é-re-i-la-é-r̄e-
són / eŋ-kám-bjo / fo-né-maṣ-ði-fe-rén-tes // pé-ro / pé-r̄o / ká-ro / ká-r̄o //
loṣ-míṣ-mos-fo-né-ma-sa-pa-ré-θem-ba-xo-fór-maṣ-mwí-ði-βér-sas // en-r̄e-a-
li-ðáð-noáj-fo-né-ma-ke-seój-ɣaen-tó-ðoṣ-loṣ-lá-βjoṣ-ðe-la-míṣ-ma-ma-né-ra // a-
sí-ko-moel-fo-né-ma-r̄e-pre-sén-tael-tí-poj-ðe-o-ló-xi-ko / ke-ðáw-ni-ðá-ða-la-βa-
rje-ðaᵟ-ðe-loˢ-so-ní-ðos / el-so-ní-ðo-por-su-pár-te-pro-por-θjó-na-fór-ma-r̄e-á-li-
koŋ-kré-ta-laj-má-xen-te-ó-ri-ka-ðel fo-né-ma // la-βir-túð-se-mán-ti-ka-ðel-so-
ní-ðo / r̄e-sí-ðe-nel-βíŋ-ku-lo-ðe-su-fi-li-lja-θjóm̦-fo-no-ló-xi-ka / awŋ-ke-su-fi-
ɣú-ra-sen-tre-lá-θej-mul-ti-plí-ken-la-ka-ðé-na-pa-rén-te-mén-tejn-di-βi-sí-βle-ðe-
lar-ti-ku-la-θjón // laj-ðé-a-kom-plé-ta-ðel-fo-né-ma-r̄e-ú-ne-lo-r̄áṣ-ɣo-se-sen-
θjá-leṣ-ðel-so-ní-ðo-rá-len-su-kons-ti-tu-θjó-nor-ɣá-ni-ka / a-kús-ti-kaj-se-mán-ti-
ka //

ú-nos-fo-né-maˢ-són-de-ðo-mí-njo-ko-mún // ó-troˢ-só-lo-se-ko-nó-θe-nen-
de-ter-mi-ná-ðaṣ-léŋ-gwas // los-fo-né-maṣ-ðe-ka-ráɣ-ter-xe-ne-rál-nó-se-ðá-nen-
tó-ðos-lo-si-ðjó-ma-se-ni-ɣwál-pro-por-θjón // laj-má-xen-so-nó-ra-ðéw-na-léŋ-
gwa / de-pén-deŋ-gráᵐ-me-ðí-ða-ðe-la-pro-por-θjó-neŋ-ke-se-sír-βe-ðéw-no-
swó-tros-fo-né-mas / i-má-ses-pe-θjál-mén-te / de-la-mo-ða-li-ðáð-par-ti-ku-lár-
ke-ká-ða-léŋ-gwa-praɣ-tí-ka / en-tre-la-sé-rje-ðe-βa-rján-tes-ke-tá-le-su-ni-ðá-
ðes-per-mí-ten //

Tomás Navarro, 1946

2. eʎ-d͡je-íṣ-moeᵐ-mil-no-βe-θjén-toˢ-se-sén-taj-θíŋ-ko

la-koŋ-kíṣ-ta-ká-sjaβ-so-lú-ta-ðe-ma-ðrí-pa-raeʎ-d͡je-íṣ-mo / del-ke-noṣ-ðe-
fen-dé-mo-r̄o-mán-ti-ka-mén-tes-ká-so-r̄e-pre-sen-tán-tes / á-θe-po-sí-βles / a-su-
βéθ / koŋ-kíṣ-ta-ses-peɣ-ta-ku-lá-res / ko-mo-la-ke-seað-βjér-te-nal-ɣú-no-siṣ-ló-

tes-práy-ti-ka-mén-te-so-me-tí-ðo-sa-lajm-flwén-θja-ma-sí-βa-ðe-los͜-dje-ís-tas /
pe-ro-r̄o-ðe-á-ðos͟-ðe-tjé-r̄a-i-r̄e-ðén-ta // e-la-βán-θe-ðel-fe-nó-me-no-nó-se-pa-ré-
θe / ko-mo-no-sen-se-ɲá-βa-la-xe-o-ɣra-fí-a-liŋ -gw ís-ti-ka / a-la-paw-sá-ðaj-sis-
te-má-ti-ka-már-tʃa-ðe-lajm͜-fan-te-rí-a / si-noa-la-sál-to-ðe-los-pa-ra-kaj-ðís-tas //
és͟-ðe-no-tár / si-nem-bár-ɣo / la-r̄e-ay-θjón-deal-ɣú-nos͟-lo-ku-tó-res͟-ðe-r̄á-ðjoj-
pre-sen-ta-ðo-res͟-ðe-te-le-βi-sjón / ke-ðe-fjén-den-la-pro-nun-θja-θjón-de-la-é-
ʎe-iŋ-klú-so-ko-nul-tra-ko-r̄eɣ-θjó-nes // a-ká-so-ðe-téŋ-gan-la-ðe-ser-θjón-de-
kje-nes-tjén-de-na-kon-si-ðe-rár-láwn-r̄ás͟-ɣo-r̄u-rál / del-keáj-ke-ðes-pren-dér-
se-ko-mo-ðea-βár-ka-soal-par-ɣá-tas / ú-najm-bes-ti-ɣa-θjóŋ-kom-plé-ta-ðel-fe-
nó-me-no / a-βrí-a-ðejn-da-ɣár-nó-so-lo-su-ðis-tri-βu-θjóŋ-xe-o-ɣrá-fi-kaj-so-
θjál / si-no-tam-bjé-na-βe-ri-ɣwár-sjeɣ-sís-ten-di-fe-rén-θjas-xe-ne-ra-θjo-ná-les /
jeŋ-ké-am-bjén-te^s-se-ðán // em͟-fín / a-pu-rán-do-más͟-la-kwes-tjón / se-rí-ajn-
te-re-sán-tes-tu-ðjár-kwá-lé-se-lal-kán-θe-nó-tras-pár-tes͟-ðel-sis-té-ma-ðel-fe-nó-
me-no-ke-new-tra-lí-θa-lao-po-si-θjóm-pó-ʎo-i-pó-jo // si-lao-mo-ní-mja-ðe-ter-
mí-na-la-ðe-sa-pa-ri-θjón-de-le-mén-tos͟-léɣ-si-kos-ke-só-ni-nú-ti-le-so / po-rel-
kon-trá-rjo / si-nó-lo-só-njes-tám-bi-xén-tes / su-sus-ti-tu-θjóm-por-si-nó-ni-
mos //

Emilio Lorenzo, 1966

3. eŋ-ga-ɲó-sa-fa-θi-li-ðá-ði-se-ɣu-ri-ðá^ð-ðel-leŋ-gwá-xe
     bá-ʎi-r̄e-ál-θa-kel-fí-nú-ni-ko-ðel-leŋ-gwá-xe-sen-ten-dér-nos // pe-roé̀s-to-
nó-pwé-ðe-to-már-se-más-ke-ko-mo-fi-na-li-ðáð-pri-má-rja / por-kel-fí-na-ke-ðé-
βeas-pi-rár-sé-saen-ten-dér-nos͟-βjén / klá-ra-mén-tej-βé-ʎa-mén-te / jés-to-nó-
se-ló-ɣra-si-nún-dú-roa-pren-di-θá-xe // ká-ðajn-di-βí-ðwo-ðe-βí-a-fi-nár-su-pro-
pja-léŋ-gwa-ko-moe-lins-tru-mén-to-más-pre-θjó-so-ðe-su-kul-tú-ra / i-ká-ða-
pwé-βlo-ðe-βí-a-ɣwar-ðár-su-pró-pjoj-ðjó-ma-ko-mo-su-ma-jór-te-só-ro / ko^m-
má-sin-te-rés-kel-de-su-r̄i-ké-θa-ma-te-rjál // por-sé-rel-leŋ-gwá-xe-lajm-pre-θi-
sjó^m-mís-maj-laj-nes-ta-βi-li-ðáð / tó-ðoe-lin-te-ré-ses-pó-ko-pa-ra-man-te-nér-
low-ní-ðoj-per-féɣ-to // nó-kjé-re-sé-rés-taw-na-leɣ-θjón-de-pe-si-mís-mo / si-
nów-na-βóθ-ðea-lér-taen-los-pe-lí-ɣros-ðel-leŋ-gwá-xe // ko-mo-tó-ða-leɣ-θjón-
de-lajn-te-ɣrál-fla-ké-θaw-má-na / kjé-r̄e-sé-ra-la-βéθ-leɣ-θjón-dew-mi-li-ðáð / pa-
ra-ke-kon-si-ðe-ré-mos-nwés-tra-ses-ká-sas-fwér-θas / i-nwés-tras-kons-tán- te-so-
ka-sjó-nes-ðe-pe-ka-ðos͟-liŋ-gw ís-ti-kos // ko-moen-las-léŋ-gwa-ses-po-sí-βle-mos-
trár-si-nes-kán-da-lo-los-ká-sos-ðe-po-sí-βles-ka-í-ðas / djó-ki-sjé-ra-mos-trár-los-
pá-sos-ðeos-ku-ri-ðáð-ðel-leŋ-gwá-xe / i-los-pe-lí-ɣros-kons-tán-tes-ðe-ka-é-re-ne-
le-r̄ór / kon-sér-tán-tas-las-fál-tas-ðel-leŋ-gwá-xe / to-ða-βí-aes-kon-so-la-ðór-
kó-mo-nó-se-ko-mé-te^m-má-se-nǔŋ-ka-mí-nos-kú-roj-r̄es͟-βa-la-ðí-θo / don-de-la-
βi-sjó-né^s- sjém-prejm-per-féɣ-taj-las-kó-sas-sjém-pre-kon-fun-dí-βles //bjén-do-
lo-ðe-feɣ-twó-so-ðe-nwés-tro-leŋ-gwá-xe / é-sa-som-bró-so-kó-mo-no-sa-r̄eɣ- lá-
mos-ko-nél-pa-rael-ko-mér-θjo-βi-tál / i-ðe-βe-rá-som-brár-nos-kó-mojŋ-xé-njo-
su-má-nos / kon-tán-de-leθ-ná-βles-ma-te-rjá-les / án-lo-ɣrá-ðo-le-βan-tár-mo-
nu-mén-tos-ðe-ter-ni-ðáð-más-pe-rěn-nes-kel-βrón-θe //

Vicente García de Diego, 1960

4. léŋ-gwa-já-βla
la-léŋ-gwaé-su-né-tʃo-so-θjál // e-lá-βlaw-né-tʃojn-di-βi-ðwál // la-léŋ-gwa-
βár-ka-tó-ðo-loe-sen-θjál / é-súŋ-grán-tó-ðo // e-lá-βlae-βó-ka-só-lów-na-pe-ké-
ɲa-pár-te-ðes-te-sis-té-ma-to-tál / i-se-sír-βe-ðe-él-pa-ra-la-r̄e-pro-ðuɣ-θjón-déwŋ-
kon-te-ní-ðo-ðe-kon-θjén-θjajn-di-βi-ðwá-li-mo-men-tá-ne-o //

en-tre-léŋ-gwae-nés-te-sen-tí-ðo-já-βlaeɣ-sís-téw-na-r̄e-la-θjom-pe-ku-ljár / ú-naes-pé-θje-ðe-mo-βi-mjén-to-ðe-r̄o-ta-θjón // kwan-doβ-ser-βá-mos-kó-mo-se-βá-for-mán-do-pó-koa-pó-ko-la-léŋ-gwa / eŋ-ká-ða-ú-no-ðe-loˢ-sé-re-su-má-nos / kom-pren-dé-mos-ké-se-lá-βla-la-ke-kré-a-la-léŋ-gwa / éṣ-ðe-θír / e-lá-βla-ðe-loṣ-ðe-más // las-pa-lá-βra-si-frá-ses-keó-je-lin-di-βí-ðwoal-kre-θér / bá-nin-tro-ðu-θjén-do-paw-la-tí-na-mén-teaés-ten-la-ko-mu-ni-ðáð-liŋ-gwís-ti-ka-ðel-pwé-βlo // és-tas-pa-lá-βra-si-frá-seˢ-són / á-βla / ke-pro-θé-ðe-ðe-la / léŋ-gwa / de-loṣ-ðe-más // es-teá-βla / ke-se-r̄e-pí-tejⁿ-nu-me-rá-βleṣ-βé-θes / dé-xa-fi-nál-mén-téw-na-wé-ʎaen-la-kon-θjén-θja / je-nés-ta / ko-mo-fór-majm-pré-sa / se-ði-men-tá-ða / se-βá-kom-βir-tjén-do-pó-koa-pó-koen-léŋ-gwa // na-tu-rál-mén-te / és-ta-trans-for-ma-θjón-de-lá-βla / o-í-ðao-le-í-ða / en-léŋ-gwa / nó-θé-sa-tam-pó-koe-ne-lóm-brea-ðúl-to // tam-bjé-nés-te-r̄e-θi-βe-ðe-βé-θeŋ-kwán-do-nwé-βas-po-si-βi-li-ðá-ðes-ðes-pre-sjón / i-la-siŋ-kor-pó-ra-su-kon-θjén-θja-liŋ-gwís-ti-ka / de-tál-mó-ðo-ke-más-tár-ðe-pwé-ðe-ser-βír-se-ðé-ʎas // pe-roés-tas-mo-ði-fi-ka-θjó-nes-ðe-su-léŋ-gwa-són-r̄e-la-ti-βa-mén-te-nin-siɣ-ni-fi-kán-tes-ke-já-nó-se-tjé-ne / ko-moe-nel-ɲí-ɲo / lajm-pre-sjón-déw-naw-mén-tojm-por-tán-te //

W. von Wartburg, 1951

ORTHOGRAPHIC VERSIONS

1. Sonidos y fonemas

Cuando dos sonidos pueden alternar en la misma palabra sin producir efecto perceptible en la significación con que tal palabra es conocida, los sonidos indicados no son sino modificaciones de un mismo fonema. En cambio, cuando dos sonidos no pueden sustituírse mutuamente sin afectar el sentido del vocablo en que se hallan, los sonidos indicados son fonemas distintos. Es, pues, base esencial para la diferenciación entre sonidos y fonemas el efecto que los cambios fonéticos ejercen sobre el valor semántico de las palabras. Las modificaciones de articulación y sonoridad que la *n*, por ejemplo, experimenta en *confuso, encima,* y *cinco,* son sonidos de un mismo fonema. La *y* de *mayo*, con pronunciación suave, africada o rehilante, constituye igualmente una sola unidad fonológica. La *r* y la *rr* son, en cambio, fonemas diferentes: *pero – perro, caro – carro.*

Los mismo fonemas aparecen bajo formas muy diversas. En realidad no hay fonema que se oiga en todos los labios de la misma manera. Así como el fonema representa el tipo ideológico que da unidad a la variedad de los sonidos, el sonido por su parte proporciona forma real y concreta a la imagen teórica del fonema. La virtud semántica del sonido reside en el vínculo de su filiación fonológica, aunque su figura se entrelace y multiplique en la cadena aparentemente indivisible de la articulación. La idea completa del fonema reune los rasgos esenciales del sonido oral en su constitución orgánica, acústica y semántica.

Unos fonemas son de dominio común; otros solo se conocen en determinadas lenguas. Los fonemas de carácter general no se dan en todos los idiomas en igual proporción. La imagen sonora de una lengua depende en gran medida de la proporción en que se sirve de unos u otros fonemas y más especialmente, de la modalidad particular que cada lengua practica entre la serie de variantes que tales unidades permiten.

Tomás Navarro, *Estudios de fonología española,* (Syracuse, 1946), 8–10.

2. El yeísmo en 1965

La conquista casi absoluta de Madrid para el *yeísmo,* del que nos defendemos románticamente escasos representantes, hace posibles, a su vez, conquistas espectaculares, como la que se advierte en algunos islotes prácticamente sometidos a la influencia masiva de los yeístas, pero rodeados de tierra 'irredenta'. El avance del fenómeno no se parece, como nos enseñaba la geografía lingüística, a la pausada y sistemática marcha de la infantería, sino al asalto de los paracaidistas. Es de notar, sin embargo, la reacción de algunos locutores de radio y presentadores de televisión, que defienden la pronunciación de la *ll* incluso con ultracorrecciones: acaso detengan la deserción de quienes tienden a considerarla un rasgo rural del que hay que desprenderse como de abarcas o alpargatas. Una investigación completa del fenómeno habría de indagar no sólo su distribución geográfica y social, sino tambien averiguar si existen diferencias generacionales y en qué ambientes se dan. En fin, apurando más la cuestión, sería interesante estudiar cuál es el alcance en otras partes del sistema del fenómeno que neutraliza la oposición *pollo* y *poyo;* si la homonimia determina la desaparición de elementos léxicos que son inútiles o, por el contrario, si no lo son y están vigentes, su sustitución por sinónimos.

Emilio Lorenzo, 'El español en 1965', in *El español de hoy, lengua en ebullición* (Madrid, 1966), 26.

3. Engañosa facilidad y seguridad del lenguaje

Bally realza que el fin único del lenguaje es entendernos; pero esto no puede tomarse más que como finalidad primaria, porque el fin a que debe aspirarse es a entendernos bien, claramente y bellamente, y esto no se logra sin un duro aprendizaje. Cada individuo debía afinar su propia lengua como el instrumento más precioso de su cultura, y cada pueblo debía guardar su propio idioma como su mayor tesoro, con más interés que el de su riqueza material. Por ser el lenguaje la imprecisión misma y la inestabilidad, todo el interés es poco para mantenerlo unido y perfecto. No quiere ser ésta una lección de pesimismo, sino una voz de alerta en los peligros del lenguaje. Como toda lección de la integral flaqueza humana, quiere ser la vez lección de humildad, para que consideremos nuestras escasas fuerzas y nuestras constantes ocasiones de pecados lingüísticos. Como en las lenguas es posible mostrar sin escándalo los casos de posibles caídas, yo quisiera mostrar los pasos de oscuridad del lenguaje y los peligros constantes de caer en el error. Con ser tantas las faltas del lenguaje, todavía es consolador cómo no se cometen más en un camino oscuro y resbaladizo, donde la visión es siempre imperfecta y las cosas siempre confundibles. Viendo lo defectuoso de nuestro lenguaje, es asombroso cómo nos arreglamos con él para el comercio vital, y deberá ásombrarnos cómo ingenios humanos con tan deleznables materiales han logrado levantar monumentos de eternidad más perennes que el bronce.

Vicente García de Diego, 'La imprecisión, sino fatal del lenguaje', in *Lecciones de lingüística española* (Madrid, 1960), 174.

4. Lengua y habla

La lengua es un hecho social; el habla un hecho individual. La lengua abarca todo lo esencial, es un gran todo; el habla evoca sólo una pequeña parte de este sistema total y se sirve de él para la reproducción de un contenido de conciencia individual y momentáneo.

Entre lengua en este sentido y habla existe una relación peculiar, una especie de movimiento de rotación. Cuando observamos cómo se va formando poco a poco la lengua en cada uno de los seres humanos, comprendemos que es el habla la que crea la lengua, es decir, el habla de los demás. Las palabras y frases que oye el individuo al crecer van introduciendo paulatinamente a éste en la comunidad lingüística del pueblo. Estas palabras y frases son *habla* que procede de la *lengua* de los demás; este habla, que se repite innumerables veces, deja finalmente una huella en la conciencia y en ésta, como forma impresa, sedimentada, se va convirtiendo poco a poco en lengua. Naturalmente, esta transformación del habla (oída o leída) en lengua, no cesa tampoco en el hombre adulto. También éste recibe de vez en cuando nuevas posibilidades de expresión y las incorpora a su conciencia lingüística, de tal modo que más tarde puede servirse de ellas. Pero estas modificaciones de su lengua son relativamente tan insignificantes que ya no se tiene, como en el niño, la impresión de un aumento importante.

W. von Wartburg, *Problemas y métodos de la lingüística,*
tr. Dámaso Alonso and Emilio Lorenzo (Madrid, 1951), 10–11.

PART II: HISTORICAL PHONOLOGY

Language moves down time in a current of its own making. It has a drift. If there were no breaking up of a language into dialects, if each language continued as a firm, self-contained unity, it would still be constantly moving away from any assignable norm, developing new features unceasingly and gradually transforming itself into a language so different from its starting point as to be in effect a new language.

E. Sapir, *Language:an Introduction to the Study of Speech,* 1921.

10.1   Living speech, as Edward Sapir observed in the 1920s, has always been in a state of drift, growing and changing from one locality to another, from one century to another, at times from one generation to another. Sapir's 'drift', however, is determined to a very large extent by the historical context in which it occurs, and a diachronic study of the phonetic evolution of the Spanish language involves us of necessity in a brief survey of the historical background against which the changes took place.

10.2   The particular phonetic nature and phonetic structure of Modern Spanish can be traced back to a point in time when a small language community found itself called upon by accident of history to learn and use an unfamiliar language — the language of a conquering nation. Spain became a province of Rome in 197 B.C., and the Roman legionaries, settlers and administrators who came to the new Roman province brought with them the Latin language. Latin, the language taught in the schools, the language of the educated man, was soon adopted as the official language of the Peninsula. Iberians began to use it as a means of communication with their conquerors and the native languages of the Peninsula, after a bilingual period during which their social status declined constantly, eventually fell into disuse. Later accidents of history, which led to the Moorish invasion of the Peninsula and the leading part played in the Christian reconquest by **Castile**, a small northerly region of Spain which had learned its Latin at some distance from the main cultural centres, meant that the particular type of speech which became standard in the Peninsula was the speech of that region. This speech, although subsequently modified by chronological, geographical and social factors, derived from spoken Latin as it had been learned and pronounced, or misprounced, by a small language community in Cantabria, in the upper reaches of the valley of the Ebro.

10.3   The Latin introduced to the Iberian Peninsula was the **sermo vulgaris** (Vulgar Latin) of the bulk of the population, and not the polished and highly refined language which owed its existence to the writings, and possibly also to the speech, of an educated and cultured minority in Rome during the hundred years which followed 87 B.C. This was the 'Classical' or 'Golden' Age of Rome when narrative prose was polished by Caesar and philosophical and rhetorical prose was polished by Cicero; this was the age which provided the standards for what is now generally referred to as 'Classical' Latin.

0.4   It is not from Classical Latin, however, but from the spoken tongue – the **sermo vulgaris** – that the Romance languages largely derive, and this presents the first major problem for the linguist who concerns himself with their evolution. Vulgar Latin was not a written language, our knowledge of it is scant and our sources of information are few. There are the occasional remarks of grammarians, who comment on the subject of 'substandard' pronunciations. One of the most important written texts of this type is the *Appendix Probi,* a list compiled by a grammarian at some time between the third and the seventh century A.D., which contains a list of 'correct' and 'incorrect' spellings and possibly pronunciations. There are the works of a few writers who are influenced by or deliberately introduce colloquial usages; there are a few forms in manuscripts and inscriptions which betray the influence of popular speech. These are the only useful sources. Later, however, the prose style of early Christian writers such as St Jerome and St Augustine and, even more important, the early Romance translations of the Bible, provide much more plentiful and informative evidence about the Latin vernacular of their times. These sources apart, the great bulk of our information is derived from the evidence of the Romance languages themselves. Where there is a large measure of agreement among those languages which derive from Latin, or among the Western Romance group (which includes Catalan, Spanish, Portuguese, Provençal and French), it is always possible to reconstruct a hypothetical colloquial Latin form (conventionally marked with an asterisk). On the basis of Catalan *cavall,* Spanish *caballo,* Portuguese *cavalo,* Provençal *caval* and French *cheval,* the prototype **kaβállus** could be reconstructed for the **sermo vulgaris** even if there were no other evidence of its existence, and contrasted with the Classical Latin form EQŬŬS which it evidently replaced in popular speech. On the basis of the way in which some vowels have diphthongized in these languages and others not, the Vulgar Latin vowel-system which differentiated between open and close vowels can be easily reconstructed.

0.5   The scantiness of our direct knowledge of colloquial Latin, however, becomes even more evident when we consider that it is extremely unlikely that what is generally termed 'Vulgar Latin' was ever a unified linguistic system. The term is used as a convenient label to describe the colloquial language of all social groups from the educated man to the farm labourer, and of all geographical areas from the Balkans in the East to Lusitania in the West. Evidence for the variety of usage throughout the social hierarchy is almost non-existent. Evidence of geographical variation tends to be concealed in the documents of the time, compiled by men with training not only in the arts of reading and writing but also in spelling and grammar, but it would be difficult not to believe that by the time of the late Empire there were at least as many 'accents' and varieties of vocabulary as there were provinces of Rome.

10.6   A study of diachronic sound-change in Spain should therefore depend upon Peninsular evidence where that can be discovered, and in the chapter of this book which deals with the vowels and consonants of Vulgar Latin (Ch. 11) only those developments which have direct relevance to the subsequent development of the Spanish language are discussed. Many of the differences between Classical and Vulgar Latin (e.g. the development of the fricatives β, ð, ɣ described in 11.17) are changes which can be deduced from the subsequent history of these sounds. For others (e.g. the appearance of the affricate sound t͡s described in 11.18) there is more direct evidence in the form of contemporary spelling and comment.

10.7   Some developments in Castilian may be due to reasons of history or geography which are peculiar to the Peninsula. In the Iberian Peninsula the situation rose in which a large number of non-Latin speakers (the **linguistic substratum**) slowly learned the language of their Roman conquerors. In this situation it would be surprising if the struggles of the native speech community to master the new language, with its unfamiliar phonetic system, did not lead to new ways of pronouncing at least some sounds in the new language. The evolution of initial *F* to *h* in Castilian is the most frequently quoted example of substratal influence: FABA > *haba*, FACĚRE > *hacer*, FĪLĬU > *hijo*, FŪMU *humo* etc. Although *h* is no longer pronounced in modern Castilian, it was articulated as an aspirated sound in the medieval period, as it was and still is to the north of the Pyrenees, in Gascony. The fact that both Gascony and the original County of Castile adjoined the Basque country, taken together with the fact that the phoneme /f/ is absent from the Basque language, suggest that Latin F came to be pronounced as an aspirated *h* by a linguistic community which was unfamiliar with the /f/ phoneme and who replaced it by a more familiar aspirated *h*. It is also true, however, that h was a rustic alternative to f in Vulgar Latin (it survives in Arumanian, Daco-Rumanian and in some French place-names), and it may well be that in this case the effect of the Iberian substratum was to favour one of two possible alternatives rather than to initiate a change: the absence of *f* and the presence of *h* in the local speech favoured the adoption of Latin forms with *h* rather than *f*. The absence of labiodental v in the greater part of Spain and Gascony may have a similar explanation: Latin V, pronounced w in the Classical period, came to be pronounced β and then v in the vulgar tongue, and the absence of labiodental v from Spain and Gascony seems to indicate not the introduction of a new sound but the favouring of one of two already established alternatives in an area where labiodental v was an unfamiliar sound. The substratal theory, however, can only account for changes which occurred during the time when the new tongue was being learned as a second language. More exotic and mystical versions of substratal theory which ascribe changes which took place centuries later, during the creation of Romance standards, to 'latent tendencies' or 'hereditary predispositions' of an Iberian substratum which had long since forgotten its pre-Roman speech-habits belong more to the field of philosophy than linguistics; from a purely linguistic standpoint they seem unlikely.

10.8   In view of the lack of direct evidence about Vulgar Latin, and of its undoubted social and geographical diversity, it has become customary in the study of historical phonology to use Classical Latin forms as the starting-point for the study of individual sound-histories or word-histories. This is not an ideal situation, but the practice is justifiable, provided that we always bear in mind the phonetic developments which would be expected to have taken place in Vulgar Latin. Where a Spanish form has descended from a phonetic variant of Vulgar Latin peculiar to the Peninsula (e.g. *enero*, which depends, to judge from the initial vowel, on V.L. JENUARIUS, documented in a number of Peninsular inscriptions and based on C.L. JANUARIUS), the relevant Peninsular form is given as the root, prefixed by the abbreviation V.L. When a Spanish form depends on a Late Latin word (e.g. *enjugar*, based on Late Latin EXSŪCARE, a derivative of C.L. SŪCUS), the Late Latin form is given, prefixed by the abbreviation L.L. When the Vulgar Latin form has to be deduced from the evidence of the Romance languages but is not documented, the postulated root is prefixed by the abbreviation V.L. and an asterisk: e.g. *culebra* < V.L *COLŎBRA.

0.9   The Romans occupied Spain from the beginning of the second century B.C. until the beginning of the fifth century A.D. Latin became the prestige language, the language taught in the schools, the language of administration, law, inscriptions, magistracy, and it had to be acquired by anyone who wanted to make a career for himself in any of these spheres. The native languages had no social value or usefulness; the modern feeling for language as a symbol of national 'pride just did not exist, the country was full of 'ideal' Latin speakers on whom a man could model his speech, and all of these factors taken together meant that within a remarkably short time Latin completely dominated the native languages. It would be reasonable to suppose a fairly long bilingual period, during which the native languages came increasingly to mark out the uneducated man who had no contact or dealings with the legislators and administrators. By the beginning of the fifth century A.D., however, the native languages seem to have been completely forgotten, and with the exception of the Basque country in the north it is likely that a form of Vulgar Latin was spoken over the whole of the Peninsula.

0.10   As the Roman Empire decayed and crumbled, so Spain became more and more isolated by the Pyrenees, and this may help to account to some extent for the differentiation of the Peninsular languages from those of Gaul. New habits, new fashions in language were slow to reach the Iberian Peninsula, if they ever did, and Spain in the course of the third and fourth centuries A.D. became increasingly remote from the new trends and innovations which were still going on fast in Gaul.

0.11   At the beginning of the fifth century the Roman domination of Spain came to an end. Germanic tribes – among them the Swabians, the Alans and the Vandals – poured over the northern frontier and overran the Peninsula. These were followed by the Visigoths, eastern Germans who were already partly Romanized and who had adopted Christianity before their invasion of Spain; during the sixth century Toledo became the official capital of Spain and the seat of the Visigothic kings. Although the Visigoths succeeded in establishing themselves and in achieving a degree of political unity in the Peninsula, they remained during their three centuries of rule a somewhat aloof military caste, living in the country rather than in the cities as the Romans had done, and making little attempt at integration. This lack of social contact between conquerors and conquered, allied to the fact that the Visigoths were considerably Romanized before they even entered Spain and had even adopted the practice of using Latin as the language of their official documents, has meant that the number of words which have entered the Spanish language as a direct result of the Visigothic occupation is strikingly small.

10.12   Some of the most common proper names in Spanish are Gothic in origin – for example *Fernando, Ramiro, Alfonso, Gonzalo, Rodrigo* – and some Spanish place-names provide reminders of the apartheid of the period – *Godos, Godojos, Gotones* against *Romanos, Romancos, Romanillos.* In addition to these there is a very small number of terms which have no corresponding forms in other Romance languages and which it is therefore reasonable to attribute directly to the Visigothic occupation of Spain: *sayón* < Goth. **sagjis, ganso* < Goth. **gans, ropa* < Goth. **raupa, ganar* < Goth. **ganan, escanciar* < Goth. **skankjan.* The majority of Germanic loan words which have entered Spanish, however, were introduced to Latin by Gothic legionaries or crossed the frontiers between the Roman colonies and the Gothic tribes; these were already assimilated into Latin before the final fall of the Empire in 476 and appear in the works of Late Latin writers. Words such as *guerra* < Germ. *werra, guardar* < Germ. *wardôn, toalla* < Germ. *thwahljo, espía* < Goth. **spaíhôn, rico* < Goth. *reiks, espuela* < Goth. **spaúra* all entered Spanish, and other Romance languages, via Late Latin. The Germanic invasions appear to have had little influence on the phonetic development of Spanish; the sounds of Gothic words were simply adapted to the nearest corresponding Latin sounds and usually, once introduced, went through the same phonetic changes as did the Vulgar Latin words in Spain.

10.13   The period of Visigothic domination in Spain came to an end in A.D. 711 when a comparatively small Moorish expeditionary force under the leadership of Tāriq landed at what is now Gibraltar, defeated Roderick, the last king of the Goths, near Jerez de la Frontera, and very quickly overran the rest of the Peninsula. Just seven years later the whole country, with the exception of a few scattered pockets of resistance in the North, was under Moorish domination. The Moorish and the Peninsular peoples achieved a degree of coexistence that the Visigoths and the Hispano-Romans never seem to have achieved. Moorish rule, until the end of the eleventh century at least, was remarkably tolerant; there was little religious or racial persecution; inter-marriage was permissible; the Christians who did not flee to the north were left to follow their own customs, religion and way of life provided that they did not make religious or political difficulties. There was a time when linguists believed that Peninsular Romance had virtually died out in this period, but it is obvious now, from the numerous references made to the Romance tongue in both Arabic and Hebrew texts, and from the recent deciphering of the *jarchas* (short two-line Romance tail-pieces appended to Arabic and Hebrew lyrics) that this was by no means the case. The upper classes soon became bilingual, Arabic continued to be the official speech, but there were many – those who did not come into direct contact with official circles – who would never have felt the need to acquire it, and there are references to men of some consequence who could speak nothing but Romance.

0.14 Much of the population of the Peninsula, Moors and Spaniards, came to be bilingual, and the interchange of words and ideas from one language to the other provided few problems. Romance words were incorporated into Arabic and Arabic words into Romance with great ease, so that against the mere handful of Germanic words which have survived into modern Spanish there are over 4,000 Arabic words in the modern lexicon, making up the second greatest fund of terms after Latin itself. Most items of vocabulary entered Peninsular Romance via the *Mozárabes* (Christians living under Arabic rule, but retaining their own customs and language), who needed for their own use a large number of terms dealing with society, with administration, with commerce and industry, with things new to or developed in Andalusia. Words such as *acequia* < Ar. *sâqiya*, *arroz* < Ar. *ruzz*, *zanahoria* < Ar. *safunâriya*, *jazmín* < Ar. *yāsamîn*, *arrabal* < Ar. *rabad*, *alcalde* < Ar. *qâdî*, *atalaya* < Ar. *talâyi^c*, *carmesí* < Ar. *qarmazî* were introduced to Hispano-Romance at this period, with the degree of phonetic adaption necessary to accommodate them to the developing sound system of Romance. The influence of Arabic is almost entirely confined, however, to the introduction of new items of vocabulary; the influence of Arabic on the Spanish phonemic system is very small. One legacy of the Arabic occupation is the rare adjectival suffix *-í*, in *Marroquí, Alfonsí* etc. and in other words such as *jabalí, carmesí, baladí*, where its adjective function has been obscured. Occasionally Mozarabic pronunciation led to the substitution of Latin s by ʃ in words such as O.Sp. *ximio* < SĪMĬU, O.Sp. *xabón* < L.L. SAPŌNE, O.Sp. *enxiemplo* < EXĔMPLU (16.6c).

0.15 The reconquest of the Peninsula, shared by the Christian kingdoms of the north but spearheaded by Castile, meant that the particular dialect of Romance which acquired prestige and subsequently became 'standard' over the bulk of the Peninsula from the fourteenth century onwards was that of Castile. The language has continued, however, to borrow items of vocabulary from other languages and from its own dialects from medieval times down to the present day. Such borrowings, or **loan words,** are generally subject to some modification at the moment of their introduction in order to bring them into line with the phonetic structure of the language at the time of borrowing; once they have become an accepted part of the language they are subject to the same phonetic changes as subsequently affect wholly popular words.

0.16 From the thirteenth to the fifteenth century French literature was widely read in Spain and many French terms were borrowed into Spanish at this time; *giga, jaula, paje, reproche, estandarte, ardido* and many others date from the medieval period. The process has gone on continuously up to the present day, with the seventeenth and the twentieth centuries proving a particularly fertile period for the introduction of French loan words. Large numbers of words were borrowed from Italian during the Renaissance, among them *soneto, pianoforte, centinela, piloto, charlatán;* the discovery of America led to the introduction from the native languages of the New World of a number of terms describing local conditions or products: *huracán, maíz, tomate, cacao, pampa, cancha;* the influence of English has been comparatively small until the present century, which has seen the acceptance into common usage of such words as *mitin, party, récord, bridge, barman, film, esnob, gangster, hall, laborista, líder.*

10.17   By far the richest source of loan words in Spanish is Classical Latin. Classical Latin words borrowed at a late period, when the major phonetic changes had taken place, are subject only to the small degree of adaption necessary to make them conform to the phonetic or morphological patterns of the language. Final -US and -UM > *-o* in the medieval borrowings *tributo* < TRĬBUTŪM, *magnífico* < MAGNĬFĬCUS, *tácito* < TACĬTUS; final -ATEM > *-ad* in *voluntad, capacidad, multiplicidad, simultaneidad* etc; the final -T of the Latin -ATUM ending becomes a voiced *-d* in *dictado* < DĬCTATU, *ducado* < DŪCATU; the final -E of OPTARE, OCCŬPARE is dropped when they are borrowed into Spanish as *optar, ocupar;* but apart from these minor modifications the words are introduced to Spanish in a phonetic form as close as possible to their original Latin form. Cultural borrowings which suffer only the minimum amount of adaption necessary to make them phonetically acceptable in their new language are **learned words.**

10.18   Some words borrowed at an early stage in the history of the language can be described as **semi-learned;** these words do not display all of the sound changes which have taken place in the language up to the time of their introduction. Until well into the medieval period Latin continued to be the common language of cleric, lawyer, administrator, natural philosopher and man of letters; Church Latin and written Latin exerted a continuous influence on the spoken language. *Ángel,* an early loan word from Church Latin ANGĔLUS, is clearly semi-learned in that the intervocalic group -NG- has not palatalized to ɲ as it did in purely popular developments like CĬNGIT > *ciñe* (16.3), and in that the post-tonic vowel, which is normally effaced, is here retained. But once established in the language, O.Sp. *ángel,* pronounced án͡ʒel, is subject to the same phonetic changes as affect purely popular words: during the sixteenth and seventeenth centuries ʒ > x as in popular words (18.5–7), and the modern form ánxel resulted. In the thirteenth century the form *peligro* < PERĬCŬLU is documented in Spanish texts: *peligro* is semi-learned in that it does not undergo the popular development k'l > ʒ, as in OCULU > *ojo* (17.11) but it is nevertheless subject to metathesis of *l* and *r*, so that it cannot be considered a wholly learned word. The same can be said of *molde* < MŎDŬLU, where Ŏ does not diphthongize as in popular words (13.1–2), but metathesis of *l* nevertheless takes place.

10.19   In a number of cases a Latin word which has been transmitted by popular development has been reborrowed at a later date in a learned or semi-learned form. Occasionally the two phonetic forms remain fairly close in meaning:

INFLĀRE > *hinchar, inflar*
VĬGĬLĀRE > *velar, vigilar*
ĬNTĔGRU > *entero, íntegro*
RŬGĪTU > *ruido, rugido.*

More frequently the two words diverge semantically, with a marked tendency for the popular word to preserve a more concrete sense than the loan word:

FĬNGĔRE > *heñir* 'to knead', *fingir* 'to pretend'
CAUSA > *cosa* 'thing', *causa* 'cause, case'
CONCĬLIU > *concejo* 'town council', *concilio* 'meeting'
CATHEDRA > *cadera* 'hip', *cátedra* 'university chair'.

A popular word and a learned derivative of the same root may have strikingly dissimilar phonetic forms in the modern language:

hijo-filial	*ojo-oculista*
tamaño-magnífico	*igual-ecuable*
pobre-paupérrimo	*hierro-ferrugíneo*

0.20 The popular phonetic development of a word may be arrested or modified at some stage in its development by the pronunciation of the more educated classes. For example, the dark *l* which occurred before a consonant in Classical Latin normally vocalized and combined with a preceding *a* to produce Spanish *o* (12.8b); thus ALTU > *oto* in the place-names *Montoto, Colloto,* and in the derivative *otero.* But in more educated pronunciation Classical Latin L was retained in ALTU > *alto,* and it is this form of the adjective which has become standard. Similarly, C.L. DŬLCE produced the Old Spanish popular forms *duz, duce;* the more learned form *dulce* (with retention of *l*) gradually came to predominate in the medieval period, and of the three forms current in the Middle Ages it is the least 'popular' form *dulce* which has become established in the modern language. In some cases both the more educated and the less educated forms have survived: in educated pronunciation Latin initial F was retained during the Middle Ages, so that FĬDEM > O.Sp. and M.Sp. *fe;* in more popular pronunciation F – was replaced by an aspirate h which was later dropped: FĬDEM > *he,* and hence the expression *a la he* which coexists with *a la fe.*

0.21 The foregoing paragraphs are intended to provide a brief outline of the historical context in which the phonetic evolution of Spanish took place. The remainder of the second part of this manual concentrates on what can be regarded as the central element of the Spanish language – the Vulgar Latin basis – with a description of the sound-changes which have given popular words their present form in Modern Spanish. Learned introductions are generally mentioned only in the notes for comparison and contrast.

0.22 **FURTHER READING.** A. Alonso (1941), 185–218. K. Baldinger (1963).
W. D. Elcock (1960), ch. 2. W. J. Entwistle (1936), chs. 1 and 2.
V. García de Diego (1951), 10–31, 166–201. D. Gifford (1973), 1–15.
F. Jungemann (1955). R. Lapesa (1942), chs. 1–5. F. Lázaro (1949). Y. Malkiel (1953). R. Menéndez Pidal (1950), 1–8; (1952), ch. 1. J. Orr (1936), 10–35.
M. K. Pope (1934), I.1, II.2. R. Posner (1966), chs. 1–3. R. K. Spaulding (1943).

11 CLASSICAL LATIN AND VULGAR LATIN

VOWELS

CLASSICAL LATIN

11.1 The vowel system of Classical Latin consisted of ten vowels *(i, e, a, o* and *u,* each of which could be either long or short, with phonemic distinction) and three diphthongs *(oe, ae, au)*. There is some evidence that the *quality* of the vowels varied slightly with their length, the long vowels being rather more close than the short ones, but *quantity* was apparently the main distinctive feature. The long/short phonemic opposition can be seen in the following minimal pairs:

LĀTŬS la:tus 'broad'   LĂTŬS latus 'side'
LĒUŌ le:wo: 'I polish'   LĔUŌ lewo: 'I lift'
LĪBĔR li:ber 'free'   LĬBĔR liber 'book'
ŌS o:s 'mouth'   ŎS os 'bone'

In the conjugation, the opposition long/short was capable of distinguishing tense:

VĒNĬT we:nit 'he came'   VĔNĬT wenit 'he comes'
LĒGĬT le:git 'he read'   LĔGĬT legit 'he reads'

In the declension, the same opposition was capable of distinguishing case or number:

MĒNSĀ me:nsa: ablative   MĒNSĂ me:nsa nominative
MANŪS manu:s nominative pl.   MĂNŬS manus nominative sing.

11.2 The thirteen vowel and diphthong phonemes of Classical Latin were thus:

LONG VOWELS		SHORT VOWELS	
/i:/	FĪLUM fi:lum	/i/	PĬLUS pilus
/e:/	TĒLA te:la	/e/	MĔL mel
/a:/	CĀRUS ka:rus	/a/	MĂRE mare
/o:/	FLŌRA flo:ra	/o/	MŎLA mola
/u:/	MŪRUS mu:rus	/u/	LŬTUM lutum

DIPHTHONGS

/oe/ POENA poena
/ae/ CAELUM kaelum
/au/ CAUSA kausa

VULGAR LATIN

11.3 Early in Vulgar Latin, if not in Classical Latin itself, vowel oppositions based on *quantity* came to be associated with oppositions based on *quality*. Except for /a/, where the long and short forms fused into a single phoneme, the short vowels of Classical Latin tended to open, while the long vowels closed slightly or remained at the same point of articulation. Furthermore, the Classical Latin diphthongs /ae/ and /oe/ fused with their neighbouring sounds: /ae/ with /ẹ/ and /oe/ with /ẹ/. These changes can be summarized as follows:

11.4 Subsequently, /i̭/ was absorbed by the neighbouring phoneme /e/, thereby losing its distinctive value, and /ṷ/ was absorbed by /o/. In some parts of the Romance area the diphthong /au/ fused with /o/, but not usually in the Latin of Spain. We can thus take our scheme a stage further:

```
i   i̭   ẹ   ẹ   a   au   ọ   ọ   ṷ   u
|    \  |   |   |   |   |   |   /    |
i       ẹ   ẹ   a   au  ọ   ọ        u
```

It appears probable that by the time the Romans withdrew their forces from Spain in the fifth century, the ten vowel phonemes and the three diphthongs of Classical Latin had been reduced in normal speech to seven vowels and one diphthong.

11.5 The vowel changes so far outlined, in so far as they affect the tonic vowel, can be summarized in diagram form (figs. 34–5). They are also illustrated in the following examples:

1. Ī i: > i fi:lum > fílo
2. Ĭ i ⎫ > ẹ pilum > pẹ́lo
   Ē e: ⎭   te:la > tẹ́la
3. Ĕ e > ẹ mel > mẹ́l
4. Ā a: ⎫ > a ka:rum > káro
   Ă a ⎭   mare > máre
5. Ŏ o > ọ mola > mọ́la
6. Ō o: ⎫ > ọ flo:rem > flọ́re
   Ŭ u ⎭   lutum > lọ́to
7. Ū u: > u mu:rum > múro

NOTES

1. For the further development of unstressed vowels see 11.7
2. For the loss of final *m* see 11.14.

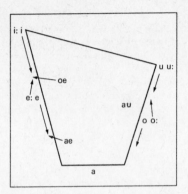

FIG. 34 CLASSICAL LATIN VOWELS AND DIPHTHONGS. The arrows indicate movement towards Vulgar Latin.

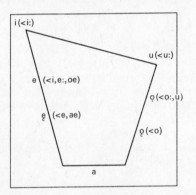

FIG. 35 VULGAR LATIN VOWELS AND DIPHTHONGS. Classical Latin sources are in brackets.

11.6   In Classical Latin, although scholars still disagree about this, the main accent on a word appears to have been musical, or melodic. Later, an *expiratory accent* gradually came to be associated with the Classical Latin musical accent, and by the fourth century at the latest had become dominant.

NOTE
The musical accent which may have fallen on one syllable of a Classical Latin word is not marked in phonetic transcripts. The expiratory accent of Vulgar Latin, however, is always marked Thus:

C.L. POENA poena > V.L. pẹ́na
C.L. MĔL mel > V.L. mẹ́l

11.7   The expiratory accent of Vulgar Latin was a strong one, and its influence considerably intensified the stress which was accorded the tonic syllable of a word. The stress which fell upon other syllables of a word diminished in proportion. From the point of view of their subsequent development into Castilian it is essential to recognise four principal degrees of stress in Vulgar Latin.

(a) **Tonic vowels.** Here the phonetic oppositions /ę/ – /ẹ/ and /ǫ/ – /ọ/ were clearly maintained. When the main stress accent of a word fell on one of the half-open vowel phonemes /ę/, /ǫ/, the vowel tended to lengthen in Vulgar Latin and create a situation which was to give rise to a diphthong in Old Spanish.

C.L. SĔRRA > V.L. sęrra > O.Sp. *sierra* sjére
C.L. PŎRTA > V.L. pǫrta > O.Sp. *puerta* pwérta

When the main stress fell on one of the half-close vowel phonemes /ẹ/, /ọ/, however, no lengthening took place in Vulgar Latin and the half-close vowel survived undiphthongized into Old Spanish:

C.L. TĒLA > V.L. tẹla > O.Sp. *tela* téla
C.L. SŌLA > V.L. sọla > O.Sp. *sola* sóla

(b) **Initial vowels.** Provided that the tonic accent did not fall upon the vowel of the first syllable in a word, that vowel bore a secondary accent. This secondary accent ensured that initial vowels were largely preserved in Old Spanish, but the phonemic distinctions /ę/ – /ẹ/ and /ǫ/ – /ọ/ were obscured. In phonetic transcripts these vowels are represented without diacritical marks, as e and o respectively:

C.L. LĒGŪMEN > V.L. leyúmen   C.L. CŎRTĬCĔA > V.L. kortę́tsa
C.L. SĒCŪRU > V.L. sekúro   C.L. SŬBĪRE > V.L. soβíre

(c) **Final vowels.** In the last syllable of a word the vowel was still more weakly stressed. Not only were the distinctions /ẹ/ – /ę/ and /ọ/ – /ǫ/ obscured, but also the distinctions /i/ – /e/ and /u/ – /o/:

C.L. MĪSĪ miːsiː > V.L. míse
C.L. NŎVEM nowem > V.L. nǫ́βe
C.L. ANNŬM annum > V.L. ánno
C.L. AMBŌ ambo: > V.L. ámbo

Final Ī occasionally proved resilient, for example in the first person singular ending of strong preterites, where in some cases it survived long enough to affect a preceding tonic vowel (see 12.4a 2).

(d) **Unstressed vowels.** Vowels interior in a word, both preceding and following the tonic accent, were unstressed in Vulgar Latin and (with the exception of *a*) subject to effacement.

C.L. CĂLĬDU > V.L. kálðo
C.L. TĂBŬLA > V.L. táβla
C.L. ŎCŬLU > V.L. óklo
C.L. AURĬCŬLA > V.L. aurę́kla

NOTE
In VĔTŬLU and CAPĬTŬLU the fall of the post-tonic vowel led to the
production of the group t'l, which rapidly developed to k'l, aided by the
analogy of AURĬCŬLA > aurękla, OVĬCŬLA > oβękla etc.

C.L. VĔTŬLU > V.L. βęklo
C.L. CAPĬTŬLU > V.L. kapęklo

The Vulgar Latin stress hierarchy can be illustrated in the six-syllable
proparoxytone *recuperaverat:*

2   4   4   1   4   3
R E C U P E R A V E R A T

11.8   In Vulgar Latin, even after the differences of quality among vowels had
ceased to be distinctive in many positions and all traces of the melodic or
'pitch' accent of Classical Latin had disappeared, the *position* of the main
accent, with very few exceptions, remained unaltered. One exception
involved a group of words stressed in Classical Latin on the antepenultimate
syllable. In words which had a short penultimate vowel in Classical Latin
followed by a plosive consonant plus *r*, the stress shifted to the
penultimate syllable in Vulgar Latin:

C.L. ĬNTĔGRUM > V.L. entęγro
C.L. TĔNĔBRAS > V.L. tenéβras
C.L. CŌLŬBRAM > V.L. kolǫ́βra

NOTES
1. Compound verbs such as RĔTĬNET and DĬSPLĬCET which were regularly
stressed on the first syllable in Classical Latin were treated in Vulgar Latin as
derivatives of the simple verbs TENĒRE and PLACĒRE. The stress
accordingly moved to the stem syllable: V. L. reténet, desplát͡set.
2. In the Vulgar Latin of Spain the Latin -ĔRE conjugation (with unstressed
Ĕ) was absorbed into either the -ĒRE or the -ĪRE conjugation. As a result the
stress moved from the stem to the infinitive ending in these verbs:

C.L. CAPĔRE > V.L. kapę́re
C.L. SAPĔRE > V.L. sapę́re
C.L. VĔRTĔRE > V.L. βertę́re
C.L. LŪDĔRE > V.L. luðíre
C.L. PARĔRE > V.L. paríre
C.L. DĪCĔRE > V.L. dit͡síre

SEMIVOWELS

CLASSICAL LATIN

11.9   Classical Latin had no semivowels.

VULGAR LATIN

11.10   A stressed front vowel, in hiatus with a following vowel in Classical Latin,
became the semivowel j in Vulgar Latin, and the stress shifted on to the

following vowel:
    C.L. MŬLĬERĔM muli:erem > V.L. moljére
    C.L. *VARĪŎLA wari:ola > V.L. βarjóla
    C.L. FĪLĬŎLUM fi:liolum > V. L. filjólo

.11   Unstressed Ĕ and Ĭ, in hiatus with a following vowel in Classical Latin, also closed to become the Vulgar Latin onglide j:
    C.L. ĀLĔA a:lea > V.L. álja
    C.L. FĪLĬUM fi:lium > V.L. ffljo
    C.L. LĬNĔA li:nea > V.L. línja
    C.L. CĀSĔUM ka:seum > V.L. kásjo
Similarly Ŭ and Ŏ, in hiatus with a following vowel, became Vulgar Latin w:
    C.L. VĂCŬO wakuo > V.L. βákwo
    C.L. LĬNGŬA lingua > V.L. léngwa
    C.L. VĬDŬA widua > V.L. βéдwa
    C.L. CŎAGULARE koagulare > V.L. kwayláre

CONSONANTS

.12   In general the consonants of Classical Latin persisted into Vulgar Latin:
    C.L. POENA > V.L. péna
    C.L. DŪRU > V.L. dúro
    C.L. FAMA > V.L. fáma
    C.L. CASA > V.L. kása
    C.L. LĔNTĬSCU > V.L. lentísko

.13   **Prosthesis.** Classical Latin S, when it was initial in a word, was pronounced with strong breath force before a consonant. The effect was that of an extra syllable:
        SCŪTU s-ku:tu   SPARTU s-partu   STĀRE s-ta:re
This led to the introduction in Vulgar Latin of a *prosthetic* or prefix vowel (usually *i* until the seventh century, and later *e*) before the combination *s* + consonant:
    C.L. SCŪTU > V.L. iskúto > eskúto
    C.L. SPARTU > V.L. ispárto > espárto
    C.L. STĀRE > V.L. istáre > estáre

.14   **Fall.** Classical Latin final m ceased to be pronounced in words of more than one syllable:
    MĒNSEM > mése   DĔCEM > détse
    MŪRUM > múro   TĂBŬLAM > táβla
Classical Latin h ceased to be pronounced in all positions:
    HŎSTĬA > óstja   PRĔHĒNDO > préndo
    HĔDĔRA > éд(e)ra   CŎHŎRTEM > kórte

.15   **Gemination.** Some consonants in an implosive position (8.15) were *assimilated* to the following sound (i.e. attracted to its point of articulation), and a *geminate* (or double) consonant was produced:

(a)   pt > tt   SCRĬPTUM > skrítto
                       SĚPTEM > sę́tte
                       APTARE > attáre

(b)   ps > ss   ĬPSE > ę́sse
                       GȲPSUM > ję́sso

(c)   rs > ss   ŬRSUM > ósso
                       VĚRSUM > βę́sso

11.16   Reduction

(a)   In two consonant groups the first element was lost.
When final in a syllable:

ks > s   SĚXTUM > sę́sto
                 DĚXTER > dę́ster
                 FĒLIX > fę́lis

When intervocalic:

ns > s   ANSA > ása
                 MĒNSA > mę́sa
                 MENSŪRA > mesúra

(b)   In the groups **dj, gj** the combination consonant + palatal glide was
simplified to a single palatal sound **j.**

C.L. PŎDĬUM **podium** > V.L. **pǫ́djo** > **pójo**
C.L. RADĬUM **radium** > V.L. **rǎdjo** > **rǎjo**
C.L. EXAGĬUM **eksagium** > V.L. **ekságjo** > **eksájo**

11.17   Changes in manner of articulation.

(a) In Classical Latin, B was pronounced as the bilabial plosive **b** in all positions,
and V as the velar **w** in all positions.
   BĚNE **bene**   BIBĚRE **bibere**
   VĪTA **wi:ta**   CŪRAVIT **ku:rawit**
In Vulgar Latin:
1. Plosive **b** remained unchanged at the beginning of a rhythm group.
   C.L. BĚNE > V.L. **bę́ne**
   C.L. BASĬUM > V.L. **básjo**

2. Elsewhere, all sounds written B and V came to be pronounced as the
bilabial fricative β.
   Intervocalic B:
   C.L. CŬBĬTU > V.L. **kóβeto**
   C.L. BĬBĚRE > V.L. **beβére**
   Intervocalic V:
   C.L. CŪRAVIT > V.L. **kuráβet**
   C.L. AVĒNA > V.L. **aβéna**

Initial V:

C.L. VĪTA > V.L. βíta

C.L. VALĔO > V.L. βáljo

The result was a temporary situation in which **b** was the pronunciation of *b* at the beginning of a rhythm group, and β was the pronunciation of both *b* and *v* elsewhere; the phonemes /b/ and /w/ of Classical Latin had become the phonemes /b/ and /β/ of Vulgar Latin. The confusion of the time is reflected in contemporary spellings: *serbus* for *servus, solbit* for *soluit, rogabimus* for *rogavimus, biginti* for *viginti, cabia* for *cavea* etc.

SUMMARY

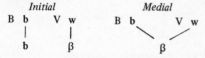

NOTES

1. In some parts of the Empire confusion was later lessened as the bilabial fricative β which had developed from Latin V came to be pronounced as a labiodental **v**, and the new opposition /b/ — /v/ was established. Castilian Spanish, however, reflects the earlier stage described above.

2. Particularly in popular speech, Classical Latin V tended to be lost before the velar vowel **u**: RĪVU > r̄ío.

(b) Between vowels, Classical Latin D and G developed, in the same way as B, to fricatives: **d** > ð, **g** > γ.

C.L. VĪDĔRE wi:de:re > V.L. βiðére

C.L. NĔGĀRE nega:re > V.L. neγáre

D and G also became weak fricatives before R:

C.L. QUADRUM kwadrum > V.L. kwáðro

C.L. NĬGRO nigro > V.L. néγro

(c) The intervocalic groups **kt** and **ks** provided problems of articulation in Vulgar Latin. In each case, the syllable-final velar stop **k** weakened to the velar fricative **x**: **kt** > **xt, ks** > **xs**.

C.L. LACTE > V.L. láxte

C.L. ŎCTU > V.L. óxto

C.L. TAXU > V.L. táxso

C.L. MATAXA > V.L. matáxsa

NOTE

The developments described in 11.17 are not revealed by Vulgar Latin orthography and cannot therefore be regarded as certain. On the evidence of the subsequent development of the Western Romance Languages, however, it is reasonable to conclude that these changes took place within the Latin period.

11.18   **Changes in point of articulation.**

(a) **lj > ʎ, nj > ɲ**. The groups **lj, nj** palatalized to ʎ and ɲ respectively. This was the result of a process of *coalescent assimilation*, whereby the sequence of two sounds, one alveolar and one palatal, coalesced and gave rise to a single new sound:

    C.L. FĪLĬUM fiːlium > V.L. fíljo > fíʎo
    C.L. PALĔA palea > V.L. pálja > páʎa
    C.L. VĪNĔA wiːnea > V.L. βínja > βíɲa
    C.L. ĂRĀNĔA araːnea > V.L.aránja > aráɲa

(b) **ǵ > j**. Before the palatal vowels E and I, Classical Latin G, articulated in a forward, post-palatal position, was attracted further forward towards the point of articulation of the following vowel and by the fourth century was pronounced as a palatal fricative j:

    C.L. GĔLU ǵelu > V.L. jélo
    C.L. GĔNTEM ǵentem > V.L. jẹ́nte

In an intervocalic position this j was assimilated to a following palatal vowel.

    C.L. MAGĬSTER maǵister > V.L. majẹ́ster > maẹ́ster
    C.L. REGĪNA reːǵina > V.L. r̄ejína > r̄eína
    C.L. FRĪGĬDUM friːǵidum > V.L. fríjeðo > fríeðo
    C.L. SAGĬTTA saǵitta > V.L. sajétta > saétta
    C.L. VAGĪNA waǵiːna > V.L. βajína > βaína
    C.L. VĪGĬNTĪ wiːǵinti: > V.L. βijénti > βiénti

NOTE
The sound written J or I in JACET, JAM, JUSTUS, CUJUS, MAJU etc. was also pronounced j in Vulgar Latin.

(c) **tj, kj, k̂ > t͡s**. During the second and third century A.D. both **t** and **k**, when followed by the palatal glide j which had developed from C.L. Ĕ or Ĭ in hiatus (11.11), became themselves slightly palatalized – t̂j, k̂j – and from this point onwards the two sounds were regularly confused with each other. By the fourth century coalescent assimilation had taken place in the Latin of northern Spain: t̂j > t͡s. By the fifth or sixth century t͡s was also the regular pronunciation of the group k̂j:

    C.L. FŎRTĬAM fortiam > V.L. fọ́rtja > fọ́rtsa
    C.L. TRĪSTĬTĬAM triːstitiam > V.L. tristẹ́tja > tristẹ́tsa
    C.L. MĬNACĬAM minakiam > V.L. menákja > menátsa
    C.L. CORTĬCĔAM kortikeam > V.L. kortẹ́kja > kortẹ́tsa

Before the front vowels E and I the tongue position for k was also palatal (of. 8.11 n. l). During the third century an onglide developed between this palatal k̂ and the following vowel: CĔNTUM k̂entum > k̂jẹ́nto; the palatal articulation of k̂ caused the point of articulation to shift forward until it reached that of t̂, and from this point k̂j shared the development of t̂j in the Latin of northern Spain. By the sixth or seventh century the pronunciation t͡s, already established in other words, had become standard in this position: t͡sẹ́nto.

    C.L. CENTUM kentum > V.L. k̂jẹ́nto > t̂jẹ́nto > t͡sẹ́nto
    C.L. CIRCA kirka > V.L. k̂jérka > t̂jérka > t͡sérka
    C.L. PLACĒRE plakeːre > V.L. plakjẹ́re > plat̂jẹ́re > plat͡sẹ́re

11.19 **Consonant system: Proto-Romance.** Proto-Romance is the term used by many scholars to designate the form of Vulgar Latin spoken immediately prior to the break-up into the separate regional varieties which we now call Romance languages. It is generally agreed that the break-up had occurred by the end of the eighth century. Table III summarizes the developments described in Chapter 11 and represents, insofar as it can be reconstructed, the consonant system of the Vulgar Latin spoken in Spain during the sixth and seventh centuries.

TABLE III   THE CONSONANTS OF PROTO-ROMANCE

	Labial		*Dental*	*Alveolar*	*Palatal*	*Velar*
	Bilabial	*Labiodental*				
Plosive	p b		t d			k g
Affricate				$\widehat{ts}\left(\left\langle\begin{array}{l}tj\\<kj\\ḱ\end{array}\right.\right)$		
Fricative	β (<b, w)	f	ð (<d)	s z		x (<k)
						ɣ (<g)
Nasal	m			n	ɲ (<nj)	
Lateral				l	ʎ (<lj)	
Vibrant				r		
Semi vowel	w				j	

11.20 **FURTHER READING.** E. Alarcos (1965), paras. 141–2, 146. W. S. Allen (1965). W. D. Elcock (1960), ch. 1. W. J. Entwistle (1936), ch. 3. C. H. Grandgent (1934), ch. 3. J. Herman (1966). R. Lapesa (1942), chs. 2 and 3. R. Menéndez Pidal (1952), paras. 1–2, 5 bis – 8, 34. M. K. Pope (1934), I.1, II.2. E. B. Williams (1962), paras. 1–12.

11.21 **EXERCISES ON CHAPTER 11**
1. Write a phonetic transcription of the following words (i) for Classical Latin and (ii) for Vulgar Latin: DĒBĔT , TĔNĔRŬ, HĂSTĪLE, PŎSSĬDĒRE, DŌNĂT, TAURŬ, MAURŬ, NŎVŬ, FĔRŬ, SĪBĬLĀRE, PĂRĂBŎLĂ, PRAESTŌ, FOEDŬ, MŪTĂT, PŬLLŬ.
2: Which sounds in the following words were pronounced as semivowels in Vulgar Latin? CĪLĬA, MĔLĬŌRE, SAPŬI, BASĬU, TENUERAT, COĀGŬLŬ, HĬSPANĬA, SĔNĬŌRE, V.L. *MĬNUA, V.L. *QUASSIARE. What effect did this development have on the number of syllables in each word?
3. What phonetic developments occurred in Vulgar Latin among the consonants of the following words? HŌRA, VERSŪRA, CAPTĀRE, SPŌNSŬ, EXPLŌDĔRE, FASTĪDĬU, HABĒRE, LĔVĀRE, STŬPPA, SCRĪPSĬT.

4. What new consonant sounds developed in Vulgar Latin in the following words? MĚLIŌRE, MĬLĬU, EXTRANĔU, SĔNĬŌRE, GERMĀNU, GĔLÁRE, TĪTIŌNE, CONCĬLĬU, CAELU, JACĒRE. Write a phonetic transcription for each word in its Vulgar Latin pronunciation.

5. The *Appendix Probi* (compiled at some time between the third and the seventh century A.D.) was a word list in which the compiler presented a 'correct' Latin pronunciation or spelling followed by what he considered an 'incorrect' form. Comment on the phonetic information provided by the following entries:

> *vacua* non *vaqua*
> *calida* non *calda*
> *vinea* non *vinia*
> *ansa* non *asa*
> *tabes* non *tavis*
> *puella* non *poella*
> *meretrix* non *menetris*
> *persica* non *pessica*
> *capitulum* non *capiclum*
> *vapulo* non *baplo*

12 STRESSED VOWELS AND VOICED SINGLE CONSONANTS

STRESSED VOWELS

12.1 In general the stressed vowels of Vulgar Latin survived unaltered into Old Spanish. The half-open vowels ẹ and ọ are the major exceptions: these usually became the diphthongs *ie* jé and *ue* wé respectively (see 13, 1–2). The vowel-changes from Classical Latin to Spanish can be summarized in the following table:

C.L.	Ī	Ĭ	Ē	Ĕ	Ā	Ă	Ŏ	Ō	Ŭ	Ū
V.L.	i		ẹ	ę		a	ǫ	ọ		u
O.Sp.	i		e	je		a	we	o		u

Examples:

C.L.	PĪLA	SĬCCU	TĒLA	VĔNTU	CĀRU
V.L.	píla	sékko	téla	βę́nto	káro
O.Sp.	píla	séko	téla	βjénto	káro

C.L.	MĂNU	BŎNU	TŌTU	LŬTU	MŪRU
V.L.	máno	bǫ́no	tóto	lǫ́to	múro
O.Sp.	máno	bwéno	tódo	lódo	múro

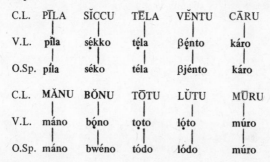

V.L. i	V.L. u

12.2 V.L. i (< C.L. Ī) > Sp. i
V.L. u (< C.L. Ū) > Sp. u

Examples:

PĪLA > *pila*   CRŪDU > *crudo*
SCRĪPTU > *escrito*   MŪRU > *muro*
FĪCU > *higo*   FŪMU > *humo*
VĔNĪRE > *venir*   CŪRA > *cura*

V.L. ẹ	V.L. ọ

12.3   V.L. ẹ (< C.L. Ĭ, Ĕ, OE) > Sp. e
V.L. ọ (< C.L. Ō, Ŭ) > Sp. o

Examples:

CRĬSTA > *cresta*	CŎLŌRE > *color*
SĬCCU > *seco*	CŎRŌNA > *corona*
TĒLA > *tela*	LŬTU > *lodo*
POENA > *pena*	CŬRTU > *corto*

12.4   **Raising of ẹ to i**

(a) By attraction, ẹ was raised, in certain phonetic contexts, towards the high point of articulation of a following palatal vowel or semivowel, closing one stage to **i**. This happened:

1. Before Vulgar Latin **j**:
    VĬTRĔU > *vidrio*   VĬNDĒMĬA > *vendimia*
    SĒPĬA > *jibia*   NAVĬGĬU > V.L. naβẹ́jo > *navío*

NOTE
Exceptions to this are *berza* < V.L. VĬRDĬA, *correa* < CORRĬGĬA, where V.L. ẹ remained unaffected by the following palatal sound.

2. Before a surviving final Ī:
    VĒNĪ > *vine*   VĪGĬNTĪ > *veinte*
    FĒCĪ > *fize*   SĬBĪ > *sí*
3. Before the semivowels **j** and **w** in:
    LĬMPĬ(D)U > *limpio*   VĬDŬA > *viuda*

(b) By dissimilation, a stressed ẹ was raised to **i** in hiatus with a following **a**:
    VĬA > *vía*   MĒA > *mía*
The hiatus might already be present in the Classical Latin form, as in the above examples, or might arise after the loss of an intervocalic consonant:
    HABĒ(B)AM > *había*   DEBĒ(B)AM > *debía*

12.5   **Raising of ọ to u.**
By attraction, ọ was also raised, in certain phonetic contexts, towards the high point of articulation of a following semivowel, closing one stage to **u**. This happened:
1. Before a velar glide produced by the vocalization of a lateral (12.8b).
V.L. ọ́l + consonant > ọ́w + consonant > ú + consonant:
    CŬLMĬNE > *cumbre*
    SŬLPHŬR > *azufre*

NOTE
DŬLCE > O.Sp. *duz, duce,* and also *dulce,* where the L̇ of Classical Latin was retained in the pronunciation of the more educated classes. Similarly SŬLCU

> O.Sp. *suco,* with the more learned variants *sulco* and *surco,* of which the last has become the accepted form.

2. Before Vulgar Latin **j**:

FŬGĬO > *huyo*
PLŬVĬA > *lluvia*
RŬBĔU > *rubio*

3. Before a semivowel produced by the fall of an intervocalic consonant:

CŌ(G)ĬTO > *cuido*
TŬRBĬ(D)U > *turbio*

4. The raised vowel of *cuño, puño, lucha, trucha, mucho, cuchillo* etc. will be dealt with later; see 16.3a, n., 16.3c, n. 1., 16.4a, n. 1., 16.4b, n.

V.L. a

12.6   V.L. a (< C.L. Ă, Ā) > Sp. a

Examples:

PRĀTU > *prado*	PĂTRE > *padre*
CĀRU > *caro*	MĂRE > *mar*

12.7   **Raising of a to e.**

When **a** came into contact with a following **i** the resulting diphthong was reduced, by a process of mutual assimilation, to the half-close vowel **e**:

ái > áj > éj > é

The group **ai** might already be present in Classical Latin: LAĬCU > *lego.* It might come into being with the loss of an intervocalic consonant:

SARTA(G)ĬNE > V.L. sartá(j)ine > sartájne > *sartén*
*BŬRRA(G)ĬNE > V.L. borrá(j)ine > borrájne > *borrén*
CANTAVĪ > V.L. kantáj > *canté*

It might also be the result of metathesis of **j** in the groups **apj, arj** and **asj,** which became **ajp, ajr** and **ajs** respectively:

SAPĬAT > sájpa > sépa *sepa*
CAPĬAT > kájpa > képa *quepa*
V.L. *CARRARĬA > karrájra > kaŕéra *carrera*
BASĬU > bájso > béso *beso*

NOTES

1. Against BASĬU > *beso,* the semivowel **j** was not subject to metathesis in the group -SSJ-, where it had the effect of palatalizing the preceeding sibilant (16.6b) and sporadically raising a preceding **a** to **e**:

C.L. LAXĬUS > V.L. *LASSĬUS > O.Sp. *lexos*
C.L. QUASSO > V.L. *QUASSĬO > O.Sp. *quexo*

But

V.L. *BASSĬO (a derivative of C.L. BASSUS) > O.Sp. *baxo.*

2. The raised vowel of *leche* < LACTE, *hecho* < FACTU, *tejo* < TAXU, *madeja* < MATAXA, *eje* < AXE etc. will be discussed later; see 16.4a, n. 1, 16.6a, n. 1.

12.8   **Reduction of aw diphthong.**
(a) áw > o
When a came into contact with a following u a compromise was effected, and
the result was the intermediate half-close vowel o:

áw > ów > óo > o

Examples:

CAUSA > *cosa*   AURU > *oro*
MAURU > *moro*   TAURU > *toro*

Although there is ample evidence that monophthongization of the group AU
had already begun in Vulgar Latin, the development came late to the Iberian
Peninsula, where the Western regions preserve the intermediate stage ou:
Northern Portuguese *cousa, mouro* etc., Western Leonese *cousa, pouco* etc.

(b) aɫ > o
Before a consonant the *l* of Classical Latin was pronounced as a 'dark' sound,
with the resonance of a back vowel (see 9.4). This velar pronunciation made
the transition from lateral to velar glide a common one. Where a preceded a
vocalized velar ɫ the combination áw was reduced to o:

BALBU baɫbu > báwbo > bóβo *bobo*
ALT(Ĕ)RU áɫt(e)ru > áwtro ≥ ótro *otro*
CALCE káɫke > káw͡tse > kód͡z *coz*
V.L. *TALPU taɫpu > táwpo > tópo *topo*

The development áw > o was characteristic of popular pronunciation; in the
pronunciation of the educated classes C.L. al was retained: ALTU > *alto*,
PALPARE > *palpar*, SALTARE > *saltar*. For each of these, more popular
forms are to be found in Old Spanish – *oto, popar, sotar* – but in each case
the pronunciation of the more literate speakers has determined the final
choice of variants. The group -ALC- shows similar indecision – thus CALCE
'the kick of a horse' developed to *coz*, with vocalization of l, while the
lateral was retained in V.L. *CALCĔA 'stocking' > *calza*.

(c) á–u > o
A diphthong was also produced by metathesis of the semivowel w in preterite
forms. Again the diphthong was regularly reduced to o in Old Spanish:

CAPUI kapui: > káwpe > kópe O.Sp. *cope (cupe)*
HABUΊ habui: > áwbe > óβe O.Sp. *obe (hube)*
SAPUΊ sapui: > sáwpe > sópe O.Sp. *sope (supe)*
JACUΊ jakui: > jáwge > jóge O.Sp. *yogue*
PLACUΊ plakui: > pláwge > plóge O.Sp. *plogue*

Some of these preterites survived into Modern Spanish with the raised vowel u,
analogical on preterites such as *pude* < PŎTUΊ, *puse* < PŎSUΊ, where u was
etymological; others, such as *yogue* and *plogue,* did not survive the medieval
period and were replaced by preterites based on the infinitive stem: *yací,
plací* etc.

VOICED SINGLE CONSONANTS

.9   The form in which voiced and voiceless consonants of Vulgar Latin developed into Spanish depended to a very large extent on the position of the consonant in relation to the syllabic nucleus. Latin consonants initial in a syllable were articulated with considerable breath force and proved most resistant to change in this position:

PĔRNA > *pierna*   ĬNTĔR > *entre*

RANA > *rana*   TARDARE > *tardar*

Between vowels consonants were articulated more weakly, and tended to be modified slightly or in some cases lost:

V.L. CATA > *cada*   SABŪCU > *saúco*

SĒCŪRU > *seguro*   DĒBĒBAM > *debía*

Consonants final in a syllable were articulated extremely weakly, and tended to be lost:

AUT > *o*   ANSA > *asa*

SĔPTEM > *siete*   ŬRSU > *oso*

V.L. **b**	V.L. **β**

10   The situation in Old Spanish was confused, but it seems most likely that Castilian perpetuated the Vulgar Latin pattern whereby a plosive **b** represented Classical Latin initial B and a fricative **β** represented Classical Latin B elsewhere and V in all positions (11.17). In an initial position, Latin B was usually represented orthographically as *b*, and Latin V as *v* or *u:*

BARBA > *barba*   VĪNU > *vino*

BŎNU > *bueno*   VŎLARE > *volar*

BŬCCA > *boca*   VACCA > *vaca*

Intervocalically, both B and V were usually represented in Old Spanish by *u*, occasionally by *v:*

BĬBĔRE > O.Sp. *beuer* > M.Sp. *beber*

CAVARE > O.Sp. *cauar* > M.Sp. *cavar*

V.L. AVIŎLA > O.Sp. *auuela* > M.Sp. *abuela*

The Vulgar Latin combination βj remained unaltered:

PLŬVĬA > V.L. **plúβja** > *lluvia*

L.L. LABIU **láβjo** > *labio*

In a small number of words Vulgar Latin intervocalic β weakened still further and was lost:

SABŪCU > *saúco*   RĪVU > *río*

VENDĒBAM > *vendía*   CANTAVĪ > *canté*

PRĪVATU > O.Sp. *priado*   V.L. VACĪVU > *vacío*

Medieval texts make it clear that there was a great deal of confusion between the two sounds, especially in the North of the Peninsula, with a strong tendency for initial β to be pronounced as a plosive **b** (cf. the spellings *boda* < VŌTA, *barrer* < VERRĔRE, *berza* < V.L. VĬRDĬA). This confusion continued well into the sixteenth century, when there is evidence that although the two speech-sounds of Old Spanish continued to be differentiated the

tenuous phonemic opposition between /b/ and /β/ was dropped, and b and β
became simple positional variants of the phoneme /b/ (18.4). Modern
orthography dates from the efforts of the Spanish Academy in the
eighteenth century to impose some sort of order on the spelling practices
of the time; in general, words which had the graph B in Classical Latin were
required to be written with *b* in Spanish and words with the graph V in
Classical Latin to be written with *v*. There are, however, a considerable
number of anomalies: cf. *boda*, *barrer* and *berza* quoted above, all of which
were written with V in Latin, and *bermejo* < VERMĬCŬLU, *basura* < V.L.
*VERSŪRA, *bodigo* < VŌTĪVU etc.

NOTE
C.L. VĔHĔMĔNTĬA produced the doublets *vehemencia* and O.Sp. *femençia*.
fimençia. The first is a cultural borrowing, introduced in the sixteenth
century; the most likely explanation for the initial *f*- of the Old Spanish semi-
learned forms *femençia*, *fimençia* is that it is the result of contamination with
other words with initial *f*-: O.Sp. *fee* < FĬDE, and possibly *firmeza*, a derivative
of *firme* < V.L. FĬRMIS.

> **V.L.   r**

12.11   The Latin *r* sound was almost certainly a vibrant, and was regularly preserved
in all positions:

RŎTA > *rueda*   HŌRA > *hora*
RAMU > *ramo*   CARU > *caro*

When initial, the evidence is that *r* was pronounced in Old Spanish as a fully
rolled vibrant, a pronunciation which medieval scribes generally represented by
the graphs *R*, *Rr* or *rr*: *Rueda*, *Rrueda*, *rrueda*; *Ramo*, *Rramo*, *rramo* etc. The
vibrant was fully rolled after a nasal: HONŌRARE > O.Sp. *onrrar* onṝár. By
metathesis, final -*r* became interior in ĬNTER > *entre*, SĔMPĔR > *siempre*,
SŬPĔR > *sobre*, MAGĬSTĔR > *maestre*, SŬLPHŬR > *azufre*.

> **V.L.   l**

12.12   The lateral was preserved in initial, intervocalic and final positions:

LŪNA > *luna*   ALA > *ala*   MĔL > *miel*
LŬTU > *lodo*   PĬLU > *pelo*   FĔL > O.Sp. *fiel*

Final -*l* became internal in O.Fr. *ensemble* < IN + SIMUL, which was
introduced into Spain in the thirteenth century as a loan-word.

> **V.L.   m**

12.13   Initial and intervocalic m remained:

MAGU > *mago*   RAMU > *ramo*
MĪCA > *miga*   CȲMA > *cima*

The combination **mj** remained in VINDĒMIA > *vendimia*.
In polysyllables, final *-m* was regularly lost:

    NŎVEM > *nueve*   CABALLUM > *caballo*   ŬNDĔCIM > *once*

In monosyllables the nasal was retained as alveolar **n,** most probably to strengthen a form that would otherwise be phonetically weak:

    QUĔM > *quien*   CŬM > *con*   TAM > *tan.*

Exceptionally, SŬM > O.Sp. *so,* where it is likely that the nasal was dropped in order to bring the form into line with other first person singulars and to preserve the distinction between the first person singular and the third person plural of the present indicative of *ser* (where SUNT > *son*). In JAM > *ya* the nasal was lost early, in Vulgar Latin – cf. French *déjà,* Portuguese *já.*

V.L. **d, g**		V.L. **ð, ɣ**

2.14 The two voiced plosives developed along parallel lines.

(a) In an initial position both remained as plosives:
    DŎMĄRE > *domar*   GALLU > *gallo*
    DŪRU > *duro*   GŬTTA > *gota*

(b) Intervocalically, both consonants were articulated as the weak fricatives ð and ɣ in Vulgar Latin (11.17); these fricatives generally remained in Old Spanish and survived to Modern Spanish:

    NĪDU > *nido*   PLAGA > *llaga*
    SŪDARE > *sudar*   NĔGARE > *negar*
    CRŪDU > *crudo*   RŎGAT > *ruega*

The changes d > ð, g > ɣ cannot be considered **regular phonetic changes,** however, since in a large number of words the intervocalic fricatives weakened still further and were lost:

    TĔPĬDU > *tibio*   RĒGALE > *real*
    CRĔDĬT > *cree*   LĒGALE > *leal*
    SĔDĒRE > *ser*   LĪTĬGARE > *lidiar*

This type of change, where it is not possible on the basis of observed data to predict in a given phonetic context which of two or more possible Romance results can be expected of a Classical Latin sound or group of sounds, can be described as a **weak phonetic change** (Y. Malkiel, 1962a, para. 12.5, and 1963).

NOTE
Final *-d* was lost in the monosyllable AD > *a.* For Classical Latin *g* before the palatal vowels *e* and *i,* see 14.12.

2.15 **FURTHER READING.** E. Alarcos (1965), para. 143. A. Alonso (1955), chs. 1 and 2. V. García de Diego (1951), 58–62, 86, 87, 92, 93, 95–98, 101–3. Y. Malkiel (1955), 161–4; (1962b), 153–62. R. J. Penny (1976), 149–59. R. Menéndez Pidal (1952), paras. 9, 11, 12, 14, 37, 41, 43, 62.

12.16   **EXERCISES ON CHAPTER 12**

1. Give the Spanish result of: CŪNA, FOEDU, GRĀNU, GŬRDU, HASTĪLE, LĬNGUA, MĂNU, MŬSCA, PĬLU, SŌLU.

2. Account for the phonetic development of the tonic vowels in:

CĂBALLĀRIU > *caballero*	CĒRĔU > *cirio*
FALCE > *hoz*	ŌRDIO > *urdo*
PLANTĀGĬNE > *llantén*	RŌSCĬDU > *rucio*
SĬBĪ > *sí*	TENĒBAM > *tenía*
THESAURU > *tesoro*	TĬNĔA > *tiña*

3. Give the Spanish result of each of the following Latin forms, paying particular attention to the development of the voiced intervocalic consonants: AESTĪVU, CĂVARE, CŪRA, LAUDARE, LIXĪVA, NAVĬGARE, PROBARE, SĬGĬLLU, TĬMĒRE, VĂDU.

4. What evidence is there of learned influence in the following words? DĬSTRĬCTU > *distrito;* PAUSA > *pausa;* MŬNDU > *mundo;* SALARĬU > *salario;* TŬNĬCA > *túnica.* What phonetic form might these words have taken if their development had been along purely popular lines?

5. Devise as many further examples as you can to illustrate the regular phonetic development C.L. Ĭ, Ŭ > Sp. *e, o* when accented in a word.

13 STRESSED VOWELS, VOICELESS SINGLE CONSONANTS, GEMINATE CONSONANTS

STRESSED VOWELS

V.L. ę	V.L. ǫ

.1

V.L. ę (< C.L. Ĕ, AE) > Sp. jé
V.L. ǫ (< C.L. Ŏ) > Sp. wé

Examples:

VĔNTU > *viento*	BŎNU > *bueno*
NĔBŬLA > *niebla*	FŎCU > *fuego*
CAECU > *ciego*	RŎTA > *rueda*
QUAERO > *quiero*	SŎLU > *suelo*

3.2   **Diphthongization process.** This diphthongization, which occurs only when the tonic accent falls on the V.L. vowels ę and ǫ, is to be attributed partly to the influence of the Vulgar Latin stress accent, which tended to be unevenly distributed over the vowel, and partly to a more energetic utterance of these two vowel sounds, a feature which is apt to lead to a lengthening of the vowel, and this in turn to a closing of part of it. The more energetic utterance of the Vulgar Latin vowel phonemes /ę/ and /ǫ/ (but not /e̩/ and /o̩/) probably owes its origin to an attempt to distinguish clearly between the half-open and the half-close vowels by a language community not accustomed to making this distinction: increased emphasis on the half-open vowels led to lengthening and to unevenness of timbre over the length of the vowel. The process of diphthongization generally accepted by Romance linguists is the following:

C.L. Ĕ   e > ę > ę̣ę > ę̣ę > íe > jé
C.L. Ŏ   o > ǫ > ǫ̣ǫ > ǫ̣ǫ > úo > úe > wé

In each case the short vowel of Classical Latin became the open vowel of Vulgar Latin and acquired an expiratory accent:

e > ę   o > ǫ

Both vowels lengthened as they were pronounced with increased energy:

ę > ę̣ę   ǫ > ǫ̣ǫ

Then in each case the first part was progressively closed:

ę̣ę > íe   ǫ̣ǫ > úo

As the first element closed still further, from vowel sound to glide, the accent became dislodged and fell on the second, vocalic, element:

íe > jé

In the case of úo, the point of articulation of the second and less distinct part of the diphthong was moved forward, and subsequent dislodgement of the accent produced the diphthong wé, which was firmly established as the norm in Castile by the eleventh century:

úo > úe > we

NOTE
For an alternative account of the diphthongization process see R. Menéndez Pidal (1964), para. 22 ff. Menéndez Pidal denies that either diphthong was ever stressed on its first element, and insists that throughout the diphthongization process the accent fell upon the second, more open, of the elements of a 'naturally rising' diphthong. Short summaries of the principal arguments against this contention are conveniently grouped in E. Alarcos (1958), 1–4, and (1965), 221–5.

13.3   **Dialectal variants.** There was considerable indecision in the Peninsular dialects over the value of the second element of the diphthong during the early medieval period: *uo* and *ua* are found as variants in forms such as *fuort, puode, uostro; ia* is found for *ie* less commonly in forms such as *ciarta, diaz, niata, piadra.* Once the indecision over variants had been resolved in Castile, however, with *ue* wé and *ie* jé established as the standard forms, these diphthongs ceased to be independent phonemes, and the constituent parts became equated with the phonemes /u/ + /e/ and /i/ + /e/ respectively (see 7.13) to produce the vocalic system of modern Castilian, based on the five phonemes /a/, /e/, /i/, /o/, /u/.

13.4   **Reduction of *ie* diphthongs.** In certain contexts the diphthong written *ie* was reduced to *i*. This happened:

(a) Before *ll*:
ANĚLLU > *aniello* > *anillo*   CASTĚLLU > *castiello* > *castillo*
SĚLLA > *siella* > *silla*   V.L. MARTĚLLU > *martiello* > *martillo*
The *-illo* forms did not become regular in the literary language of Toledo until the fourteenth century, but the process started much earlier in the north of Castile and in Burgos, where *-illo* forms are found as early as the tenth century (R. Menéndez Pidal, 1964, para. 27). Reduction, if due to phonetic causes, must have taken place when the diphthong was stressed on its first element: *-íello* > *-illo;* the second element of the diphthong, weakly articulated between the palatal vowel i and the following consonant, was eliminated.

(b) Before *s* + consonant:
VĚSPA > *aviespa* > *avispa*   VĚSPĚRA > *viéspera* > *víspera*
PRĚSSA > *priessa* > *prisa*   V.L. *NĚSPĬRU > *niéspero* > *níspero*
RĚSTE > *riestra* > *ristra*   V.L. *APPRĚSSĬCO > *apriesco* > *aprisco*
Here the circumstances were similar to those described in 13.4a above: the half-close vowel e, between a palatal vowel and the slightly palatalized s of Castilian, was eliminated, but in this case the development was not consistent and the diphthong was retained in a number of words:
FĚSTA > *fiesta*   TĚSTU > *tiesto*
SĚXTA > *siesta*   V.L. GĚNĚSTA > *hiniesta*

NOTES
1. Reduction of a triphthong at a time when the stress fell on the first element accounts for MĔU > *mío* (where V.L. ę̞o > O.Sp. íeo > ío, with no dislocation of accent) and for ĔGO > *yo*, DĔUS > *dios* (where V.L. mę̞o > O.Sp. míeo > mío > mjó, with dislocation of accent). In MULIĔRE > O.Sp. *mugier* > *mujer* the palatal onglide was absorbed by the preceding palatal consonant: V.L. molję́re > O.Sp. muʒjér > muʒér. Similarly DĪXĒRUNT > O.Sp. *dixieron* > M.Sp. *dijeron.*
2. Reduction also occurred sporadically before groups such as *rl* and *gl:*
   MĔRŬLA > *mierla* > *mirlo* (with change of gender)
   SAECŬLU > *sieglo* > *siglo* (semi-learned)
3. An alternative explanation for the development *ie* > *i* is offered by Y. Malkiel (1968c), 55–63, who suggests that at first *-iello* was replaced by *-illo* under the influence of other diminutive suffixes *(-ico, -ito, -ino)* and that the innovation later spread to affect the vowel before *s* + consonant and before consonant groups such as those exemplified by n. 2 above. Malkiel also proposes that eventually the drive towards symmetry produced the partially parallel shift *ue* > *e*, as in *fr(u)ente* (for which see 13.5).

.5 **Reduction of *ue* diphthongs.** The diphthong written *ue* was in some circumstances reduced to *e:*
   FRŎNTE > O.Sp. *fruente* > *frente*
   FLŎCCU > O.Sp. *flueco* > *fleco*
   V.L. *CŎLŎBRA > O.Sp. *culuebra* > *culebra*
The process took place in Old Spanish later than the reduction of *ie* to *i*, and at a time when the accent had shifted to the second element of the diphthong, so that in the case of wé it was the onglide w which was eliminated: wé > é. Since in each case the labial onglide was preceded by a labial consonant *(f)* or a labial vowel *(u)* plus *l* or *r*, it is possible that the loss of w was aided by a tendency towards dissimilation of the two labial sounds.

.6 **Effect of a following nasal.** In a syllable closed by a nasal, C.L. Ŏ diphthongized normally in some words:
   FŎNTE > *fuente*   CŎMPŬTAT > *cuenta*
Sporadically, however, the nasal had the effect of closing C.L. Ŏ to ǫ and diphthongization was prevented in:
   MŎNTE > *monte*   CŎMPĔRAT > *compra*
In a third group of words, diphthongized and undiphthongized forms coexisted for some time in Old Spanish:

   CŎNTRA > O.Sp. *cuentra, contra*
   CŎM(Ĭ)TE > O.Sp. *cuende, conde*
   HŎM(Ĭ)NE > O.Sp. *uemne, uembre, omne, ombre*

In each of the last three cases it is the undiphthongized variant – *contra, conde, ombre* – which proved the more resilient and became standard in modern Spanish. In the case of *dueño, don* < DŎM(Ĭ)NU both forms have survived in the modern language, the first in a stressed and the second in an unstressed position in the rhythm group.

13.7   **Non-diphthongization.** Both C.L. Ĕ and Ŏ were affected by a following
palatal semivowel. Each was attracted slightly towards the higher point of
articulation of the following sound, and became a half-close vowel which did
not diphthongize. This happened:

(a) Before Vulgar Latin j:
   SĔDEAT > O.Sp. *seya* > *sea*   HŎDIE > *hoy*
   V.L. NĔRVIU > *nervio*   V.L. NŎVIU > *novio*
   SŬPĔRBIA > *soberbia*   FŎVEA > *hoya*
With metathesis of the **rj** group (see 12.9), MATĔRIA > **maðéjra** > **madera**.
Similarly CŎRIU > **coero* which, by analogy with words containing the
more common *ue* diphthong was remodelled to *cuero*.

(b) Before a semivowel produced by the fall of an intervocalic consonant:
   GRĔ(G)E > *grey*   COLLĬ(G)O > *cojo*

(c) The non-diphthongization of Ĕ, Ŏ before O.Sp. ɲ, t͡ʃ, ʒ will be discussed
later: see notes to 16.3a, 16.4a, 16.5b, 16.6a, 17.10.

VOICELESS SINGLE CONSONANTS

13.8   As a general rule the voiceless consonants of Classical Latin remained
unaltered in an initial position, were lost in a final position, and voiced when
they occurred between vowels. Intervocalically, the voicing usually took
place before the fall of a post-tonic vowel. The earliest undisputed case of
voicing is in an inscription of A.D. 691 *(eglesie* for *ecclesiae)*, but the voicing
of intervocalic consonants does not seem to have become general, at least in
the south, until some considerable time after the Arabic invasion of the eighth
century (W. Meyer-Lübke, 1924). In the north, the earliest written evidence
of Romance, the *Glosas Emilianenses* of the early tenth century, still shows
no evidence of the voicing of single intervocalic consonants – *salbatore, faca,
sieculos* etc. – although this could well be a dialectal (Navarrese) feature; by
the late twelfth century, however, when the first Castilian literary text, the
Poema de mío Cid, was probably composed, the voicing process was complete.

> V.L. p, t, k

13.9   (a) In an initial position all three voiceless plosives remained:
   PAVU > *pavo*   TĒLA > *tela*   CŌLŌRE > *color*
   PĬNNA > *peña*   TŬRDU > *tordo*   CŪNA > *cuna*

(b) In a final position -*p* does not appear in Latin; -*t* and -*c* weakened and
were lost:
   AUT > *o*   AMAT > *ama*   NEC > *ni*

(c) In an intervocalic position:
   V.L. p > O.Sp. b
   V.L. t > O.Sp. d
   V.L. k > O.Sp. g

Each consonant voiced as the result of assimilation to the voiced vowel-sounds which preceded and followed.

CAPŬT > *cabo*	V.L. CATA > *cada*	FŎCU > *fuego*
LŬPU > *lobo*	CATĒNA > *cadena*	MĪCA > *miga*
ŎPUS > O.Sp. *huebos*	VĪTA > *vida*	PACARE > *pagar*

At first these were voiced stops in Old Spanish, coexisting with the voiced fricatives β < B, ð < D, γ < G. By the sixteenth century, however, the distinctions between b and β, d and ð, g and γ in an intervocalic position had become obscured and the fricative articulation for all intervocalic sounds which derived from Classical Latin B, V, P, D, T, G, C was established (18.4).

NOTES
1. Latin intervocalic *t* was the weakest of these sounds: the verbal endings -ATIS, -ETIS, -ITIS were preserved in Old Spanish as *-ades, -edes, -ides* until the fifteenth century, when the intervocalic consonant weakened still further and was lost, initially in paroxytones:

AMĀTĬS > O.Sp. *amades* > 15th century *amáis*
TENĒTĬS > O.Sp. *tenedes* > 15th century *tenéis*
VENĪTĬS > O.Sp. *venides* > 15th century *venís*

The intervocalic g of O.Sp. *cogombro* < CŬCŬMĔRE also weakened further between back vowels and was lost: M.Sp. *cohombro*.

2. Voicing took place regularly only when a voiceless single consonant occurred between full vowels. In the combinations *vowel + voiceless consonant + semivowel* and *semivowel + voiceless consonant + vowel* there was some indecision. Intervocalic C voiced in some words:

JACŪĪ > O.Sp. *yogue*   PLACŬĪ > O.Sp. *plogue*.

More commonly the consonant did not voice:

CAPĬAT > *quepa*	V.L. AUCA > *oca*
PAUCU > *poco*	V.L. *TALPU > *topo*

A fuller account of the phonetic development of these words is given in 12.7–8.

3. For the voicing of V.L. *p, t, k* before *r* and *l* see 15.11b.

> V.L. s

3.10   (a) In initial and final positions the Latin sibilant became the retroflex tip-alveolar s characteristic of Castilian:

SĬCCU > *seco*	MĬNŬS > *menos*
SĔPTE > *siete*	VĔNĬS > *vienes*
SŬRDU > *sordo*	PĔCTŬS > *pechos*

(b) Intervocalically, s was subject in the same way as other voiceless intervocalic consonants to assimilation by the surrounding voiced vowel sounds, and voiced in Old Spanish to z, written s:

CAUSA > O.Sp. *cosa* kóza
CASA > O.Sp. *casa* káza
THESAURU > O.Sp. *tesoro* tezóro
PĒNSARE > V.L. pesáre > O.Sp. *pesar* pezár
MĒNSA > V.L. mésa > O.Sp. *mesa* méza

NOTE
Intervocalic -*s*- continued to be articulated as a voiced fricative until the
sixteenth century when, along with other voiced sounds of Old Spanish, it
was again devoiced to s (18.5). This tip-alveolar and voiceless s, which occurs
in initial, final and intervocalic positions, can now be considered the principal
member of the Spanish phoneme. A slightly voiced version occurs only as a
positional variant before voiced consonants (8.27). The replacement of s by
t̂s, ʃ, will be discussed later; see 14.10c, n. 1, 16.6c.

> V.L. f

13.11   (a) Initial V.L. **f** (< C.L. F) > O.Sp. **h** > ø
This development may have been influenced by the linguistic substratum of
the Peninsula (10.7).
Examples:
  FABULARE > O.Sp. **haβlár**
  FACTU > O.Sp. **hét̂ʃo**
  FĒNU > O.Sp. **héno**
Although words with Latin initial F were written with the graph *f* in Old
Spanish – *fablar, fecho, feno* etc. – this graph does not provide an accurate
picture of the popular phonetic development. R. Menéndez Pidal (1964),
para. 41, shows how early evidence of aspirate h appeared in the North-
West, in eleventh-century Cantabria, as a pronunciation confined to the speech
of the lower classes. From that point its diffusion is the story of a slow
spread upwards through the social hierarchy and geographically downwards
through the Peninsula, with the rise of Castile as a political power. By the
twelfth century aspirate h had spread south to Burgos in the pronunciation of
the lower classes, while the upper classes continued to use the more 'educated'
pronunciation f. The development thus provides an example of weak
phonetic change (cf. 12.14b); during this period some words – e.g. *hablar,
hecho, heno, haba, hieno, hilo* – became established in the language in their
popular form, with initial h, while others – e.g. *falta, fiar, fiero, fiebre, falso,
fe* etc. – became established in their more literary form, with initial f. From
the twelfth to the fifteenth century the pronunciation h continued to gain in
popularity among the more educated classes and to spread southwards; by
the fifteenth century it was general in Toledo. Throughout the Middle Ages,
however, *f* continued in literary texts to be the normal graph used to
represent the sound which derived from Latin initial F-; it was not generally
replaced by the graph *h* until towards the end of the fifteenth century.
Initial h continued to be aspirated until well into the following century, when
it was finally dropped (18.3). Modern orthography retains the graph *h* only as
a relic of earlier pronunciation.
  FABULARI > O.Sp. *fablar* **haβlár** > M.Sp. *hablar* **aβlár**
  FACTU > O.Sp. *fecho* **hét̂ʃo** > M.Sp. *hecho* **ét̂ʃo**
  FĒNU > O.Sp. *feno* **héno** > M.Sp. *heno* **éno**

Words established in Old Spanish with initial *f-* retain the labio-dental consonant to the present day.

FĔRU > O.Sp. *fiero* fjéro > M.Sp. *fiero* fjéro

V.L. *FĪDARE > O.Sp. *fiar* fjár > M.Sp. *fiar* fjár

V.L. *FALLĬTA > O.Sp. *falta* fálta > M.Sp. *falta* fálta

(b) Intervocalic V.L. **f** (< C.L. F, PH) > Sp. β

The Latin intervocalic **f**, in common with other voiceless single intervocalic consonants, voiced in Old Spanish to a sound written *b* or *v*, and probably pronounced β:

AURĬFĬCE > O.Sp. *orebze*

(FĪCU) BĬFĔRA > O.Sp. *bebra*

During the sixteenth century the pronunciation β became standardized, and in modern Spanish orthographic practice varies. The graph *b* is used in some words:

STEPHANU > *Esteban*   V.L. *ACĪFU > *acebo*

The graph *v* appears in others:

CŎPHĬNU > *cuévano*   PROFĔCTU > *provecho*

O.Sp. *bebra* > *breva* (with metathesis of *r*)

NOTES

1. Initial F- was retained in popular words before the rising diphthong wé, where the influence of the labial onglide was probably the decisive factor in determining the choice between labial **f** and glottal or pharyngeal **h**:

FŎCU > *fuego*   FŎNTE > *fuente*

FŎRU > *fuero*   FŎLLE > *fuelle*

2. Initial F- is regularly retained in cultural borrowings:

FACŬNDU > *facundo*   FĬNGĔRE > *fingir*

FERTĬLE > *fértil*   FŌRMA > *forma*

3. For alternative accounts of the origins of the initial *f* of O.Sp. *finchar* < INFLARE, O.Sp. *fenchir* < IMPLĒRE and O.Sp. *fallar* < AFFLARE, see Y. Malkiel (1955), 164–85 and J. Corominas (1954–7), II, 871, 900, 921.

GEMINATE CONSONANTS

12 **Vulgar Latin geminate consonants.** The greater energy required in the articulation of double consonants maintained the phonetic distinction between these and the weaker single intervocalic consonants. Although voiceless geminate consonants were simplified to single consonants in Spanish, they resisted the voicing process:

ABBATE > *abad*   MĬTTĔRE > *meter*

SABBATU > *sábado*   GLŬTTŌNE > *glotón*

BŬCCA > *boca*   V.L. CŬPPA > *copa*

FLAMMA > *llama*   V.L. *INADDĔRE > *añadir*

Latin -SS- simplified to Old Spanish s, generally written *ss* to distinguish it from O.Sp. z, written *s* (13.10):

MASSA > O.Sp. *massa*   PASSU > O.Sp. *passo*

SPĬSSU > O.Sp. *espesso*   AMAVĬSSEM > O.Sp. *amasse*

ĬPSE > O.Sp. *esse*   ŬRSU > O.Sp. *osso*

Latin -RR- became a rolled vibrant in Old Spanish, generally written *rr*:
    CARRU > *carro*   SĔRRA > *sierra*
    TŬRRE > *torre*   CŬRRĔRE > *correr*
The palatalization of Latin -LL- and -NN- will be discussed later: see 16.2c,
16.3d.

13.13   **FURTHER READING.** E. Alarcos (1958), 1–4; (1965), paras. 143–5, 153.
A. Alonso (1955–1969), ch. 4. C. Blaylock (1964), 16–26. V. García de Diego
(1951), 58–9, 60–1, 85, 87–9, 91, 93–5, 101–6. F. Lázaro (1949).
Y. Malkiel (1955), 164–85; (1962b), 153–62, (1968c), 55–63. A. Martinet
(1951), 141–5. R. Menéndez Pidal (1952), paras. 10, 13, 37, 38, 40, 42, 45,
46, 62; (1964), paras. 22–8. W. Meyer-Lübke (1924), 1–32. J. Orr (1936),
10–35. R. J. Penny (1972), 463–82. G. Salvador (1957), 418–25.

13.14   **EXERCISES ON CHAPTER 13**
    1. Trace into Spanish: AMĪCU, V.L. LŎCO, MĔTU, MŎLA, PRĀTU,
RĀPU, SĔPTE, SĔRVU, SŎLU, TĔRRA.
    2. Account for the development of the tonic vowel in each of the following:
        BALLAENA > *ballena*   V.L. *ROSĔLLU > *rosillo*
        BALLĬSTA > *ballesta*   SARMĔNTU > *sarmiento*
        CAMĒLLU > *camello*   SCŬTĔLLA > *escudilla*
        COSTĔLLA > *costilla*   V.L. *SĬNĔXTER > *siniestro*
        MERĔNDA > *merienda*   VĔSPĔRA > *víspera*
    3. Account for the development of the tonic vowel in each of the following:
        ABSCŎNDO > *escondo*   FRŎNTE > *frente*
        BŬRSA > *bolsa*   HŎMĬNE > *hombre*
        CŎNSTAT > *cuesta*   PŎNTE > *puente*
        CŎNTRA > *contra*   RECŬPĔRO > *recobro*
        FŎRTE > *fuerte*   RESPŎNDO > *respondo*
    4. Which six of the following words show learned influence? Explain your
choice.
        agudo < ACŪTU   *ocupar* < OCCŬPARE
        apodar < L.L. APPŬTARE   *repetir* < REPĔTĔRE
        épico < EPĬCU   *saco* < SACCU
        excitar < EXCĬTARE   *seguro* < SECŪRU
        fútil < FŪTĬLE   *sofocar* < SUFFŌCARE
    5. Transcribe into phonetic script:
        O.Sp. *forca* (<FŬRCA)   O.Sp. *huebos* (<ŎPUS)
        O.Sp. *fuera* (<FŎRAS)   O.Sp. *huesso* (<ŎSSU)
        O.Sp. *fuerte* (<FŎRTE)   O.Sp. *losa* (<*LAUSA)
        O.Sp. *fumo* (<FŪMU)   O.Sp. *posar* (< L.L. PAUSARE)
        O.Sp. *gruesso* (<GRŎSSU)   O.Sp. *vienes* (< VĔNĬS)

FINAL VOWELS

4.1 Whereas the stressed vowels of Classical Latin were always preserved, either as
Castilian vowels or diphthongs, unstressed vowels tended to weaken and in
many cases to be lost completely. Even where they were preserved the finer
distinctions of timbre became obscured: against the five vowels and two
diphthongs which survived in a stressed position (12.1) only three contrasting
vowel sounds regularly survived in a final position:

V.L. e (< C.L. Ī, Ĭ, Ē, Ĕ) > Sp. e
V.L. a (< C.L. Ā, Ă) > Sp. a
V.L. o (< C.L. Ŏ, Ō, Ŭ, Ū) > Sp. o

NOTE
For final *-i, -y, -u* in Spanish see 14.5, 14.6.

4.2 | V.L. e |
| --- |

In a final position, V.L. e (< C.L. Ī, Ĭ, Ē, Ĕ) > Sp. e.

| ILLĪS > *les* | AVĔM > *ave* |
| DĪCĬT > *dice* | SĔPTĔM > *siete* |

Early in Old Spanish, final *-e* was lost after /d/, /n/, /l/, /r/, /s/, /d͡z/:

VĬRTŬTE > *virtud*	MŎVĒRE > *mover*
PĔDE > *pie*	TŬSSE > *tos*
FĪNE > *fin*	MENSE > *mes*
FĬDĒLE > *fiel*	LŪCE > *luz*

After these consonants, final *-e* was preserved only in special circumstances.
It survived as a characteristic verbal ending in:

VĒNĪ > *vine*   FĒCĪ > *hice*   QUAESĪ > *quise.*

It also survived as a support vowel for difficult consonant groups, whether
these were of Latin origin or whether they came together as the result of the
fall of a post-tonic vowel in Romance:

ARTE > *arte*	HŎM(Ĭ)NE > *hombre*
MATRE > *madre*	CAL(Ĭ)CE > *cauce*
ĬNDE > O.Sp. *ende*	PĔCT(Ĭ)NE > *peine*

$\boxed{\text{V.L. a}}$

14.3   In a final position, V.L. a (< C.L. Ā, Ă) > a
        CĬRCĀ > *cerca*   MĒNSĂ > *mesa*
        AMĀS > *ama*   CANTĂNT > *cantan*

$\boxed{\text{V.L. o}}$

14.4   In a final position, V.L. o (< C.L. Ŏ, Ō, Ŭ, Ū) > Sp. o
        QUAERŎ > *quiero*   VĪNŬ > *vino*
        QUANDŌ > *cuando*   PĬLŬ > *pelo*

14.5   **Spanish final -i, -j.** Final j evolved spontaneously only when, as the result of the fall of an intervocalic consonant, final *-e* came into hiatus with the tonic vowel. In these circumstances final *-e* closed in syneresis to the semivowel **j**, written *y:*
        RĒ(G)E > *r̄ée > r̄éj *rey*
        LĒ(G)E > *lée > léj *ley*
        BŎ(V)E > *bwée > bwéj *buey*

    This type of hiatus was resolved in the same way even as late as the fifteenth and sixteenth century, when intervocalic *d* was lost from the second person plural verb-endings:
        O.Sp. *amades* > *amáes* > *amáis* **amájs**
        O.Sp. *amábades* > *amábaes* > *amabais* **amáβajs**

NOTES
1. The offglide of *hay* **áj** originated in the C.L. adverb IBI: HA(BET) + IBI > *hay*. Possibly by analogy with *hay*, the offglide was extended to the first person singular of *ser, estar, ir,* and *dar* during the late medieval period: SŬM > *so* > *soy*, STO > *estó* > *estoy*, VO > *vo* > *voy*, DO > *do* > *doy*.
2. Final *-i, -y* appear only in very restricted circumstances in Modern Spanish. They are to be found among medical terms such as *bronquitis, apendicitis, conjuntivitis* etc., and among cultural borrowings (e.g. *áspid* < ASPIDE, *metrópoli* < METROPOLIS, *tesis* < THESIS) and loan-words from other languages (e.g. *dandi* < Eng. *dandy*, *party* < Eng. *party*, *mitin* < Eng. *meeting, yoquey* < Eng. *jockey*, *panoli* < Valencian *pa en oli*, *coy* < Dutch *kooi*). Otherwise *-i* only appears in pet names or popular slang words such as *Luci, Pili, la mili, las bicis* etc.

14.6   **Spanish final** *-u.* Final *-u* in modern Spanish is found only in cultural borrowings (e.g. *ímpetu* < IMPETUS, *ángelus* < ANGELUS, *virus* < VIRUS, *campus* < CAMPUS), in loan words (e.g. *status* < Eng. *status*), in a few onomatopoeic creations (e.g. *miau, guau*) and in pet names such as *Maru, Joselu, Asun(ción)*.

CONSONANTS FINAL IN ROMANCE

4.7   As a result of the fall of final *-e*, seven consonants which had been interior in Classical Latin became final in Old Spanish. Of these, *n, l, r* and *s* remain:

PANE > *pan*   MARE > *mar*

SALE > *sal*   TŬSSE > *tos*

The Vulgar Latin alveolar consonants t and t͡s both voiced, to d and d͡z respectively, before the fall of the final vowel; d was preserved as a weak fricative ð – SALŪTE > *salud*, RĒTE > *red*, VENĪTE > *venid* – but there is some doubt about the value of the sound written *z* in the syllable-final position in Old Spanish – PACE > *paz*, VĬCE > *vez*, LŪCE > *luz*.

R. Menéndez Pidal (1952), 168, describes the Old Spanish sound as voiced; J. D. M. Ford (1900), 94–7, argues for devoicing of the affricate to t͡s at the end of a word, in line with the general tendency of Old Spanish for final consonants to devoice after the fall of final *-e* (14.8). Most probably, however, the degree of voicing depended in Old Spanish upon the position of the sound in a rhythm group, word-final *-z* being pronounced as the voiceless affricate t͡s in the final position in a rhythm group and before a voiceless consonant, and as the voiced affricate d͡z between vowels in a rhythm group: *luz* lút͡s and *luz trasera* lút͡s traséra, but *luz amarilla* lúd͡z amaríʎa (H. Gavel (1920), 255–62 and A. Alonso, 1955–69, II, 165). Classical Latin intervocalic D had already become the fricative ð of Vulgar Latin. After the fall of the final vowel this weakened still further and was lost: FĬDE > *fe*, PĔDE > *pie*, PRŌDE > *pro*, VĬDET > *ve*.

APOCOPE IN OLD SPANISH

4.8   During the twelfth and thirteenth centuries the tendency for final *-e* to be dropped continued to increase, and a much wider range of final consonants was tolerated. Forms with final *-e* and forms without the final vowel existed side by side:

noche – noch	*suerte – suert*
leche – lech	*dixe – dix*
monte – mont	*conduxe – condux*
puente – puent	*dulçe – dulz*
este – est	*creçe – crez*
veniste – venist	*viniesse – vinies*
arte – art	*amasse – amas*

After the fall of final *-e* the final consonant tended to devoice in Old Spanish:

verdad – verdat	*linaje – linax*
humilde – humilt	*homenage – homenax*
nueve – nuef	*nube – nuf*

When, after the fall of final *-e*, a lateral or nasal closed the last syllable of a word, the distinctions between l and ʎ, and between m, n and ɲ were neutralized (cf. 9.6, 9.14). A lateral or nasal which closed the final syllable of a word became an alveolar:

valle – val	*no me – non*
elle – él	*que me – quen*
calle – cal	*si me – sin*
lueñe – luen	*págame – pagan*

During the fourteenth century the tendency towards apocope was arrested and forms with final *-e* became increasingly the more popular of the alternatives. By the fifteenth century apocopated forms were rare, and since then Spanish has admitted only the final consonants *-d, -n, -l, -r, -s, -z* and, sporadically, *-j* (in *reloj, balaj, boj, troj, borraj, cambuj* etc.).

> ### V.L. t͡s

14.9   V.L. t͡s (< C.L. CE, CI, TE + vowel, TI + vowel) > O.Sp. t͡s, d͡z
The alveolar affricate t͡s of Vulgar Latin which developed from t, k followed by a palatal onglide and from k before palatal vowels (11.18c) was preserved in Old Spanish as an affricate sound. The affricate remained voiceless (pronounced t͡s and written *ç*) in some positions, and became a voiced sound (pronounced d͡z and written z) in others.

14.10   Old Spanish t͡s, d͡z

(a) Initial in a word, V.L. t͡s > O.Sp. t͡s:
  CĒNA: V.L. t͡séna > O.Sp. t͡séna *çena*
  CAELU: V.L. t͡sélo > O.Sp. t͡sjélo *çielo*
  CĬRCA: V.L. t͡sérka > O.Sp. t͡sérka *çerca*

(b) Intervocalically, V.L. t͡s > O.Sp. d͡z:
  VĪCĪNU: V.L. βit͡síno > O.Sp. βed͡zíno *vezino*
  DĪCĬT: V.L. dít͡set > O.Sp. díd͡ze *dize*
  PLACĒRE: V.L. plat͡sére > O.Sp. plad͡zér *plazer*
  RATĬŌNE: V.L. rat͡sóne > O.Sp. r̄ad͡zón *razón*
  CORTĬCĔA: kortét͡sa > O.Sp. kortéd͡za *corteza*
  V.L. MĬNACĬA menát͡sa > O.Sp. menád͡za *menaza*

(c) After a consonant, V.L. t͡s > O.Sp. t͡s:
  CONCĬLĬU: V.L. kont͡séʎo > O.Sp. kont͡séʒo *conçejo*
  LANCĔA: V.L. lánt͡sa > O.Sp. lánt͡sa *lança*
  TERTĬARIU: V.L. tert͡sárjo > O.Sp. tert͡séro *terçero*
  V.L. LĔNTĔU lɛnt͡so > O.Sp. ljént͡so *lienço*
When the consonant which preceded V.L. t͡s was a sibilant, the group st͡s was reduced, by dissimilation of the first sibilant from the second, to t͡s:
  MĬSCĒRE: V.L. mest͡sére > O.Sp. met͡sér *meçer*
  CRĒSCĬT: V.L. krést͡set > O.Sp. krét͡se *creçe*
  V.L. CARĒSCĒRE karest͡sére > O.Sp. karet͡sér *careçer*

NOTES
1. Occasionally, initial V.L. s > O.Sp. t͡s (written ç):
    SERRATŬLA > O.Sp. t͡será͡ʒa *çerrają*
    L.L. SERARE > O.Sp. t͡serár *çerrar*
    V.L. (CRIBRUM) SAETACĔUM > O.Sp. t͡sedá͡dzo *çedazo*
The process was aided by assimilation in V.L. CARO *SĬCCĪNA > O.Sp.
t͡set͡sina *çeçina*.
2. Since the semivowel which developed in LANCĔA, VĬTĬU, V.L. LĔNTĔU
etc. disappeared in the Vulgar Latin period, it had no effect on the development of a preceding tonic vowel: A remained in LANCĔA > *lanza*, Ĭ > *e* in
VĬTĬU > O.Sp. *vezo*, Ĕ > *ie* in V.L. LĔNTĔU > *lienzo* etc.
3. After a consonant, V.L. dj devoiced to tj in the syllable-initial position
and then assibilated normally to O.Sp. t͡s:
    HŎRDEŎLU > O.Sp. *orçuelo*   V.L. VĬRDĬA > O.Sp. *berça*
    VĔRĒCŬNDĬA > O.Sp. *vergüença*   V.L. *ADMŎRDĬU > O.Sp. *almuerço*
In the case of GAUDĬU, the semivowel w which preceded the dj group gave
rise to some indecision in Old Spanish: both *goço* gót͡so and *gozo* gó͡dzo are
found.

4.11 As a result of these developments Old Spanish contained two alveolar
affricate sounds – a voiceless t͡s, written ç, and a voiced d͡z, written z. These
affricate consonants can be considered phonemes, since they were capable in
an intervocalic context of distinguishing a very small number of minimal
pairs such as:
    deçir < V.L. DĬSCEDĔRE 'to go down, descend' / *dezir* < DĪCĔRE 'to
    tell, say'
    façes < FASCĒS 'faggots' / *fazes* < FACĪS 'you do'.
In practice, however, the distinction between the two sounds was neutralized
in an initial position, where only t͡s occurred. It was also neutralized to some
extent in a final position, where there was a tendency to devoice the final d͡z
of *cruz, luz* etc. (14.7). Consequently confusion between the voiced and the
voiceless affricates was common in Old Spanish. The development t͡s, d͡z >
M.Sp. θ will be considered later: see 18.5–9.

      | V.L. j |

4.12 V.L. j (< C.L. GE, GI) > Sp. ø, j, d͡j

(a) V.L. j > Sp. ø.
The palatal j of Vulgar Latin which developed from Classical Latin g before
palatal vowels (11.18b) was weakly articulated, assimilated to the following
front vowel, and lost. It is frequently represented in modern orthography by
the graph h (cf. the graph h in *cohombro* < CŬCŬMERE, 13.9 n. 1).
    GĔLARE > *helar*   RĒGĪNA > *reina*
    GERMANU > *hermano*   SAGĬTTA > *saeta*
    V.L. GENŬCŬLU > O.Sp. *inojo*   V.L. FŬLLĪGINE > *hollín*
    RŬGĪTU > *ruido*   CŌGĬTARE > *cuidar*

(b) V.L. j > Sp. j, d͡j.
When strengthened by the first element of the diphthong jé < C.L. Ĕ, the
Vulgar Latin palatal sound remained, articulated as the semivowel j between
vowels and as the affricate d͡j in an initial or post-consonantal position:

GĔNĔRU > *yerno*   GĔMMA > *yema*
GĔNTE > O.Sp. *yente*   · GĔLU > *hielo*

NOTES
1. In learned and semi-learned words, C.L. g was retained in Spanish
orthography, and pronounced ʒ or d͡ʒ in Old Spanish:

GĔNTE > *gente*   RĔGĔRE > *regir*
GĔNĬU > *genio*   RŪGĪTU > *rugido*
GȲRU > *giro*   VĬGĬLARE > *vigilar*

2. Exceptionally, initial j is retained in GȲPSU > *yeso*, a word which may
have been borrowed early into Castilian from one of the Central Mozarabic
dialects (E. Alarcos, 1954, 339).
3. The non-etymological *f-* of O.Sp. *finojo* 'knee' was introduced during the
medieval period, most probably by attraction from the verb *fincar* as a
result of constant use in the phrase *fincar los inojos* 'to kneel': *fincar los
inojos* > *fincar los finojos* (Y. Malkiel, 1954–55, 164–85). For an alternative
explanation (contamination with *hinojo* 'fennel' < L. L. FENŬCŬLU) see
J. Corominas (1954–7), 922–3.

14.13   **FURTHER READING.** E. Alarcos (1954), 330–42; (1965), paras. 148, 149.
A. Alonso (1949), 20–52; (1951d), 51–3; (1955–69), chs. 3 and 4.
V. Garcia de Diego (1951), 72–8, 89–91, 99, 100, 129–31, 136. R. Lapesa
(1951), 185–226. Y. Malkiel (1955), 164–85. R. Menéndez Pidal (1952),
paras. 27–9, 37, 38, 42, 43, 47, 53, 63. W. Meyer-Lübke (1921), 225–51.
J. Saroihandy (1902), 198–214.

14.14   **EXERCISES ON CHAPTER 14**
1. After which consonants was V.L. final *-e* lost in Old Spanish? Explain the
reasons for the retention of final *-e* in each of these forms: AMAVERĬT >
amare; ĬSTE > *este;* SALĬCE > *sauce;* SALĬT > *sale.*
2. Which final consonants are normally admissible in Modern Spanish? Give
an example of each, with its etymon. In what circumstances is it possible for a
word which does not end in one of these consonants (e.g. *coñac, club, film,
argot*) to be accepted into the language?
3. Trace into Old Spanish, and write both an orthographic version and a
phonetic transcription of the Old Spanish form: L.L. ASCĬŎLA, CAECU,
V.L. CALCĬATA, CĬPPU, ERĪCĬU, FŎRTĬA, PŬNCTĬŌNE, PŬTĔU, V.L.
RACĪMU, SATĬŌNE.
4. List three possible sources for the Spanish group d͡je- at the beginning of a
word. Trace the etyma of the following: *hiedra, hiel, hielo, hiena, hierba,
hierro, yegua, yema, yero, yesca.*
5. Account for the following doublets:

DĬGĬTALE > *digital, dedal*
GĔNTE > *gente,* O. Sp. *yente*
MALĬTĬA > *malicia, maleza*
SĬGĬLLU > *sigilo, sello*
VĬTĬU > *vicio,* O.Sp. *bezo*

15 INITIAL VOWELS, CONSONANT CLUSTERS

INITIAL VOWELS

15.1 In an initial position the five vowel sounds of Vulgar Latin i, e, a, o, u survived.

> V.L. i, u

15.2
V.L. i (C.L. Ī) > Sp. i
V.L. u (< C.L. Ū) > Sp. u
When initial, the long close vowels of Classical Latin became i, u in Vulgar Latin, and both remained unaltered in Spanish:

MĪRARĪ > *mirar*   MŪTARE > *mudar*
SĪBĬLARE > *silbar*   CŪRARE > *curar*
CĪVĬTATE > *ciudad*   DŪRACĬNU > *durazno*

> V.L. e

15.3
V.L. e (< C.L. Ĭ, Ē, Ĕ, AE, OE) > e
When initial, Vulgar Latin e from all sources remained in Spanish:

MĬNŪTU > *menudo*   LĔGŪMEN > *legumbre*
CĒPŬLLA > *cebolla*   PRAECŌNE > *pregón*
SĒCŪRU > *seguro*   FOETĒRE > *heder*

> V.L. o

15.4
V.L. o (< C.L. Ŏ, Ō, Ŭ) > Sp. o
When initial, Vulgar Latin o from all sources remained in Spanish:

CŎRTICĔA > *corteza*   CŬCŬLLU > *cogollo*
COTŬRNĬCE > *codorniz*   SŬPĔRBĬA > *soberbia*
NŌMĬNARE > *nombrar*   LŌRĪCA > *loriga*

V.L. a

15.5   V.L. a (< C.L. Ā, Ă) > Sp. a
When initial, Classical Latin Ā and Ă coincided in Vulgar Latin a, which was
preserved in Spanish:
      MĀJORE > *mayor*   ĂMĪCU > *amigo*
      PĀRĔRE > *parir*   CĂNALE > *canal*

NOTE
In the same way as in a tonic syllable (12.8), the diphthong AU was reduced
to o in:
      LAUDARE > *loar*   V.L. CAULĬCŬLA > *colleja*
      AUDIRE > *oír*   HABUIMUS > O.Sp. *ovimos*
      AURĬFĬCE > O.Sp. *orebze*   ALTĔRU + SIC > O.Sp. *otrosí*

15.6   **Assimilation.** Initial *e* > *a* by assimilation to the tonic vowel in:
      SĬLVATĬCU > *salvaje*
      V.L. *BILANCĬA > *balanza*
      V.L. *TRIPALĬARE > *trabajar*

15.7   **Dissimilation.** Occasionally, initial *i, o* > *e* by dissimilation from the tonic
vowel:
      VĪCĪNU > *vecino*
      ROTŬNDU > *redondo*
      FORMŌSU > *hermoso*

15.8   **Raising.**
(a) V.L. e > Sp. i. A following palatal or velar glide had the effect of closing
initial e to i in:
      V.L. *RĔNĬŌNE > *riñón*   CAEMĔNTU > *cimiento*
      GENĔSTA > *hiniesta*   V.L. *SĬNĔXTER > *siniestro*
There was also, in a number of popular and semi-learned words, some
indecision about the value of the Old Spanish initial vowel:
      Popular   *Semi-learned*
      MELIŌRE > O.Sp. *mejor, mijor*   LECTIŌNE > O.Sp. *lección, lición*
      AEQUALE > O.Sp. *egual, igual*   VĬRTŪTE > O.Sp. *vertud, virtud*
      V.L. *MEDŬLLU > O.Sp. *meollo,*   EXĔMPLU > O.Sp. *ensiemplo, insiemplo*
      miollo
In each case only one of the variants — *mejor, igual, meollo, lección, virtud* and
ejemplo — survived the medieval period in Castile. For the raised vowel of *mejilla*
see 16.6a, n. 1.

(b) V.L. o > Sp. u. Initial o was similarly affected by a following palatal or
velar glide; o > u in:
      DORMIAMUS > *durmamos*   MŬLIERE > *mujer*
      MORIAMUS > *muramos*   V.L. *COLŎBRA > *culuebra, culebra*

There was also some indecision about the timbre of the initial back vowel in Old Spanish:

JOCARĪ > O.Sp. *jogar, jugar*
RŬGĪTU > O.Sp. *roido, ruido*
COOPERIRE > O.Sp. *cobrir, cubrir*
MOLLIRE > O.Sp. *mollir, mullir*
CŌ(G)ĬTARE > O.Sp. *coidar, cuidar*

In each case it is the form with the raised vowel which has survived into the modern language, although in other words – e.g. *hogar* < FOCARE, *rogar* < RŎGARE, *lograr* < LŬCRARĪ – there is no evidence of raising. For the raised initial vowel of *cuchillo, cuchara*, see 16.4b and 16.5b, n. 2.

15.9 **Aphaeresis.** In the vast majority of popular and learned words the Latin initial vowel was preserved as Spanish *i, e, a, o,* or *u.* Rare examples of its loss include:

V.L. *GEMELLICIU > O.Sp. *emellizo* > *mellizo*
EPĬTHĒMA > *bizma* (semi-learned)
V.L. *ECĬFĔRU > *cebra*
HORŌLOGĬU (via Catalan *relotge*) > *reloj.*

In APŎTHĒCA > *bodega* and V.L. ĪLĬCĪNA > *encina* the initial vowel has been lost as a result of syntactic phonology: **la abodega* > *la bodega*, O.Sp. *el le(n)zina* > *el encina.*

CONSONANT CLUSTERS

15.10 **Prosthesis.** The prosthetic *e-* which developed before *s* + consonant in later Vulgar Latin (11.13) was retained in Spanish:

SCHŎLA > *escuela*	SPĔCŬLU > *espejo*
SCUTĔLLA > *escudilla*	STARE > *estar*
SPATHA > *espada*	STRATU > *estrado*

V.L. Consonant + **r, l**

15.11 (a) In an initial position, V.L. voiced consonants remained before *r* and *l:*

BRACCHIU > *brazo*	BLANDU > *blando*
DRACŌNE > *dragón*	GLŬTTŌNE > *glotón*

The voiceless consonants *c, f* and *p* remained before *r*:

CRAS > O.Sp. *cras*	FRĪGĬDU > *frío*
CRĬSPU > O.Sp. *crespo*	PRATU > *prado*
FRĒNU > O.Sp. *freno*	PRĪMATU > *primado*

NOTES

1. The group *pre-* was particularly subject to metathesis in Old Spanish:

PRAELATU > O.Sp. *prelado, perlado*
V.L. *PRAECUNCTARE > O.Sp. *preguntar, perguntar*

Conversely, *per-* frequently underwent metathesis to *pre-*:
> PERSŌNA > O.Sp. *persona, presona*
> PĔRSĬCU > O.Sp. *prisco*

2. The palatalization of initial *cl-, fl-, pl-* will be considered in 16.2.

(b) In an intervocalic position, the first element of a cluster which consisted
of consonant + *r, l* developed as when intervocalic.
Voiceless plosives voiced:

CAPRA > *cabra*	V.L. SŎCRA > *suegra*
ŬTRE > *odre*	DŬPLU > *doble*

Voiced plosives became fricatives or were lost:

QUADRU > *cuadro*	NĬGRU > *negro*
QUADRAGINTA > *cuarenta*	PĬGRĬTĬA > *pereza*

V.L. intervocalic clusters

15.12   In an intervocalic position, many Classical Latin combinations survived both
in Vulgar Latin and in Spanish:

ALBU > *albo*	TĔMPU > *tiempo*.
CALĔNTE > *caliente*	PŎRTU > *puerto*
CĬSTA > *cesta*	GŬRDU > *gordo*

Other groups were subject to assimilation of one consonant by the other.

(a) V.L. *-mb-* > Sp. *-m-*
The process was one of progressive assimilation, whereby the speech-organs
for the second sound of the cluster were adjusted to a position more like
that of the preceding sound. In this instance the assimilation of *b* to *m* was
total.

LŬMBU > *lomo*	AMBŌ > O.Sp. *amos*
V.L. PALŬMBA > *paloma*	L.L. CAMBIARE > O.Sp. *camiar, camear*

The intervocalic group *-mb-* was preserved in the West of the Peninsula (cf.
Leonese *ambos, lombo, palomba*), and the combined effect on popular
pronunciation of this, and on educated pronunciation of the Latin forms,
resulted in the restoration of the *-mb-* group to some words by the end of the
medieval period: *amos > ambos, camiar, camear > cambiar* etc.

(b) V.L. *-ss-* (< C.L. *-RS-, -PS-*) > Sp. *-s-*
Vulgar Latin geminate *-ss-* (11.15b, c) was reduced to a single voiceless s
(written *ss*) in Old Spanish:

ŬRSU > O.Sp. *osso* óso	GȲPSU > O.Sp. *yesso* d͡jéso
VĔRSU > O.Sp. *viesso* βjéso	ĬPSE > O.Sp. *esse* ése

(c) V.L. *-tt-* (< C.L. *-PT-*) > Sp. *-t-*
Vulgar Latin geminate *-tt-* (11.15a) was reduced to a single voiceless t (written
t) in Spanish:

SĔPTE > *siete*	CAPTARE > *catar*
SCRIPTU > *escrito*	RŬPTU > *roto*

(d) V.L. -s- (< C.L. -NS-) > Sp. -z-
The Classical Latin -NS- group had simplified to -s- early in the Vulgar Latin period (11.16a), and V.L. voiceless s voiced to z (written s) in Old Spanish:
>ANSA > O.Sp. *asa* **áza**
>SĒNSU > O.Sp. *seso* **sézo**
>V.L. PĪNSARE > O.Sp. *pisar* **pizár**

> V.L. kw

5.13   V.L. kw (< C.L. QU) > Sp. k, g, kw

(a) V.L. kw > Sp. k
The semivowel of the group kw was lost in an initial position and after a consonant:

QUĬD > *que*	NUMQUAM > *nunca*
QUAERO > *quiero*	SQUAMA > *escama*
QUĔM > *quien*	V.L. *TORQUACĔU > *torcaz*

(b) V.L. kw > Sp. g
Between vowels the semivowel was also lost, and the velar plosive voiced to **g**:
>V.L. SĔQUO > *sigo*
>AQUĬLA > *águila*
>ALĬQUOD > *algo*

(c) V.L. kw > Sp. kw
The semivowel survived only in two contexts. It was retained before a stressed **a** when kw was initial:
>QUALE > *cual*   QUANDO > *cuando*   QUADRU > *cuadro*

It also survived before **a** (stressed or unstressed) when kw was intervocalic:
>AQUA > *agua*   ANTĪQUA > *antigua*   ĔQUA > *yegua*

NOTES
1. In some words the semivowel was lost early. Between a consonant and a front vowel the group developed kw > k̂ > t͡s:
>TŎRQ(U)ĒRE > V.L. *TORCĒRE > O.Sp. *torçer* **tort͡sér**

Intervocalically, V.L. t͡s voiced to d͡z before a front vowel:
>CŎQ(U)ĔRE > V.L. COCERE > O.Sp. *cozer* **kod͡zér**
>LAQ(U)EU > V.L. *LACIU > O.Sp. *lazo* **lád͡zo**

2. The fact that the semivowel was preserved after initial k only before stressed **a** produced alternations of the type *cuatro* (< QUATTUOR) – *catorce* (< QUATTUORDECIM). The w of *cuarenta* **kwarénta** is analogous on the w of *cuatro* **kwátro**. In Old Spanish *casi* (unstressed) and *cuasi* (stressed) coexisted for some time as semi-learned descendants of C.L. QUASI; of these only the unstressed form *casi* has survived to the modern literary language.

QUŌMŎDO > O.Sp. *como* (unstressed); in a stressed position the result was
O.Sp. *cuomo,* and then *cuemo* as the wé diphthong became standardized in
Castile (13.2); the unstressed form *como* eventually prevailed.

15.14   **Clusters of three consonants.** Latin groups which presented no problems
of articulation were preserved:
    RŌSTRU > *rostro*   ĬNTRARE > *entrar*
    STRATU > *estrado*   V.L. *CALANDRIA > *calandria*
In an implosive position, K and P were weakly articulated and easily
eliminated:
      CAMPSARE > *cansar*   DĔXTRU > *diestro*
      PUNCTA > *punta*   V.L. EXCALDARE > *escaldar*
      SANCTU > *santo*   V.L. *EXCAPPARE > *escapar*
Less frequently, other consonants initial in the group of three were lost:
      CŎNSTARE > *costar*   ABSCONDĔRE> *esconder*

15.15   **FURTHER READING.** E. Alarcos (1965), para. 150. V. Garcia de Diego
(1951), 62–7, 108, 109, 113, 114, 116–18, 123, 138–9. F. González-Ollé
(1972), 285–318. R. Menéndez Pidal (1952), paras. 17–22, 39, 47–9,
51, 52.

15.16   **EXERCISES ON CHAPTER 15**
1. Plot the regular popular development from Classical Latin to Spanish
(i) of the vowels Ĕ and Ŏ in the tonic and initial positions, (ii) of the
vowels Ĭ and Ŭ in the tonic and final positions, and (iii) of the vowels Ī
and Ū in the initial and final positions.
2. Account for the appearance of the initial vowel *i* in the followin.* words:
discrepar (< DĬSCRĔPARE); *midamos* (< MĒTĬAMUS); *simiente*
(< SĒMĔNTE); *tinieblas* (< TĔNĔBRA); *tizón* (< TĪTIŌNE).
3. Account for the appearance of the initial vowel *u* in the following words:
cuchara (< CŎCHLEARE); *culantro* (< CŎRIANDRU); *pulgar*
(< POLLĬCARE); *pulmón* (< PŬLMONE); *sudar* (< SŪDARE).
4. Trace into Spanish: APRĪCARE, APTAVI, CAPĬSTRŬ, V.L.
*EXCARSŬ, GRŎSSŬ, MACRŬ, PLŬMBŬ, SPĪCA, SPŌNSŬ, V.L.
*STRAGĀRE.
5. Which of the following developments can be considered wholly popular?
Explain your choice.
     ARCŬATIONE > *arcuación*   PERSĔQUI > *perseguir*
     CASĔU > *queso*   QUAESTIŌNE > *cuestión*
     CŎQUĪNA > *cocina*   QUALĬTATE > *cualidad*
     LŎQUĀCE > *locuaz*   QUATĔRNU > *cuaderno*
     QUĬD > *qué*   SEQUESTRARE > *secuestrar*

16 THE PALATAL SOUNDS OF OLD SPANISH

Medieval Spanish contained a number of palatal sounds which were unknown to Classical Latin. The relationship of these to the alveolar sounds discussed in earlier chapters can be seen in the following table:

	Alveolar		Palatal	
	Voiceless	Voiced	Voiceless	Voiced
Laterals		l		ʎ
Nasals		n		ɲ
Affricates	t͡s	d͡z	t͡ʃ	d͡ʒ
Fricatives	s	z	ʃ	ʒ

In addition to these new palatal sounds, the palatal j of Vulgar Latin (11.18) was preserved in many positions, with a tendency to be strengthened to the palatal affricate d͡j in an initial position and after a consonant, so that Old Spanish contained a total of eight palatal sounds – ʎ, ɲ, ʃ, t͡ʃ, ʒ, d͡ʒ, j, d͡j.

The phonemic distribution of these palatal sounds in Old Spanish was the following:

In the remainder of this section the Latin sources for each of these sounds are considered in detail. The secondary clusters which produced these Old Spanish palatal sounds will be considered in Chapter 17.

O.Sp. ʎ

(a) V.L. initial kl-, fl-, pl- > Sp. ʎ-.
In these initial groups the most popular result was for the lateral to palatalize early. V.L. kl- > kʎ-, V.L. fl- > ʾfʎ-, V.L. pl- > pʎ-. The first element of each was then lost in Castilian, so that all three coincided in ʎ:

| CLAMARE > llamar | FLAMMA > llama | PLANCTU > llanto |
| CLAVE > llave | FLŎCCU > lleco | PLŌRARE > llorar |

NOTES

1. The Castilian development shows an affinity with Italian, where palatal ʎ vocalized to the onglide j (*chiamare, fiamma, piangere* etc.). This suggests that in some areas the tendency to palatalize *l* in these initial groups originated in Vulgar Latin. In other Romance areas, however, such as France, Catalonia and Aragon, kl-, fl- and pl- remained unaltered, while in the pronunciation of a small area between Aragon and Catalonia, the Esera valley,.the intermediate stage kʎ-, fʎ-, pʎ- has been preserved down to the present day. West of Castile (in the Leonese dialect, and in Galicia and Portugal) the development continued further as ʎ delateralized to t: ʎj > t͡j > t͡ʃ (see W. D. Elcock, 1960, 432). The voiceless affricate t͡ʃ remained in Portuguese until the seventeenth century, when it was reduced to the simple fricative ʃ: CLAMARE > Ptg. *chamar*, FLAMMA > Ptg. *chama*, PLORARE > Ptg. *chorar* etc.

2. The development kl-, fl-, pl- > ʎ represents only one of the possible results in Castilian. This is an example of weak phonetic change, for in many words of undeniably popular origin the initial groups were preserved:

CLAVU > *clavo*	FLŬXU > *flojo*	PLACĒRE > *placer*
CLARU > *claro*	FLACCU > *flaco*	PLŬMBU > *plomo*
CLAVĬCŬLA > *clavija*	FLŌRE > *flor*	PLANGĔRE > *plañir*

Such examples of preservation in forms which do not have the appearance of cultural borrowings can be attributed in many cases to the influence of more educated medieval pronunciation. However, as observed by Y. Malkiel (1963), 154, since each of the initial groups kl-, fl-, pl- could be regarded as occurring in Old Spanish in free, or almost free, variation with palatal ʎ, the final choice of a non-palatal initial group in some words could have been influenced by a number of isolated non-cultural factors, including a tendency towards the dissimilation of palatal sounds in the syllable-initial position:

PLANGĔRE > *pʎa-ɲír > pla-ɲír *plañir*
PLATĔA > *pʎá-tja > plá-t͡sa O.Sp. *plaça*

The reduction of initial FL- to l in FLACCĬDU > *lacio* is unusual. The word has the appearance of a dialectalism, but the final choice of initial alveolar, rather than palatal, *l* could well have been influenced by the type of dissimilation of palatal sounds just described:

FLACCĬDU > *lacio* (to avoid *llacio ʎá-t͡sjo).

3. In cultural borrowings the initial groups are regularly maintained:

CLASSE > *clase*	FLEXĬBĬLIS > *flexible*	PLANĒTA > *planeta*
CLĪNĬCU > *clínico*	PHLĔGMA > *flema*	PLĬNTHU > *plinto*

(b) V.L. intervocalic -ffl- > Sp. -ʎ-.
Intervocalic -ffl- was treated in the same way as initial fl-, and palatalized to ʎ in:

AFFLARE > O.Sp. *fallar* faʎár
RE + SŪFFLARE > O.Sp. *resollar* r̄ezoʎár

Confusion in Vulgar Latin between the derivatives of PLĒRE 'to fill' and those of FLARE 'to blow' led to the replacement of ffl by pl in SUFFLARE > *soplar*, which eventually superseded the variant, phonetically regular, Old Spanish form *sollar*.

(c) V.L. intervocalic -ll- > Sp. -ʎ-.
During the Old Spanish period geminate intervocalic ll palatalized to ʎ. The
development came comparatively late, after the palatalization of intervocalic
lj (16.5b); between the tenth century and the thirteenth it is most likely
that the alternative pronunciations ll and ʎ coexisted in the Peninsula. In
Castile ʎ predominated and was standard by the beginning of the thirteenth
century:

VALLE > *valle*	SĚLLA > *silla*
MOLLE > *muelle*	CABALLU > *caballo*

NOTE
By the beginning of the thirteenth century, ʎ had become a recognized
alternative to rl in the combination *infinitive + weak pronoun:*
   rl > ll > ʎ in *cantarlo > cantallo, decirle > decille* etc.

Although losing ground steadily, ʎ survived as an alternative pronunciation to
rl in this position until well into the seventeenth century.

O.Sp. ɲ

.3   (a) V.L. intervocalic -ɲ- > Sp. -ɲ-.
Palatal ɲ, which had developed in Vulgar Latin from the combination nj
(11.18a), was preserved in Old Spanish:
   ARANĚA > V.L. a-rá-nja > a-rá-ɲa > Sp. a-rá-ɲa *araña*

Similarly:

VĪNĚA > *viña*	EXTRANĚU > *extraño*
SENIŌRE > *señor*	BA(L)NĚU > *baño*

NOTE
The palatal glide j was absorbed early into the nasal, and only rarely, as in
cuño < CŬNĚU, had the effect of attracting a preceding vowel towards its
point of articulation. In O.Sp. *engeño* < ĬNGĚNĬU, *vengo* < VĚNIO, the
palatal glide closed the tonic vowel sufficiently to prevent diphthongization.

(b) V.L. intervocalic -ng- > Sp. -ɲ-.
Between the consonant *n* and a front vowel, Vulgar Latin ǵ was in some words
attracted to the point of articulation of the following vowel, and pronounced
as the semivowel j (11.18b). The combination nj remained in QUINGENTŌS
> *quinientos,* but more commonly developed further: by coalescent
assimilation, nj > ɲ:
   TANGĬT > V.L. tán-jet > tá-njet > tá-ɲe *tañe*

Similarly:

CĬNGĬT > *ciñe*	LŎNGE > O.Sp. *lueñe*
JŬNGĚRE > *uñir*	FRANGĚRE > O.Sp. *frañer, frañir*

NOTE
An alternative development occurred in words where the syllable division
was made between n and j. In these circumstances, the combination developed:
n + j > n + d͡j > n + d͡z
Examples:
    FRANGĔRE > O.Sp. **frand͡zír** *franzir*
    JŬNGĔRE > O.Sp. **und͡zír** *unzir* (M.Sp. *uncir*)
    GĪNGĪVA > O.Sp. **end͡zía** *enzía* (M.Sp. *encía*)
    V.L. *SĬNGĔLLU > O.Sp. **send͡zíʎo** *senzillo* (M.Sp. *sencillo*)
    V.L. *UNCĬCULA > O.Sp. **ond͡zéʒa** *onzeja* (M.Sp. *onceja*)

(c) V.L. intervocalic -gn- > Sp. -ɲ-.
In Vulgar Latin a forward variety of ǵ was used before a nasal sound. As
the point of articulation moved slightly forward on the palate the
combination developed:
    ǵn > jn > ɲ
Examples:
    STAGNU > *estaño*   COGNATU > *cuñado*
    LĬGNA > *leña*   V.L. PRAEGNATA > *preñada*

NOTES
1. The palatal glide which developed from V.L. ǵ had the effect of raising a
preceding o̧ to u:
    PŬGNŬ > *puño*   ŬNGŬLA > *uña*   COGNATU > *cuñado*
2. The Classical Latin group -GN- is retained in cultural borrowings, with the
first element articulated as a weak fricative ɣ:
    DĬGNU > *digno*   RĔGNU > O.Sp. *regno*
    MALĬGNU > *maligno*   MAGNĬFĬCU > *magnífico*
In the Golden Age the group ɣn was frequently simplified to n: *dino, malino,
manífico* etc. C.L. REGNARE > *reinar,* C.L. REGNU > *reino* under the
influence of *rey* < REGE.

(d) V.L. intervocalic -nn-, -mn- > Sp. -ɲ-.
Between vowels V.L. nn palatalized to O.Sp. ɲ. In the group -mn- the first
nasal was assimilated to the second, and the resulting geminate consonant
also palatalized to ɲ:
    ANNU > *año*   DAMNU > *daño*
    PĬNNA > *peña*   AUTŬMNU > *otoño*

> O.Sp. t͡ʃ

16.4   (a) V.L. intervocalic -xt- > Sp. t͡ʃ.
The velar fricative x articulated between vowel and consonant in Vulgar
Latin and originating from the C.L. group kt (11.17c) was drawn slightly
forward to produce the semivowel j. As in French, Catalan, Aragonese,
Leonese and Galician-Portuguese, kt > xt > jt.

The subsequent development jt > t͡ʃ is one of the most characteristic linguistic features of Castilian. The consonant t, attracted towards the place of articulation of the preceding palatal glide, itself became palatalized and developed an element of affrication to become t͡j, articulated most probably with the tip of the tongue raised to stop the air-flow at the hard palate. A process of coalescent assimilation, whereby the affricate sound was articulated with the blade instead of the tip of the tongue against the hard palate, produced the final development t͡j > t͡ʃ. Summary:

kt > xt > jt > t͡j > t͡ʃ

Examples:

LACTE > *leche*   LĔCTU > *lecho*
FACTU > *hecho*   ŎCTU > *ocho*
LACTŪCA > *lechuga*   LŪCTARĪ > *luchar*
JACTARE > *echar*   L.L. TRŬCTA > *trucha*

NOTES
1. The glide which developed from Vulgar Latin x combined with a preceding stressed or initial a to produce e in *leche, hecho, lechuga, echar* etc.
Thus:
    LACTE lákte > láxte > lájte > lájt͡je > léjt͡ʃe > lét͡ʃe *leche*
2. When the glide j which developed from Vulgar Latin x was preceded by a high front vowel, the two sounds were reduced to the single vowel i and the development jt > t͡j occurred only sporadically:
    V.L. FĪCTU fíktu > fíxto > fíj̃to > fíto O.Sp. *fito*
    DĪCTU díktu > díxto > díj̃to > dít͡jo > dít͡ʃo *dicho*
3. A stressed half-open vowel ę or ǫ which preceded the glide was assimilated towards it and closed slightly, preventing diphthongization in *lecho, ocho* etc.
4. Of the stressed half-close vowels, ǫ was raised one stage to u in *lucha, trucha* etc., but ę remained unaffected by the palatal glide: STRĬCTU > *estrecho*, DĪRĒCTU > *derecho*.
5. The palatal affricate pronunciation t͡ʃ was established in Castile by the eleventh century, when it was generally represented by the graphs *g, gg: Sango Pedrez, Lop Sanggeç* etc. The graph *ch* first appeared at the end of that century and became standardized during the course of the twelfth century.

(b) V.L. -olt- > Sp. -ut͡ʃ-.
In the group -olt- the 'dark' or velar *l* which occurred before a consonant in Latin vocalized, to produce the velar semivowel w (cf. 12.8b):
    MŬLTU > V.L. mólto > mówto
Thereafter, the diphthong ow was simplified to the high vowel u (cf. O.F. *mut*), and in Castile and Leon a palatal glide developed after the following t sound:
    mówto > mút͡jo
The combination t͡j then developed an increasing amount of affrication and evolved, by the process described in 16.4a, t͡j > t͡ʃ:
    mút͡jo > mút͡ʃo.

Similarly:
> AUSCŬLTARE > *escuchar*
> CŬLTĔLLU > *cuchillo*
> PŬLTES > *puches*

NOTE

In the Iberian Peninsula this development is typical of Castile and Leon. In other areas, such as Aragon, Navarre and the south, the palatal glide appeared *before* the dental t, to produce the dialectal form *muito*. This pre-consonantal glide also appeared in Castilian in the rare cases where t was followed by a consonant – VŬLTŬRE > *buitre* – or where t became final (after the irregular loss of final -*o*) in the variant development MŬLTU > O.Sp. *muyt* > *muy*.

(c) V.L. nasal + kl, fl, pl > Sp. t͡ʃ.
In the syllable-initial position, after a nasal consonant, V.L. kl, fl, pl developed, in the same way as when initial in the western dialects (16.2a, n. 1), ʎj > t͡ʃ > t͡ʃ:
> ĬNFLARE > O.Sp. *(f)inchar*
> AMPLU > *ancho*
> ĬMPLĒRE > O.Sp. *(f)enchir*

In learned and semi-learned words the group remained:
> COMPLĒXU > *complejo*   AMPLIARE > *ampliar*   INFLARE > *inflar* etc.

NOTES

1. For the initial *f-* of O.Sp. *finchar, fenchir* see 13.11, n. 3.
2. In a few words in which Latin C preceded a front vowel (where it normally produced Castilian t͡s (14.10a), the affricate sounds t͡s and t͡ʃ tended to be confused: t͡ʃ was established in CĬCCU > *chico*, CĪMĬCE > *chinche*.

O.Sp. ʒ, d͡ʒ

16.5   (a) V.L. initial j- > O.Sp. ʒ-, d͡ʒ-.

Before the back vowels o, u, the palatal j of Vulgar Latin took on an increasing amount of friction and strengthened in Old Spanish to the phoneme /ʒ/. Since the phoneme is represented by the graph *j* in Old Spanish, it is not easy to determine its precise value in differing phonetic contexts. The probability is that the fricative allophone ʒ occurred between vowels in a rhythm group, with the affricate allophone d͡ʒ as a positional variant in a post-consonantal and initial position:
> JŎCU > d͡ʒwégo   but   DE + JŎCU > de ʒwégo

Examples:
> JŎVIS > *jueves*   JŪDAEU > *judío*
> JŬNCU > *junco*   JŪSTU > *justo*

NOTES

1. Before **a**, initial j was preserved as **j**, **d͡j** (16.7).
2. The loss of initial J in JŬNGĔRE > *uñir* is due to dissimilation: **junjére** > **unjére** > **uɲir**.
3. In Aragon the affricate **d͡ʒ** became standardized, and later devoiced to **t͡ʃ** in the modern dialects:

    JŎCU > *chuego*   JŬNCU > *chungo*   JŬVĔNE > *choven* etc.

(b) V.L. intervocalic -lj- > O.Sp. -ʒ-, -d͡ʒ-.

In the Burgos area, from where it spread with the rise of Castilian to become a standard feature of Spanish, the Vulgar Latin intervocalic group **lj** became a fricative ʒ or affricate **d͡ʒ**, written *j*. The affricate **d͡ʒ** survived for some time as an alternative to ʒ, but as the sound became equated with the phoneme /ʒ/ (< V.L. j + back vowel, 16.5a), the allophone ʒ became the norm between vowels.

    FŎLĬA > *hoja*   CŎNSĬLĬU > *consejo*
    MĚLĬŌRE > *mejor*   MŬLĬERE > *mujer*

This change is peculiarly Castilian, and distinguishes Castilian from the neighbouring dialects. In medieval Aragonese the ʎ which developed in Vulgar Latin from **lj** remained unchanged: *folla, mellor, consello, muller* etc. In medieval Leonese it either remained as ʎ or delateralized to j: *folla* or *foya*, *mellor* or *meyor*, *consello* or *conseyo*, *muller* or *muyer*. If V.L. ʎ remained in the formative stages of Castilian, the reasons which set in motion the sound-change ʎ > (d͡)ʒ may have been structural: as geminate intervocalic **ll** palatalized to ʎ (16.2c), intervocalic ʎ was replaced by ʒ or d͡ʒ in order to maintain a contrastive difference between the two sounds. The contrast between the geminate **ll** of *valle* βálle and the palatal ʎ of *consello* konséʎo gave way to a contrast between the palatal ʎ of *valle* βáʎe and the palatal fricative or affricate of *consejo* konsé(d͡)ʒo:

    C.L. LL > O.Sp. **ll** > ʎ
      ↕   ↕   ↕
    C.L. LJ > O.Sp. ʎ > (d͡)ʒ

But against this explanation is the evidence of the other Northern dialects, where the two phonemes coincided in ʎ: Aragonese, Leonese *valle* < VALLE, *consello* < CŎNSĬLĬU; and the parallel situation in Castilian where **nn** and **nj** coincided in ɲ: *año* < ANNU, *extraño* < EXTRANEU (16.3). The need to maintain distinctive phonemes did not seem to have been felt in either of these cases.

It is more likely that the characteristic Castilian fricative ʒ evolved spontaneously in the Burgos area from the **lj** of Vulgar Latin without ever being reduced to a single palatal ʎ, by a purely phonetic process. The palatal glide j had the effect of palatalizing a preceding l to ʎ without being assimilated to it:

    lj > ʎj.

Delateralization of the first consonant produced the affricate **d͡j** (pronounced with the tip of the tongue on the hard palate), which then strengthened to **d͡ʒ**:

    ʎj > d͡j > d͡ʒ.

In an intervocalic position the affricate became a simple fricative:
$\widehat{d\mathsf{3}}$ > ʒ.
Summary:
lj > ʎj > $\widehat{dj}$ > $\widehat{d\mathsf{3}}$ > ʒ
ALIU > áljo > áʎjo > ádjo > á$\widehat{d\mathsf{3}}$o > áʒo O.Sp. *ajo*

NOTES
1. This process, with a voiced affricate resulting in the first instance between
vowels, is comparable to the process of palatalization of initial CL-, FL- PL-
in the western dialects (16.2) and of the same sounds after a nasal in
Castilian: in the syllable-initial position a voiceless affricate was produced, by
the process ʎj > $\widehat{tj}$ > $\widehat{tʃ}$. The development whereby ʒ developed by a similar
process from the secondary clusters -k'l-, -g'l- will be considered in 17.10.
2. The semivowel j had the effect of closing a preceding Ŏ by one stage to ǫ
and preventing diphthongization in FŎLĬA > *hoja*, V.L. MŎLLĬAT > *moja*
etc.
3. The voiced palatal $\widehat{d\mathsf{3}}$ or ʒ was produced only between vowels: where a
consonant preceded the V.L. lj group the result was the **voiceless** affricate $\widehat{tʃ}$:
CŎCHLĔARE > O.Sp. *cuchar, cuchara,* with raising of the initial vowel.

O.Sp. ʃ

16.6   (a) V.L. intervocalic -xs- > O.Sp. -ʃ-.
The palatal fricative ʃ was written *x* in Old Spanish. Between vowels the -KS-
group of Classical Latin developed along lines similar to the -KT- group
(16.4a). The point of articulation of V.L. syllable-final x (11.17c) moved
forward towards palatal j, which attracted the following s to a palatal point
of articulation and then was lost or assimilated to the preceding vowel:
ks > xs > js > jʃ > ʃ.
Examples:
TAXU > O.Sp. *texo* téʃo   V.L. CŎXU > O.Sp. *coxo* kóʃo
DĪXĪ > O.Sp. *dixe* díʃe   MATAXA > O.Sp. *madexa* madéʃa
After a nasal the group developed in the same way:
CĪNXĪ > O.Sp. *cinxe* t͡sinʃe
TĪNXĪ > O.Sp. *tinxe* tínʃe
V.L. *TANXĪ > O.Sp. *tanxe* tánʃe

NOTES
1. The glide which developed from V.L. x combined with a preceding initial
or tonic a to produce e in:
TAXU: tákso > tájso > tájʃo > téjʃo > téjo O.Sp. *texo*
Similarly MATAXA > O.Sp. *madexa*
           MAXĬLLA > O.Sp. *mexilla*
           AXE > O.Sp. *exe*
In O.Sp. *coxo* < V.L. CŎXO, the glide had the effect of preventing
diphthongization of the tonic vowel by closing C.L. Ŏ to V.L. ǫ.

2. Old Spanish *visque* βíske < VĪXĪ shows learned influence. Intervocalic -KS-
did not palatalize, but was subject to metathesis: VĪXĪ wi:ksi: > O.Sp.
visque βíske.

(b) V.L. intervocalic -ssj- > O.Sp. -ʃ-.
By a process of coalescent assimilation, geminate **ss** and a following palatal
glide produced the Old Spanish voiceless palatal fricative ʃ:

  RŬSSĔU > O.Sp. *roxo*
  V.L. *BASSĬARE > O.Sp. *baxar*
  V.L. *QUASSĬARE > O.Sp. *quexar*
  V.L. *LASSĬUS > O.Sp. *lexos*

(c) In a few words V.L. initial s- > O.Sp. ʃ-.
  SŪCU > O.Sp. *xugo*   SĬMĬU > O.Sp. *ximio*
  SȲRĬNGA > O.Sp. *xeringa* L.L. SAPŌNE > O.Sp. *xabón*
Initial ʃ in these words is the result of confusion in Old Spanish between
palatal ʃ and tip-alveolar s, with its retroflex and slightly palatal quality, aided
by the pronunciation of the Moors of the Peninsula, who articulated Spanish
alveolar **s** as a palatal ʃ. Further examples of confusion are particularly
evident after a nasal (cf. 16.6a): Old Spanish had the variants:
  enxugar, ensugar < ĒXSŪCARE
  enxiemplo, ensiemplo < EXĔMPLU
  enxalma, ensalma < V.L. SALMA
  enxeco, enseco < Arabic *šiqq* etc.

O.Sp. j, d͡j

5.7 (a) V.L. initial j- > O.Sp. j-, d͡j-.
    Vulgar Latin j was preserved before an **a** sound:
    JAM > *ya* JACET > *yace* JANTARE > *yantar.*
In Old Spanish it was most probably articulated as a fricative j between
vowels in a rhythm group – *para yantar* **para jantár** – and as an affricate d͡j
in a post-consonantal and initial position – *el yantar* **el d͡jantár,** *yantar*
d͡jantár.

NOTE
Before the back vowels **o, u,** V.L. initial j- was strengthened slightly further
to ʒ, d͡ʒ (16.5a).

(b) V.L. tonic ę > Sp. je, d͡je.
In an initial position the first element of the Romance diphthong closed to a
consonantal sound at the beginning of a syllable:
  ĔQUA > *yegua*   L.L. ĔRĔMU > *yermo*
  ĒGO > *yo*   HĔRBA > *yerba, hierba*

NOTE
In *yerno, yema, hielo* the initial consonant also represents the first element of the Romance diphthong (14.12).

(c) V.L. intervocalic -j- (< C.L. -DJ-, -GJ-) > O.Sp. -j-, -d͡j-.
Of the Old Spanish variants j, d͡j, it was the fricative allophone j which became standard between vowels:
    RADĬU > *rayo*   L.L. EXAGĬU > *ensayo*
    MŎDĬU > *moyo*   L.L. PLAGĬA > *playa*

(d) V.L. intervocalic -j- (< C.L. -J-) > Sp. -j-.
The Vulgar Latin palatal glide remained unchanged before a back vowel:
    MAJŌRE > *mayor*   CUJUS > *cuyo*
    MAJU > *mayo*   V.L. JAJŪNU > *ayuno*

NOTES
1. The intervocalic j of Vulgar Latin was absorbed by a preceding palatal vowel in:
    PEJŌRE > V.L. pejóre > O.Sp. peór *peor*
    SEDĔAT > V.L. séjat > O.Sp. sé(j)a *seya, sea*
    CORRĬGĬA > V.L. korréja > O.Sp. kor̃éa *correa*
2. Initial j was absorbed by a following palatal vowel in:
    JACTARE > V.L. *jektáre > O.Sp. et͡ʃár *echar*
    JANUARĬU > V.L. jenwárjo > O.Sp. enéro *enero*
    JŪNĬPĔRU > V.L. jenépro > O.Sp. enébro *enebro*
3. For the development GAUDĬU > O.Sp. *goço, gozo* see 14.10, n. 3.

16.8   FURTHER READING. E. Alarcos (1965), paras. 148, 149, 155, 156. A. Alonso (1947), 1–12. C. Blaylock (1968), 392–409. J. Brüch (1930), 1–17. D. Catalán (1954), 1–44. W. D. Elcock (1960), 420–3, 432. W. J. Entwistle (1936), 287–8. V. García de Diego (1951), 105–8, 110, 114, 117, 121, 122, 131–8. M. Joos (1952), 222–31. I. Macpherson (1975), 155–64. Y. Malkiel (1963), 144–73; (1968c), 21–64. R. Menéndez Pidal (1952), paras, 38, 39, 46, 47, 50, 51, 53; (1954), 165–216. E. B. Williams (1938), para. 67.

16.9   EXERCISES ON CHAPTER 16
1. Trace into Spanish: L.L. CAPPĔLLA, V.L. *FĪBĔLLA, PLAGA, V.L. PLĬCAVĪ, SUFFLĀRE.
2. Trace the source of ñ in each of the following: *otoño, piña, péñola, escaña, estameña.*
3. The following words show learned influence. Explain, and suggest what phonetic form each word might have taken if it had developed along popular lines.
    actual (< ACTUALE)   *electuario* (< L.L. ĔLĔCTUARĬU)
    adulto (< ADŬLTŬ)   *inclinar* (< ĬNCLĪNARE)
    confluir (< CONFLŬĔRE)   *nocturno* (< NŎCTŬRNU)
    culto (< CŬLTŬ)   *recto* (< RĔCTU)
    simple (< SĬMPLŬ)   *resultar* (< RESŬLTĀRE)

4. Account for these developments:

CĬLĬA > *ceja*

V.L. *JŌJO > *joyo*

LAXĀRE > O.Sp. *lexar*

MAXĔLLA > O.Sp. *mexilla*

PŎDĬU > *poyo*

PRAESĬDĬA > *presea*

V.L. *SAGĬA > *saya*

SĒPĬA > O.Sp. *xibia*

V.L. *SĬMĬLĬARE > *semejar*

V.L. TALĔARE > *tajar*

5. The closing of C.L. Ŭ to Spanish *u* in *mucho, cuchillo, luchar, trucha* etc. (where -ŬLT-, -ŬCT- > -*uch*-) is generally attributed to the influence of a yod or semivowel. Explain how this semivowel developed.

17 PRETONIC, POST-TONIC VOWELS, SECONDARY CONSONANT CLUSTERS

PRETONIC, POST-TONIC VOWELS

17.1 V.L. unstressed a (< C.L. Ă, Ā) > Sp. a.

Of the Latin internal unstressed vowels, a regularly survived:

CALAMĔLLU > *caramillo*	SABANA > *sábana*
SEXAGĬNTA > O.Sp. *sessaenta*	L.L. ŎRPHANU > *huérfano*
V.L. AMARĔLLU > *amarillo*	L.L. PARAMU > *páramo*

17.2 Other internal unstressed vowels were lost:

CATĒNATU > *candado*	V.L. CARRĬCARE > *cargar*
HŬMĔRU > *hombro*	V.L. COLUMĔLLU > *colmillo*
SPĔCŬLU > *espejo*	V.L. *CŌNSŪUTURA > *costura*

17.3 Where there were two pretonic vowels in Latin, the vowel nearer the tonic accent was lost:

ĬNGĔNĔRARE > *engendrar*	VĪCĪNĬTATE > *vecindad*
RĔCŬPĔRARE > *recobrar*	V.L. *COMĬNĬTĬARE > *comenzar*

17.4 **Raising of unstressed e to j.** When the unstressed e of Vulgar Latin came into contact with a more close vowel, it was generally assimilated towards the point of articulation of that vowel and closed to the glide j:

CŌ(G)ĬTARE > *cuidar*	TŬRBĬ(D)U > *turbio*
LĪTĬ(G)ARE > *lidiar*	LĬMPĬ(D)U > *limpio*
SŪCĬ(D)U > *sucio*	RANCĬ(D)U > *rancio*

For the raised vowel of *sartén* < SARTA(G)ĬNE see 12.7

17.5 **Retention of post-tonic vowel.** In a number of words learned or semi-learned in form the post-tonic vowel was preserved until after the fall of the final vowel:

CALĬCE > *cáliz*	APŎSTŎLU > *apóstol*
CAESPĬTE > *césped*	ANGĔLU > *ángel*
MARGĬNE > *margen*	JŬVĔNE > *joven*

Two words in which this development took place do not appear to be learned. In *árbol* < ARBŎRE the post-tonic vowel may have been preserved in order to avoid the difficult consonant cluster -rbr- (a purely popular development would have produced **arbre*). In *huésped* < HŎSPĬTE the regular phonetic development to **hueste* may have been discouraged by the possible confusion with the homonym *hueste* < HŎSTE.

In proparoxytones, many of which are semi-learned or learned in form, the post-tonic vowel and the final vowel are regularly maintained:

CARDĬNU > *cárdeno*   SYMPTŌMA > *síntoma*
AQUĬLA > *águila*   SPECTACŬLU > *espectáculo*

SECONDARY CONSONANT CLUSTERS

17.6 **General.** With the fall of unstressed internal vowels, new consonant groups came into being in the emergent Romance language: these are known as **secondary** or **Romance** clusters.

For example, the fall of the pretonic vowel in LĪBĔRARE brought together β and **r** in the formative stages of Castilian, and the secondary cluster β'**r** (where ' indicates a lost unstressed vowel) suffered no further change: M.Sp. *librar*.

In some words secondary clusters were treated in the same way as Latin groups: both **pr** and **p'r** > **br** in CAPRA > *cabra*, RECŬP(Ĕ)RARE > *recobrar*. More frequently the secondary clusters, formed at a much later date, were made up of consonants which had survived or developed before the fall of an unstressed vowel, and evolved quite differently. V.L. **mn** > ɲ in DAMNU > *daño*, whereas the secondary group **m'n** > **mbr** in FĒMĬNA > *hembra*.

Another possibility was the grouping of consonants in a sequence unfamiliar in Latin. Many of these sequences which were tolerated in early Old Spanish were subsequently modified − e.g. CATĒNATU > tenth-century *cadnado* > thirteenth-century *candado*, with metathesis of *d* and *n*.

17.7 **Order of change.** In the Latin of Spain unstressed vowels generally survived for long enough to allow the intervocalic voiceless consonants to voice before the formation of the secondary cluster. The intervocalic -T- of VĪCĪNĬTATE voiced to d before the fall of V.L. pretonic e < C.L. Ĭ, to form the secondary cluster **n'd** of *vecindad*. The intervocalic -C- of DŎMĬNĬCU voiced to g before the fall of the V.L. post-tonic e < C.L. Ĭ, to form the secondary cluster **n'g** in the semi-learned *domingo*.

NOTES

1. In a number of words, particularly after *l*, *s* and Latin consonant groups, the unstressed vowel was lost in the Vulgar Latin period, so that the second element did not voice:

PĔRS(Ĭ)CU > *prisco*   V.L. *RAS(Ĭ)CARE > *rascar*
HŎSP(Ĭ)TALE > *hostal*   V.L. *FALL(Ĭ)TA > *falta*
V.L. *CŎL(Ŭ)PU > *golpe*   V.L. *CŎNS(Ū)TURA > *costura*

2. In semi-learned words the final element of the consonant cluster was generally preserved as voiceless consonant:

LĒGALĬTATE > *lealtad*   V.L. *AMĪCĬTATE > *amistad*.

```
Consonant + r
```

17.8 The first element of the secondary cluster consonant + **r** developed as when intervocalic.

(a) Voiceless plosives voiced:
    RECŬP(Ĕ)RARE > *recobrar*   AP(Ĕ)RIRE > *abrir*

(b) Voiced plosives remained:
    LĪB(Ĕ)RARE > *librar*   HĔD(Ĕ)RA > *hiedra*

(c) Voiceless fricatives voiced:
    AC(Ĕ)RE > O.Sp. *azre* > *arce*
    JAC(Ē)RE + HAT > O.Sp. *yazdrá* (M.Sp. *yacerá*)

(d) Geminate consonants were simplified:
    LĬTT(Ĕ)RA > *letra*   QUATTUOR > *cuatro*

It is most likely that the voicing of voiceless plosives and fricatives took place before the fall of the unstressed vowel.

Consonant + l

17.9   V.L. -b'l-, -p'l- > Sp. -bl-

(a) V.L. -b'l- normally remained unaltered:
    STAB(Ĭ)LE > *estable*   NĔB(Ŭ)LA > *niebla*
    NŪB(Ĭ)LU > *nublo*   FAB(Ŭ)LARĪ > *hablar*

Occasionally, *b* and *l* suffered metathesis: SĪB(Ĭ)LARE > *silbar*.
In TRĪB(Ŭ)LU and ĬNSŪB(Ŭ)LU the secondary cluster palatalized to ʎ (possibly via geminate ll produced through assimilation of the first element to the second):
    TRĪB(Ŭ)LU > *trillo*   ĬNSŪB(Ŭ)LU > *enjullo*.

(b) V.L. -p'l- > Sp. -bl-.
The first element voiced before the fall of the post-tonic vowel in PŎP(Ŭ)LU > *pueblo*. In semi-learned words Latin -P'L- was retained:
    CŌP(Ŭ)LA > *copla*.

17.10   V.L. -k'l-, -g'l- > O.Sp. ȝ.

Between a velar and a lateral the unstressed vowel fell early, in Vulgar Latin. Both groups then palatalized to Old Spanish ȝ (written *j*):
    APĬC(Ŭ)LA > *abeja*   TĒG(Ŭ)LA > *teja*
    ŎC(Ŭ)LU > *ojo*   RĒG(Ŭ)LA > *reja*
    CŬNĬC(Ŭ)LU > *conejo*   COAG(Ŭ)LARE > *cuajar*

The process of change began when the syllable-final velars k and g came to be articulated as fricatives rather than stops, and coalesced in the voiceless velar fricative x (cf. the V.L. developments kt > xt, ks > xs described in 11.17c):
    kl, gl > xl.

The velar fricative x was then drawn slightly forward, to produce the semivowel j (cf. 16.4a, 16.6a):
    xl > jl.

The lateral was then assimilated to the place of articulation of the preceding glide, so that:
    jl > ʎ.

This remained in Aragonese and Leonese *abella, huello, cuallar* etc.

In Castilian the development continued:

$\Lambda > \Lambda j > \widehat{dj} > \widehat{d_3} > 3$.

The process is the same as that described in 16.5b.

Summary: kl, gl > xl > jl > Λ > Λj > $\widehat{dj}$ > $\widehat{d_3}$ > 3.

NOTES

1. The semivowel which developed from syllable-final x had the effect of closing a preceding stressed Ŏ by one stage to ǫ and preventing diphthong-ization in ŎCŬLU > *ojo*.

2. In late borrowings and semi-learned words, Latin C'L, G'L > Sp. gl which became gr in some words by metathesis:

REGŬLA > *regla*

SAECŬLU > O.Sp. *sieglo* > *siglo*

MĪRACŬLU > O.Sp. *miraglo* > *milagro*

PERĪCŬLU > O.Sp. *periglo* > *peligro*

7.11   V.L. -k'l- (< C.L. -T'L-) > O.Sp. -3-.

In Vulgar Latin, T'L > k'l (11.7d, n.). The group then developed regularly, as described in 17.10, to produce Old Spanish 3:

VĔT(Ŭ)LU > *viejo*

V.L. *ROT(Ŭ)LARE > *arrojar*

V.L. *MŬT(Ŭ)LŌNE > *mojon*

NOTES

1. The palatal had no closing effect on the tonic Ĕ of VĔTŬLU, which became V.L. VECLU βéklo. Tonic ę̧ most probably diphthongized to *ie* before the stage x > j, and the diphthong remained unaffected by the palatal, to give O.Sp. *viejo* βjéʒo. The development Ĕ > *ie* before k'l appears to be regular in Castilian (*espejo* almost certainly derives from V.L. *SPĬC(Ŭ)LU, which replaced the Classical form SPĔCŬLU).

Alternative explanations of the diphthong in *viejo*, which attribute the diphthong to the influence of Aragonese and Leonese *viello, vieyo,* where the diphthong was normal, or to the influence of the rare O.Sp. *viedro* < VETĔRE are difficult to accept. It is unlikely that the form of such a popular and common word would have been influenced either by dialectal forms or by the uncommon adjective *viedro,* which fell rapidly into disuse during the medieval period.

2. In semi-learned words Latin T'L, D'L > Sp. *dl, ld:*

TĬTŬLU > *tilde*

MŌDŬLU > *molde*

L.L. SPATŬLA > *espalda*

The combination dl was felt to be difficult in Old Spanish and was regularly subject to metathesis:

dadle > dalde, dezidlo > dezildo etc.

7.12   After a consonant, V.L. -p'l-, -k'l- > Sp. -$\widehat{tʃ}$-.

In V.L. *CAPP(Ŭ)LA the secondary cluster palatized, via the stages: kápla > kápʎa > kátʎja > kátja > kátʃa *cacha* (cf. the developments described in 16.2, n. 1 and 16.4c). By a similar process MASC(Ŭ)LU > *macho,*

TRŬNC(Ŭ)LU > *troncho* and CĬNG(Ŭ)LU, after devoicing of the velar in the secondary cluster, > *cincho*.

NOTE
Consonant + **g'l** developed in a variety of ways. Devoicing of the velar led to the production of a palatal affricate in *cincho,* above.
In some words **g** weakened to a palatal **j,** which palatalized a preceding nasal in:
    ŬNG(Ŭ)LA > *uña*   SĬNG(Ŭ)LOS > O.Sp. *seños.*
In others **g** was lost after the nasal, and the group developed **ng'l > nl > nd:**
    SĬNG(Ŭ)LOS > *sendos*   V.L. *CONJŬNG(Ŭ)LA > *coyunda.*

Epenthesis	Metathesis

17.13   The fall of an unstressed vowel between a nasal consonant and a liquid or vibrant led to the formation of consonant clusters such as **m'r, m'l, n'r** which were unfamiliar to Latin and which presented difficulties of articulation. Various solutions to the difficulties offered by these new secondary clusters were found.
In some words the articulatory problem was solved by metathesis of the two elements:
    CŬM(Ŭ)LU > *colmo*   GĔN(Ĕ)RU > *yerno*
In others one sound was substituted for another:
    AN(Ĭ)MA > *alma*   HŎM(Ĭ)NE > O.Sp. *omne, omre.*
A third possibility was the production of an epenthetic 'glide' consonant
– *b* or *d* – to facilitate pronunciation of the unfamiliar consonant cluster:
    HŬM(Ĕ)RU > *hombro*   ĬNGĔN(Ĕ)RARE > *engendrar.*

17.14   V.L. -m'r- > Sp. -mbr-.
Between the nasal and the vibrant of the secondary cluster **m'r** the velum had to be raised rapidly during the transition from nasal to oral consonant. When the velum, anticipating the oral consonant to come, was raised too soon after the bilabial nasal *m,* the result was a slight explosion of air at the lips – a weak *b* sound:
    HŬM(Ĕ)RU > *hombro*   MĔM(Ŏ)RARE > O.Sp. *membrar*
    CŬCŬM(Ĕ)RE > *cohombro*   COM(ĔDĔ)RE + HAT > O.Sp. *combrá*

17.15   V.L. -m'n- > Sp. -mbr-.
By a similar process, which also involved the substitution of *r* for *n* as the second element of the group, **m'n > mbr** in:
    HŎM(Ĭ)NE > *hombre*   SĒM(Ĭ)NARE > *sembrar*
    FĒM(Ĭ)NA > *hembra*   LŪM(Ĭ)NE > *lumbre*

17.16   V.L. -m'l- > Sp. -mbl-, -lm-.
An epenthetic b appeared in TRĔM(Ŭ)LARE > O.Sp. *tremblar* > *temblar,* but the group was resolved by metathesis in CŬM(Ŭ)LU > *colmo.* In Old

Spanish apocope of final -*e* among weak pronouns (14.8) led to further secondary **m'l** clusters, which also tended to produce **mbl**:

que m(e) lo > quemblo   ni m(e) la > nimbla etc.

7.17   V.L. -**n'r**- > Sp. -**ndr**-, -**rn**-.

An epenthetic **d** appeared in the **n'r** group when the velum was raised too early in the transition between alveolar nasal and oral vibrant. The result was a slight explosion of air between tongue and alveoles — a weak *d* sound:

ĪNGĒN(Ē)RARE > *engendrar*   PONERE + HAT > *pondrá*
HŎN(Ō)RARE > O.Sp. *ondrar*   TENERE + HAT > *tendrá*

Alternatively, the group was subject to metathesis:

GĒN(Ē)RU > *yerno*   PONĒRE + HAT > O.Sp. *porná*
VĚN(Ē)RIS > *viernes*   TENĒRE + HAT > O.Sp. *terná*

NOTE

Other, less popular, solutions were the retention of the **n'r** cluster, with a strengthening of the second element to a multiple vibrant: HŎN(Ō)RARE > *onrar* **onr̄ár**, or the development **n'r** > **r̄**, especially in the future tense:

PONĒRE + HAT > O.Sp. *porrá*   TENĒRE + HAT > O.Sp. *terrá*.

> Combinations of velar and dental

7.18   Early V.L. -**k't**- > Later V.L. -**t͡s't**- > O.Sp. -**d͡z**-.

In RĔC(Ĭ)TARE, V.L. **ḱ** developed normally before a front vowel to **t͡s** (11.18c.) and then O.Sp. **d͡z** (14.10b.): T voiced between vowels to **d**, and the combination **d͡z'd**, by dissimilation of the last element, was then simplified to **d͡z**, written *z* in Old Spanish.

V.L. **reḱetáre** > **ret͡setáre** > **r̄ed͡z(e)dár** > **r̄ed͡zdár** > **r̄ed͡zár** O.Sp. *rezar*

Similarly V.L. PLAC(Ĭ)TU > O.Sp. *plazdo > plazo* (where initial *pl-* was retained in the pronunciation of the educated classes, cf. 16.2a, n. 2), and V.L. *AMĪC(Ĭ)TATE produced the Old Spanish popular form *amizat* (against the semi-learned *amistad*).

NOTE

After a consonant **k't** developed to the voiceless Old Spanish affricate **t͡s**:

V.L. ACCEPTŌRE > **at͡stór** > **at͡sór** *açor*.

7.19   V.L. -**t'k**-, -**d'k**- > O.Sp. -**dg**-, -**d͡zg**-

(a) In the group -**t'k**-, alveolar **t** voiced to **d** before the fall of the unstressed vowel, and the cluster **dg** (< C.L. -T'C-, -D'C-) was the most common result until well into the fourteenth century:

JŪD(Ĭ)CARE > O.Sp. *judgar*

The group clearly provided articulatory problems, however, attested to by fourteenth-century variants such as *jugdar, jubgar, jusgar, juzgar*. Of these competing forms, *juzgar* **ʒud͡zgár** became standard in the literary language of the fifteenth century (with a syllable-final sibilant most probably analogical on *juez, juiçio, juizio*).

> PORTAT(Ĭ)CU > O.Sp. *portadgo* > *portazgo*
> V.L. *PĔD(Ĭ)CU > O.Sp. *piedgo* > *piezgo*
> PAPA + AT(Ĭ)CU > O.Sp. *papadgo* > *papazgo*

(b) In the combination **d'k** + front vowel, V.L. k̂ developed normally to O.Sp. d̂z, which assimilated the preceding dental:

> D(Ŭ)ŌD(Ĕ)CĬM > O.Sp. *dodze, doze*
> TRĒD(Ĕ)CĬM > O.Sp. *tredze, treze*

Labial + dental

17.20   V.L. β't- (< C.L. -B'T-, -V'T-), V.L. -p't-, -p'd- > O.Sp. -βd-, -bd-
Voiceless labials in these combinations voiced before the fall of the unstressed vowel to produce the clusters βd, bd in Old Spanish, usually written *bd*:

> DĒB(Ĭ)TA > O.Sp. *debda*   CĪV(Ĭ)TATE > O.Sp. *çibdad*
> BĬB(Ĭ)TU > O.Sp. *bebdo*   V.L. RECAP(Ĭ)TARE > O.Sp. *recabdar*
> CŬB(Ĭ)TU > O.Sp. *cobdo*   V.L. CUP(I)DĬTĬA > O.Sp. *cobdiçia*

In the course of the fifteenth century the first element of the cluster tended to vocalize to w, and this pronunciation became standard during the course of the sixteenth century: *deuda, recaudar* etc. The velar glide w was absorbed by a preceding back vowel and lost in *codo, codicia* etc.

17.21   V.L. l, n, r + consonant remained.
In groups where the first element was l, n or r the second element developed normally as an intervocalic consonant before the formation of the secondary cluster, which underwent no further change:

> DEL(Ĭ)CATU > *delgado*   BON(Ĭ)TATE > *bondad*
> CAL(Ĭ)DU > *caldo*   L.L. ĔR(Ĕ)MU > *yermo*

Groups of three consonants

17.22   (a) The group normally remained:

> V.L. TEMP(Ŏ)RANU > *temprano*   *PAST(Ō)RĪLIA > O.Sp. *pastrija*
> V.L. *COMP(Ĕ) RARE > *comprar*   *PAST(Ō)RANEA > O.Sp. *pastraña*

In Old Spanish, syllable-final *s* appears to have been pronounced weakly in both *pastrija* and *pastraña* (compare the weakening of syllable-final *s* described in 8.26, 8.27, 18.10c), and the O.Sp. variants *patrija* and *patraña* show simplification of the -ST'R- cluster to -tr-; *patraña* has survived to the modern language.

(b) Occasionally the middle consonant was effaced:

> VĬND(Ĭ)CARE > *vengar*   CŎLL(Ŏ)CARE > *colgar*
> ŬND(Ĕ)CIM > *once*   MŪSC(Ŭ)LU > *muslo*

(c) A nasal, liquid or vibrant was liable to be replaced by another:
ANC(Ŏ)RA > *ancla*   SANG(UĬ)NE > *sangre*
ĬNG(UĬ)NE > *ingle*   V.L. GLAND(Ĭ)NE > *landre*

(d) The lateral vocalized in ALTERU > *otro* (12.8b), VŬLTŬRE > *buitre* (16.4b, n.).

.23   Consonant system: Old Spanish. Old Spanish is a term used in its widest sense to describe the language spoken in Castile from the point at which the Vulgar Latin of Spain began to take on identifiable regional characteristics (the late eighth century) until the end of the Middle Ages. Table 4 characterizes the developments described in chapters 12–17, and represents the consonant system of Castile during the late fourteenth and early fifteenth centuries.

TABLE 4   THE CONSONANTS OF OLD SPANISH

	Labial		Dental	Alveolar	Palatal	Velar	Glottal
	Bilabial	Labiodental					
Plosive	p b		t d			k g	
Affricate				t͡s d͡z	t͡ʃ d͡ʒ		
Fricative	β	f	ð	s z	ʃ ʒ	ɣ	h
Nasal	m			n	ɲ		
Lateral				l	ʎ		
Vibrant				r r̄			
Semivowel	w				j d͡j		

.24   FURTHER READING. J. Brüch (1930), 1–17. V. García de Diego (1951), 67–72, 143–63. R. Menéndez Pidal (1952), 23–6, 54–61.

.25   EXERCISES ON CHAPTER 17.
1. Account for the development into Spanish of the following words, paying particular attention to the fate of unstressed vowels and consonant groups formed after their fall: CŎMĬTE, COMMŪNĬCARE, DECĬMARE, LĬTTERA, MASTĬCARE, PĪPĔRE, L.L. SŎLĬDŬ, V.L. TĔMPŎRANU, TȲMPĂNŬ, VĬNDĬCARE.
2. Trace the following pairs of words into Spanish, and comment particularly on the development of the consonant which precedes *r* or *l*: QUADRŬ,

HĔDĔRA; CAPRA, APĔRĪRE; DŬPLŬ, PŎPŬLŬ; SŎCRŬ, ACĔRE;
V.L. ECLĒSĪA, ŎCŬLŬ.
3. Study the following developments, state whether you think each is
popular, semi-learned or learned, and give reasons for your conclusions in
each case.

ANNĬCŬLŬ > *añejo*	JŎCŬLARE > *juglar*
COAGŬLŬ > *cuajo*	ĪNŎCŬLARE > *inocular*
LENTĬCŬLA > *lenteja*	CAPĬTŬLU > *cabildo, capitulo*
V.L. PEDŬCŬLŬ > *piojo*	MŪSCŬLU > *muslo, músculo*
L.L. CŎNCHŬLA > *concha*	SĬNGŬLOS > *seños, sendos*

4. Explain the following developments: V.L. FAMĬNE > O.Sp. *fambre;*
MAMMŬLA > *mambla;* TĔNĔRŬ > *tierno;* V.L. TEMĒRE + HAT > O.Sp.
tembrá; VĪMĬNE > O.Sp. *vimbre.* How can the change DŎMĬNŬ > *dueño*
(not **duembro*) be accounted for?
5. Describe the phonetic development of Latin k in: ACCĔPTŌRE > O.Sp.
açor; JACTARE > *echar;* JŪDĬCARE > *juzgar;* V.L. *RASĬCARE > *rascar;*
RĔCĬTARE > *rezar.* Describe the phonetic development of Latin t in:
HOSPĬTALE > *hostal;* PLACĬTU > *plazo;* PORTATĬCU > *portazgo;*
TRACTU > *trecho;* VĒRĬTATE > *verdad.*

18 SIXTEENTH-CENTURY AND SEVENTEENTH-CENTURY CHANGES

1   **Alfonso X and *castellano drecho*.** During the reign of Alfonso X *el sabio* in the second half of the thirteenth century a great increase in cultural activity, centred on Toledo, led to the emergence of a written Castilian standard which with very little modification survived as a model for 'good' Spanish for the next two centuries. The *castellano drecho* of Alfonso X was something of a social and geographical compromise – a reconciliation on the one hand between popular speech and the literary language, influenced by Latin, and on the other hand between what was considered good usage in Old Castile, characterized by the dialect of Burgos, and the more southerly dialects of New Castile, with its centre at Toledo, where the king most frequently held court. The basis of Alfonso's *castellano drecho* was the speech of the educated classes of Toledo, influenced by the more northerly dialects of Old Castile, but without the more extreme linguistic features of Burgos such as the substitution of aspirate h for initial f (13.11) or the reduction of the diminutive suffix *-iello* to *-illo* (13.4a). Until the end of the fifteenth century Toledan usage served as a model for Castilian Spanish and the language remained fairly stable, with no major phonetic changes taking place apart from a persistent advance in the popularity of initial *h-* for *f-: hijo* for *fijo, hecho* for *fecho* etc., and, during the fifteenth century, an increasing tendency for the first element of the Old Spanish *-bd-* group to vocalize to *u: deuda* for *debda, caudal* for *cabdal* etc. (17.20).

2   **Pattern of sixteenth-century and seventeenth-century change.** The sixteenth and seventeenth centuries involved a further, comparatively rapid, period of major phonetic change, in which aspirate h disappeared from the language, as did the Old Spanish phonemes /z/, /t͡s/, /d͡z/, /ʃ/, /ʒ/. Medieval confusions between the pairs b/β, d/ð and g/ɣ were resolved in favour of a system which has survived to the present day, and two new speech-sounds, x and θ, entered the language. Some of these changes, such as the loss of aspirate h, merely represented the final stage of a process which had been going on for a very long time. Others, such as the weakening and change in point of articulation of affricate sounds, are developments which were common to the whole of Western Romance, although the final results and the date of the change varied from language to language. A third type of change – the velarization of the Old Spanish palatal fricatives ʃ and ʒ – probably owes its origin to the peculiar internal phonetic circumstances of sixteenth-century Spanish.

3   **Loss of aspirate h.** Aspirate h, after a long period of rivalry with f in an initial position (it was still pronounced *hiriendo en la garganta* according to the grammarian Antonio de Nebrija, writing late in the fifteenth century), fell rapidly from favour in the second half of the sixteenth century. By the beginning of the seventeenth century initial h had disappeared from the speech of educated persons in Castile, and from the literary language (T. Navarro, 1949).

O.Sp. *fecho* > ét͡ʃo *hecho*   O.Sp. *fablar* > aβlár *hablar*

The graph *h* has survived into modern orthography, but has no phonetic value.

The old Spanish phoneme /f/, which survived before the diphthong wé in *fuego, fuero* etc. and in cultural borrowings such as *facundo fértil* etc. remained unaltered.

18.4   **The phonemes /b/, /d/, /g/.** Medieval Spanish contained a bilabial plosive b, the descendant of C.L. B in an initial position (12.10) and of C.L. P in an intervocalic position (13.9c). Alongside this, a bilabial fricative β (pronounced as a labio-dental v in some regions) had developed from Classical Latin initial V and intervocalic B, V (12.10). Not surprisingly, the two very similar sounds were frequently confused, especially in northern areas and in popular speech. During the sixteenth century the very tenuous phonemic opposition b/β disappeared and the two sounds became simple positional variants of a single phoneme /b/, realized as a plosive b in an initial position and after a nasal, and as a fricative β elsewhere.

In the same way, plosive d (12.14, 13.9) and fricative ð (12.14) became positional variants of a single phoneme /d/, and plosive g (12.14, 13.9) and fricative ɣ (13.9) became positional variants of the phoneme /g/.

18.5   **Devoicing of Old Spanish sibilants.** During the course of the sixteenth century the phonemic oppositions among sibilants which depended upon the voiced/voiceless contrast – i.e. z/s, d͡z/t͡s, ʒ/ʃ – became progressively weaker. The fricative pairs s and z, ʃ and ʒ, and the affricate pair t͡s and d͡z, had tended to be confused from an early period in the North, with a strong preference for the voiceless variant. During the sixteenth century this preference for the voiceless sibilants s, ʃ and t͡s became progressively acceptable in the educated and literary language first of Madrid (by mid-century) and then of Toledo (by the last third of the century), and consequently the norm among Castilian speakers in the Peninsula.

By the end of the sixteenth century Old Spanish *cosa* kóza was pronounced kósa, Old Spanish *viejo* βjéʒo was pronounced bjéʃo, Old Spanish *dezir* ded͡zir was pronounced det͡sír.

In common with the changes in speech habits described in 18.3 and 18.4, this represented the eventual acceptance by the literary language of a linguistic feature which was not new, but which had over a period of centuries slowly gained in acceptability socially upwards through the hierarchy and geographically downwards through the Peninsula.

18.6   **Changes in the point of articulation of sibilants.** The result of the devoicing of the Old Spanish voiced sibilants was that during the sixteenth century standard Spanish contained large numbers of voiceless sibilants which were very similar in character, and easily confused one with the other. These were:

1. s < O.Sp. s, z. A voiceless retroflex, tip-alveolar, sibilant, slightly palatal in character.
2. ʃ < O.Sp. ʃ, ʒ. A voiceless palatal fricative, with a point of articulation very close to that of retroflex s, and easily confused with it.
3. t͡s < O.Sp. t͡s, d͡z. A voiceless alveolar affricate which was to become a simple fricative s̺ by the end of the century (18.8), and which was also easily confused with retroflex s.

By the end of the seventeenth century, largely as a result of an exaggeration of the differences between the points of articulation of these three sibilants, the possibilities of confusion in Castilian Spanish had been greatly reduced:

1. Tip-alveolar s remained.
2. The point of articulation of palatal fricative ʃ moved back to the velum, to produce the velar fricative x.
3. The point of articulation of alveolar affricate t͡s moved forward, first to a dental position s̺, and then to an interdental position θ.

16th century:

17th century:

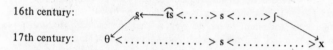

.7 **Sixteenth-century ʃ > seventeenth-century x.** A velar point of articulation for fricative ʃ < O.Sp. ʃ, ʒ was in evidence by the end of the sixteenth century, and became established as a feature of the language during the first half of the seventeenth:

	O.Sp.	16th century	17th century
DĪXĬT:	díʃo	díʃo	díxo *dijo*
FĪLĬU:	fíʒo	híʃo	íxo *hijo*

NOTE
One alternative explanation which has been put forward to account for the change ʒ > x in *hijo* etc. is that the point of articulation moved first, followed by the process of devoicing:

ʒ > *ɣ > x.

This seems unlikely, however, since if the development *ɣ > x had ever taken place, presumable the ɣ of Old Spanish *llaga* ʎáɣa, *negar* neɣár, *ruega* r̄wéɣa etc. would have devoiced at the same time to produce *ʎáxa, *nexár, *r̄wéxa etc. This clearly did not happen. Old Spanish ɣ survived unaltered into the modern language; sixteenth-century ʃ, joined by Old Spanish ʒ, became x.

.8 **Sixteenth-century t͡s > seventeenth-century θ.** By the end of the sixteenth century the affricate t͡s < O.Sp. t͡s, d͡z had lost its initial plosive element and become the simple fricative s̺, a sibilant articulated with the blade of the tongue against the upper front teeth. In Castilian Spanish, confusion between this blade-dental s̺, as in *cerca* s̺érka, *mecer* mes̺ér, *placer* plas̺ér, and the tip-alveolar s of *seco* séko, *paso* páso, *cosa* kósa was finally resolved in the seventeenth century when the point of articulation of ş moved slightly forward and the consonant was articulated as an interdental θ.

	O.Sp.	*16th century*	*17th century*	
CIRCA:	t͡sérka	şérka	θérka	*cerca*
MISCĒRE:	met͡sér	meşér	meθér	*mecer*
PLACĒRE:	plad͡zér	plat͡sér > plaşér	plaθér	*placer*

NOTE

Ceceo and seseo. In the southern part of the Peninsula and in the Spanish of Spanish America the difference between tip-alveolar s and blade-dental ş was not maintained. Both sounds came to be articulated as blade-dental ş during the sixteenth century, when the phenomenon was described as *ceceo* (then pronounced şeşéo). In some areas of the South, blade-dental ş (from all sources) developed to a dental or interdental sound θ, similar to the initial sound of modern Castilian *cena,* and the term *ceceo* (now pronounced θeθéo) has continued in use to describe this feature. *Casa* and *caza* are both pronounced káθa; *siega* and *ciega* are both pronounced θjéγa.

In other areas blade-dental ş has survived, so that *casa* and *caza* are both pronounced káşa, *siega* and *ciega* are both pronounced şjéγa. Since the eighteenth century the term *seseo* has been used to describe this feature. A third variety of *s,* articulated with the tongue flat in the mouth, and with the tip just touching the lower front teeth, is also found in Andalusia; use of this coronal *s* for the Castilian phonemes /s/, /θ/ is also described as *seseo.*

18.9   **Summary of sixteenth-century and seventeenth-century changes.**

(a) h was lost.

(b) The phonemes /b/, /d/, /g/ were established, with the allophones β, ð, γ.

(c) Six phonemes of Old Spanish were reduced to three:
1. /s/ - /z/ > /s/
2. /ʃ/ - /ʒ/ > /x/
3. /t͡s/ - /d͡z/ > /θ/.

18.10   **Developments since the seventeenth century.** The phonetic system established by the end of the seventeenth century has survived more or less intact until the present day. The only developments worthy of note since that time are the following:

(a) In educated speech -ð- has weakened in the masculine past participle ending -*ado*-, so that **tomáo** for *tomado,* **aβláo** for *hablado* are now generally acceptable. But against this there has been evidence in recent years of a tendency to restore ð to masculine past participle endings in Madrid, which could well slow or even reverse the trend towards the elimination of ð.

(b) Over extensive Spanish-speaking areas (such as Madrid, the southern half of the Peninsula and the greater part of Spanish America) palatal /ʎ/ has given way to /i/, realized as j, d͡j, ʒ, d͡ʒ etc., depending on considerations of class, dialect and phonetic context (8.34). In these areas the opposition /ʎ/–/i/ has been obscured: *pollo* and *poyo* are both pronounced /póio/, *halla* and *haya* are both pronounced /áia/. The development /ʎ/ > /i/ is described as *yeísmo*.

(c) When final in a syllable, s is weakly articulated. In Madrid it is frequently realized as a fricative ř – *esbelto* eřβélto; in Andalusia it may be articulated as an aspirate h or, in Eastern areas, lost altogether: eⁿβélto or eβélto. When a pluralizing -*s* is lost in this way, both the final and all preceding vowels of a word tend to be opened slightly, so that corresponding to the singular/ plural opposition póko/pókos of Castilian is the singular/plural opposition pǫ́kǫ/pǫ́kǫ. Since the distinction between the half-close vowels of singular forms and the half-open vowels of plural forms is accompanied by a corresponding adjustment in the length of the tonic vowel (the open vowels are longer in duration than the close vowels), the vocalic system of Eastern Andalusia can be seen to depend on two features quite alien to standard Castilian: the oppositions half-open/half-close and long/short among vowels. Singular pǫ́kǫ contrasts with plural pǫ́:kǫ; singular nę́nę contrasts with plural nę́:nę.

(d) The aspiration of *h*, four centuries after its disappearance from educated Castilian speech, has still not completely vanished from popular and rustic usage in provinces of Spain to the south, west and north-west of Castile. In areas where aspirate *h* has survived it is commonly confused with the phoneme /x/, so that although the sound may be voiced in some areas and voiceless in others no distinction is made between the pronunciation of minimal pairs such as *hoya* 'hole' and *joya* 'jewel', *hornada* 'batch' and *jornada* 'working day'. Occasionally this popular pronunciation is reflected in a word which has climbed the social ladder and been accepted into the literary language: both *jolgorio* (alongside *holgorio*, a derivative of *holgar* < L.L. FŎLLĬCARE) and *jamelgo* (alongside the purely learned *famélico* < FAMĒLĬCU) reflect the popular pronunciation of Andalusia.

3.11 **FURTHER READING.** E. Alarcos (1965), 157–63. A. Alonso (1951a), 121–72, 236–312; (1951b), 111–200; (1951c), 43–61; (1955), chs. 1–3. D. L. Canfield (1950), 233–6. G. Contini (1951), 173–82. D. Catalán (1956), 305–34; (1957), 283–322. J. Corominas (1953), 81–7. A. M. Espinosa and L. Rodríguez-Castellano (1936), 225–34, 337–78. A. Galmés (1957), 273–307. H. Gavel (1921). D. Gifford (1973), 22–39. R. Lapesa (1942), chs. 13–17; (1957–8), 67–94. E. Lorenzo (1966), 16–46. A Martinet (1951), 133–56. T. Navarro (1949), 166–9. A. Quilis and J. M. Rozas (1963), 445–9. A. Zamora Vicente (1960), 227–47. R. Spaulding and B. Patt (1948), 50–60.

8.12 **EXERCISES ON CHAPTER 18**

1. Trace the origin of the graph *h* in the following words: *haber, halcón, hálito, hermano, hiedra, hielo, hierro, hinchar, huerto, hurto.* Which of these words was pronounced with an aspirate h in Old Spanish?

2. Describe the phonetic evolution of the following words from Latin to modern Spanish, paying particular attention to the historical development of the phonemes /b/, /d/, /g/: BĬBĔRE, CATĒNA, CLAVĘ, DĒBĒRE, GŬBĔRNARE, LŬPU, PLAGA, VACARE, VADU, VŌTA.

3. Trace the origin of the graph *s* in the following words: *asa, cosa, cuerpos, masa, oso, pesar, saeta, salmo, tesoro, yeso*. In which of these words was the sibilant voiced in Old Spanish?

4. Complete the following table. (The first line provides a model.)

Latin	Old Spanish		sixteenth century	seventeenth century
VĔTŬLU	*viejo*	βjéʒo	bjéʃo	bjéxo
ALĬU				
MŬLĬERE				
RĒGŬLA				
ANNĬCŬLU				

5. Complete the following table. (The first two lines provide a model.)

Latin	Old Spanish		sixteenth century	seventeenth century
DĪCĔRE	*dezir*	dedz͡ír	det͡sír	deθír
LANCĔA	*lança*	lánt͡sa	lánt͡sa	lánθa
RATĬŌNE				
CAELU				
VĪCĪNU				
CONCĬLĬU				

BIBLIOGRAPHY

ABERCROMBIE, D. (1940), 'Syllable quantity and enclitics in English' in *In Honour of Daniel Jones*, Longmans, London, and repr. in *Studies in Phonetics and Linguistics*, Oxford, 1965
—— (1953), 'Phonetic transcriptions' in *Le Maître phonétique*, 32–4
—— (1956), *Problems and Principles in Language Study*, London
—— (1964), *English Phonetic Texts*, Faber and Faber, London
—— (1967), *Elements of General Phonetics*, Edinburgh University Press
ALARCOS LLORACH, E. (1948), 'El sistema fonológico español' in *RFE*, XXXIII, 265–96
—— (1951a), *Gramática estructural (Según la escuela de Copenhague y con especial atención a la lengua española)*, Bib. Rom. Hisp., Madrid
—— (1951b), 'Esbozo de una fonología diacrónica del español' in *Estudios dedicados a Menéndez Pidal*, II, 9–39
—— (1954), 'Resultados de $G^{e,i}$ en la península' in *Archivum*, IV, 330–42
—— (1958), 'Quelques précisions sur la diphthongaison espagnole' in *Omagiu lui Iorgu Iordan*, Bucharest, 1–4
—— (1965), *Fonología española*, 4th ed., Bib. Rom. Hisp., Madrid (1st ed., Madrid, 1950)
'ALFABETO FONETICO' in *Revista de Filología Española*, II, 1915, 374–6 (The phonetic alphabet used in *RFE* and by most Spanish linguists.)
ALLEN, W. SIDNEY (1965), *Vox Latina*, Cambridge Univ. Pr., Cambridge
ALONSO, Amado (1941), 'Substratum, superstratum' in *RFH*, III, 185–218
—— (1945), 'Una ley fonológica del español' in *Hisp. Rev.*, XIII, 91–101. Repr. in *Estudios lingüísticos; Temas españoles*, Madrid, 1961, 237–49
—— (1946), 'Las correspondencias arábigo-españolas en los sistemas de sibilantes' in *RFH*, VIII, 12–76
—— (1947), 'Trueques de sibilantes en antiguo español' in *NRFH*, I, 1–12
—— (1949), 'Examen de las noticias de Nebrija sobre antigua pronunciación' in *NRFH*, III, 1–82
—— (1951a), 'Formación del timbre ciceante en la "ç", "z" española' in *NRFH*, V, 121–72 and 263–312
—— (1951b), 'Historia del *ceceo* y del *seseo* españolas' in *Thesaurus*, Bol. del Inst. Caro y Cuervo, VII, 111–200
—— (1951c), 'Cronología de la igualización $c - z$ en español in *HR*, XIX, 43–61
—— (1951d), 'Como no se pronunciaban las "ç" y "z" antiguas' in *Hispania*, XXXIV, 51–3
—— (1955–69), *De la pronunciación medieval a la moderna en español*, completed and revised by R. Lapesa, Bib. Rom. Hisp., Madrid, Vol. I, 1955, 2nd ed., 1969; vol. II, 1969

——— (1961), "r" y "l" en España y América' in *Estudios lingüísticos: temas hispano-americanos*, Gredos, Madrid

ALVAR, M. (1953), *El dialecto aragonés*, Bib. Rom. Hisp., Madrid

BALDINGER, K. (1963), *La formación de los dominios lingüísticos en la peninsula ibérica*, Gredos, Madrid. Trans. by E. Lledó and M. Macau from the original *Die Herausbildung der Sprachräume auf der Pyrenäenhalbinsel: Querschnitt durch die neueste Forschung und Versuch einer Synthese*, Berlin, 1958

BLAYLOCK, C. (1964), 'The monophthongization of Latin AE in Spanish' in *Romance Philology*, XVIII, 16–26

——— (1968), 'Latin L-, LL- in the Hispanic dialects: Retroflexion and lenition' in *Romance Philology*, XXI, 392–409

BLOCH, B., and TRAGER, G. L. (1942), *Outline of Linguistic Analysis*, Special publication of the Linguistic Society of America, Baltimore

BLOOMFIELD, L. (1935), *Language*, Allen and Unwin, London

BOLAÑO E ISLA, A. (1959), *Manual de la lengua española*, Porrua, Mexico

BOWEN, J. D. and STOCKWELL, R. P. (1955), 'The phonemic interpretation of semivowels in Spanish' in *Language*, XXXI, 236–40. Repr. in Joos (1966), 400–2

——— (1956). 'A further note on Spanish semivowels' in *Language*, XXXII, 290–2. Repr. in Joos (1966), 405

——— (1960), *Patterns of Spanish Pronunciation*, University of Chicago Press

BRÜCH, J. (1930), 'L'évolution de l'*l* devant les consonnes en espagnol' in *RFE*, XVII, 1–17

CANFIELD, D. L. (1950), 'Spanish "ç" and "s" in the sixteenth century: a hiss and a soft whistle' in *Hispania*, XXXIII, 233–6

——— (1962), *La pronunciación del español en América: Ensayo histórico-descriptivo*, Bogotá

CATALÁN, D. (1954), 'Resultados ápico-palatales y dorso-palatales de -LL- y -NN-' in *RFE*, XXXVIII, 1–44

——— (1955), *La escuela lingüística española y su concepión del lenguaje*, Gredos, Madrid

——— (1956), 'El ceceo—zezeo al comenzar la expansión atlántica de Castilla' in *Boletim de filológia*, XVI, 305–34

——— (1957), 'The end of the phoneme /z/ in Spanish' in *Word*, XIII, 283–322

——— (1964–5), 'Nuevos enfoques de la fonología española' in *Romance Philology*, XVIII, 178–91

CONTINI, G. (1951), 'Sobre la desaparición de la correlación de sonoridad en castellano' in *NRFH*, V, 173–82

COROMINAS, J. (1953), 'Para la fecha del yeísmo y del lleísmo' in *NRFH*, VII, 81–7

——— (1954–7), *Diccionario crítico etimológico de la lengua castellana*, 4 vols., Berne

COSERIU, E. (1954), *Forma y sustancia en los sonidos del lenguaje*, Montevideo

CRYSTAL, D. (1971), *Linguistics*, Penguin Books, Harmondsworth

CUERVO, R. J. (1895 and 1898), 'Disquisiciones sobre antigua ortografía y pronunciación castellanas' in *Revue Hispanique*, II, 1–69, *Revue Hispanique*, V, 273–313

DALBOR, J. B. (1969), *Spanish Pronunciation: Theory and Practice*, Holt, Rinehart and Winston, New York

DARBYSHIRE, A. E. (1967), *A Description of English*, E. Arnold, London

DATO, D. P. (1959), 'A Historical Phonology of Castilian', Cornell University Dissertation

DELATTRE, Pierre (1966), *Comparing the Phonetic Features of English, French, German and Spanish: an Interim Report*, Harrap, London

DINNEEN, F. P. (1967), *An Introduction to General Linguistics*, Holt, Rinehart and Winston, New York

ELCOCK, W. D. (1960), *The Romance Languages*, Faber and Faber, London. Revised ed., with a new introd. by J. N. Green, 1975

ENTRAMBASAGUAS, Joaquín de (1955), *Síntesis de pronunciación española*, C.S.I.C., Madrid

ENTWISTLE, W. J. (1936), *The Spanish Language*, Faber and Faber, London

ESPINOSA, A. M. (1924), 'Synalepha and syneresis in Modern Spanish' in *Hispania* (Washington), VII, 299–309

ESPINOSA, A. M., and RODRÍGUEZ CASTELLANO, L. (1936), 'La aspiración de la *H* en el Sur y Oeste de España' in *RFE*, XXIII, 225–54, 337–78

FIRTH, J. R. (1957), '*A synopsis of linguistic theory*' in *Studies in Linguistic Analysis*, Special Volume of the Philological Society, Blackwell, Oxford

FORD, J. D. M. (1900), *The Old Spanish Sibilants*, Harvard Studies and Notes in Philology and Literature, VII, 1–182

GALMÉS, A. (1957), 'Lle-yeísmo y otras cuestiones lingüísticas en un relato morisco del siglo XVII' in *Est. ded. a Menéndez Pidal*, VII, 273–307

——— (1962), *Los sibilantes en la Romania*, Gredos, Madrid

GARCÍA DE DIEGO, V. (1946), *Manual de dialectología española*, Cultura Hispánica, Madrid. (2nd ed., Madrid, 1959)

——— (1950), 'El castellano como complejo dialectal y sus dialectos internos' in *RFE*, XXXIV, 107–24

——— (1951), *Gramática histórica española*, Madrid. (First pub. as *Elementos de gramática histórica castellana*, Burgos, 1914.)

GASSNER, A. (1897), *Das altspanische Verbum*, Niemeyer, Halle

GAVEL, H. (1920), *Essai sur l'évolution de la prononciation du castillan depuis le XIVme siècle*, E. Champion, Paris

GILI.GAYA, S. (1921), 'La "r" simple en la pronunciación española' in *RFE*, VIII, 271–80

——— (1955), *Nociones de gramática histórica española*, 2nd ed., Spes, Barcelona

——— (1958), *Elementos de fonética general*, 3rd ed., Gredos, Madrid

GIMSON, A. C. (1962), *An Introduction to the Pronunciation of English*, E. Arnold, London

GLEASON, H. A., Jr. (1955), *An Introduction to Descriptive Linguistics*, Holt, Rinehart and Winston, New York. Revised ed., 1961

GONZÁLEZ–OLLÉ, F. (1972), 'Resultados castellanos de "kw" y "gw" latinos. Aspectos fonéticos y fonológicos' in *BRAE*, LII, 285–318

GRANDGENT, C. H. (1934), *An Introduction to Vulgar Latin*, New York. Trans. F. de B. Moll: *Introducción al Latín Vulgar*, 3rd ed., Madrid, 1963

HALL, Pauline C. (1956), *A bibliography of Spanish linguistics: articles in serial publications*, Language Dissertation No. 54, Baltimore

HANSSEN, F. (1913), *Gramática histórica de la lengua castellana*, Halle
HARRIS, J. W. (1969), *Spanish Phonology*, M.I.T. Press, Research Monograph No. 54
HAUGEN, E. (1956), 'The syllable in linguistic description' in *For Roman Jakobson*, The Hague, 213–21
HEFFNER, R.-M. S. (1949), *General Phonetics*, University of Wisconsin Press
HERMAN, J. (1966), *Le Latin Vulgaire, Que sais-je?*, Paris
HOCKETT, C. F. (1942), 'A system of descriptive phonology' in *Language*, XVIII, 3–21. Repr. in Joos (1966), 97–108
—— (1955), *A Manual of Phonology*, Waverly Press, Baltimore
—— (1958), *A course in Modern Linguistics*, New York
HONSA, V. (1965), 'The phonemic system of Argentinian Spanish' in *Hispania*, XLVIII, 275–83
International Phonetic Association, *The Principles of the International Phonetic Association*, Bourg-la-Reine and London, 1912. 2nd ed., London 1949, Repr. 1962
JAMES, L. (1940), *Speech Signals in Telephony*, London
JASSEM, W. (1952), *Intonation of Conversational English*, Wroclaw
JONES, D. (1950), *The Phoneme: its Nature and Use*, Heffer, Cambridge. 2nd ed., 1962
—— (1958), *The Pronunciation of English*, 4th ed., Cambridge University Press (1st ed., Cambridge, 1909.)
—— (1960), *An Outline of English Phonetics*, 10th ed., Heffer, Cambridge (1st ed., Teubner, Leipzig, 1918.)
JONES, D., and DAHL, I. (1944), *Fundamentos de escritura fonética según el sistema de la Asociación Fonética Internacional*, University College, London
JOOS, M. (1952), 'The medieval sibilants' in *Language*, XXVIII, 222–31. Repr. in Joos (1966), 372–8
—— (ed.) (1966), *Readings in Linguistics*, 4th ed., American Council of Learned Societies, New York (1st ed., New York, 1957.)
JUNGEMANN, F. (1955), *La teoría del sustrato y los dialectos hispano-romances y gascones*, Madrid
LADO, R. (1956), 'A comparison of the sound system of English and Spanish' in *Hispania*, XXXIX, 26–9
LAPESA, R. (1942), *Historia de la lengua española*, Escelicer, Madrid. 5th, revised, ed., Madrid, 1962
—— (1951), 'La apócope de la vocal en castellano antiguo' in *Est. ded. a Menéndez Pidal*, II, 185–226
—— (1957–8), 'Sobre el ceceo y el seseo andaluces' in *Misc. Hom. a André Martinet*, 2 vols., La Laguna, I, 67–94
LÁZARO, F. (1949), 'F- > h-, ¿ fenómeno ibérico o romance?' in *Actas de la Primera Reunión Toponimia Pirenaica*, Zaragoza
LEHMANN, W. P. (1966), *Historical Linguistics: an Introduction*, Holt, Rinehart and Winston, New York
LORENZO, E. (1966), 'La lengua española en 1965. Tradición e innovación' in *El español de hoy, lengua en ebullición*, Gredos, Madrid, 16–46
LYONS, J. (1968), *An Introduction to Theoretical Linguistics*, Cambridge University Press

—— ed. (1970), *New Horizons in Linguistics*, Penguin Books, Harmondsworth.
MALKIEL, Y. (1953), 'Language history and historical linguistics' in
Romance Philology, VII, 65–76
—— (1955), 'La *f* inicial adventicia en español antiguo' in *Revue de
linguistique Romane*, XVIII, 161–91
—— (1962a), 'Etymology and General Linguistics' in *Word*, XVIII,
198–219
—— (1962b), 'Towards a unified system of classification of Latin-Spanish
vowel correspondences' in *Romance Philology*, XVI, 153–62
—— (1963), 'The interlocking of narrow sound change, broad phonological
pattern, level of transmission, areal configuration, sound symbolism' in
Archivum Linguisticum, XV, 144–73
—— (1968a), *Essays on Linguistic Themes*, Blackwell, Oxford
—— (1968b), 'Range of variation as a clue to dating (1), in *Romance
Philology*, XXI, 463–501
—— (1968c), 'The inflectional paradigm as an occasional determinant of
sound change' in *Directions for Historical Linguistics. A Symposium*, ed.
W. P. Lehman and Y. Malkiel. University of Texas Press. Austin and London,
21–64
—— (1975), 'Some late twentieth-century options open to Hispanic philology
and linguistics' in *Bulletin of Hispanic Studies*, LII, 1–11
MALMBERG, B. (1948a), 'La Structure syllabique de l'espagnole' in
Boletim de filologia, IX, 99–120
—— (1948b), *L'Espagnol dans le Nouveau Monde – problème de
linguistique générale*, Lund
—— (1962), *La Phonétique*, Paris. Also in English trans.: *Phonetics*, New
York 1963
—— (1964), *New Trends in Linguistics*, trans. E. Carney, Lund, Stockholm.
1st Swedish ed., *Nya vägar inom språkforskningen*, 1959; 2nd Swedish
ed., 1962
MARTINET, A. (1949), *Phonology as Functional Phonetics*, Oxford
University Press, London
—— (1951), 'The unvoicing of Old Spanish sibilants' in *Romance Philology*,
V, 133–56
—— (1952), 'Celtic lenition and Western Romance consonants' in *Language*,
XXVIII, 192–217
—— (1955), *Economie des changements phonétiques*, Francke, Berne
—— (1964), *Elements of General Linguistics*, trans. Elisabeth Palmer, Faber
and Faber, London. (1st ed., *Eléments de linguistique générale*, Paris, 1960.)
(MARTINET, A.), *Miscelánea Homenaje a André Martinet: estructuralismo e
historia*, 2 vols., La Laguna, 1957–8
MENÉNDEZ PIDAL, R. (1950), 'Modo de obrar el substrato lingüístico', in
RFH, XXXIV, 1–8
—— (1952), *Gramática histórica española*, 9th ed., Espasa-Calpe, Madrid
(1st ed., Madrid, 1904.)
—— (1954), 'A proposito de *ll y l* latinas. Colonización suditálica en
España' in *BRAE*, XXXIV, 165–216
—— (1961), *El dialecto leonés*, Instituto de Estudios Asturianos, Oviedo
(First publ. in the *Revista de Archivos, Bibliotecas y Museos*, 1906.)

—— (1964), *Orígenes del español,* 5th ed., Espasa-Calpe, Madrid (1st ed., Madrid, 1926.)

MEYER-LÜBKE, W. (1921), 'La evolución de la *c* latina delante de *e* e *i* en la Península Ibérica' in *RFE,* VIII, 225–51

—— (1924), 'La sonorización de las sordas intervocálicas latinas en español' in *RFE,* XI, 1–32

NAVARRO TOMAS, T. (1946), *Estudios de fonología española,* Syracuse. Trans. R. D. Abraham: *Studies in Spanish Phonology,* Miami Linguistics Series, 4, 1968

—— (1949), 'The old aspirated *h* in Spain and in the Spanish of America' in *Word,* V, 166–9. Summarized in *RFE,* XXXV (1951), 377–8

—— (1965), *Manual de pronunciación española,* 12th ed., Madrid (1st ed., Madrid, 1918.)

NEWMANN, S. S. (1946), 'On the stress system of English' in *Word,* II, 171–87

O'CONNOR, J. D. (1948), *New Phonetic Readings,* Francke, Berne

—— (1967), *Better English Pronunciation,* Cambridge University Press

—— (1973), *Phonetics,* Penguin Books, Harmondsworth

ORR, J. (1936), 'F > *h,* phénomène ibère ou roman?' in *Revue de Linguistique Romane,* XII, 10–35

PEI, M. (1965), *Invitation to Linguistics,* Allen and Unwin, London

PIKE, K. L. (1943), *Phonetics: a Critical Analysis of Phonetic Theory and a Technic for the Practical Description of Sounds,* University of Michigan Press, Ann Arbor

—— (1946), *The Intonation of American English,* University of Michigan Press, Ann Arbor

—— (1947a), 'On the phonemic status of English diphthongs' in *Language,* XXIII, 151–9

—— (1947b), 'Grammatical prerequisites to phonemic analysis' in *Word,* III, 155–72

—— (1947c), *Phonemics,* University of Michigan Press, Ann Arbor

POPE, M. K. (1934), *From Latin to Modern French,* Manchester University Press

POSNER, R. (1961), *Consonantal dissimilation in the Romance Languages,* Publications of the Philological Society, XIX, Basil Blackwell, Oxford

—— (1966), *The Romance Languages: A Linguistic Introduction,* Anchor Books, New York

POTTIER, B. (1956–7), *Introduction á l'étude de la philologie hispanique,* 2 vols., Bordeaux. 2nd ed., Paris, 1960

—— (1968), *Lingüística moderna y filología hispánica,* trans. M. Blanco Alvarez, Gredos, Madrid

QUILIS, A. (1963), *Fonética y fonología del español,* C.S.I.C., Madrid

—— (1966), 'Sobre los alófonos dentales de /s/' in *RFE,* XLIX, 335–43

QUILIS, A., and FERNÁNDEZ, J. A. (1964), *Curso de fonética y fonología españolas,* C.S.I.C., Madrid. 3rd ed., Madrid, 1968

QUILIS, A., and ROZAS, J. M. (1963), 'Para la cronología de la fricativa velar, sorda, /x/ en castellano' in *RFE,* XLVI, 445–9

ROBINS, R. J. (1964), *General Linguistics: an Introductory Survey,* Longmans, London

SALVADOR, G. (1957), 'La diptongación de Ŏ, Ĕ latinas y las cartas de un semianalfabeto' in *RFE*, XLI, 418–25

SAPIR, E. (1921), *Language, an Introduction to the Study of Speech*, Harcourt, Brace and Co., New York

SAPORTA, S. (1956), 'A note on Spanish semi-vowels' in *Language*, XXXII, 287–90. Repr. in Joos (1966), 403–4

SAPORTA, S., and CONTRERAS, H. (1962), *A Phonological Grammar of Spanish*, University of Washington Press, Seattle

SAROÏHANDY, J. (1902), 'Remarques sur la phonétique du ç et du z en ancien espagnol' in *BH*, IV, 198–214

SAUSSURE, F. de (1916), *Cours de linguistique générale*, Payot, Paris. Trans. W. Baskin: *Course in General Linguistics*, Owen, London, 1961, and by Amado Alonso, *Curso de lingüística general* (with notes), 1945

SCHOCH, A. D. (1907), 'Uniform writing or simplified alphabet, which?' in *Le Maître phonétique*, 80–4

SPAULDING, R. K. (1943), *How Spanish Grew*, University of California Press, Berkeley and Los Angeles

SPAULDING, R., and PATT, B. (1948), 'Data for the chronology of "theta" and "jota" ' in *Hispanic Review*, XVI, 50–60

STOCKWELL, R. P., and BOWEN, J. D. (1965), *The Sounds of English and Spanish*, University of Chicago Press

STOCKWELL, R. P., BOWEN, J. D., and SILVA-FUENZALIDA, I. (1956), 'Spanish juncture and intonation' in *Language*, XXXII, 641–65. Repr. in Joos (1966), 406–18

STRANG, B. M. H. (1962), *Modern English Structure*, E. Arnold, London. 2nd, revised, ed., 1968

STURTEVANT, E. H. (1917), *Linguistic Change*, University of Chicago Press
—— (1947), *An Introduction to Linguistic Science*, Yale University Press, New Haven

SWADESH, M. (1947), 'On the analysis of English syllabics' in *Language*, XXIII, 137–50

TRAGER, G. L. (1935), 'The transcription of English' in *Le Maître phonétique*, 10–13
—— (1939), 'The phonemes of Castillian Spanish' in *Travaux du Cercle Linguistique de Prague*, VIII, 217–22
—— (1942), 'The phonemic treatment of semivowels' in *Language*, XVIII, 220–3

TRAGER, G. L., and BLOCH, B. (1941), 'The syllabic phonemes of English' in *Language*, XVII, 223–46

TRAGER, G. L., and SMITH, H. L., Jr. (1956), *An Outline of English Structure*, American Council of Learned Societies, Washington

TRUBETZKOY, N. S. (1935), *Anleitung zu phonologischen Beschreibungen*, édition du Cercle Linguistique de Prague, Brno. Trans. L. A. Murray: *Introduction to the Principles of Phonological Descriptions*, The Hague, 1968
—— (1939), *Grundzüge der Phonologie*, Travaux du Cercle Linguistique de Prague, VII, Prague. Trans. J. Cantineau: *Principes de Phonologie*, Paris, 1949

TWADDELL, W. F. (1935), *On Defining the Phoneme*, Language Monographs, XVI, Baltimore. Repr. in Joos (1966), 55–80

WILLIAMS, E. B. (1938), *From Latin to Portuguese,* University of
Pennsylvania Press. 2nd ed., 1962
WISE, C. M. (1958), *Introduction to Phonetics,* Prentice Hall, Englewood
Cliffs, N. J.
ZAMORA VICENTE, A. (1960), *Dialectología española,* Gredos, Madrid.
2nd ed., expanded, Madrid, 1967

Addenda

ALONSO, Dámaso (1972), 'B=V en la peninsula ibérica', in *Obras completas,*
I, Madrid. Previously publ. in *Enciclopedia lingüística hispánica,* I
(suplemento), Madrid, 1962, 155–209
BOURCIEZ, E. (1967), *Eléments de linguistique romane,* 5th ed., Paris
CANFIELD, D. L., and DAVIS, J. C. (1975). *An Introduction to Romance
Linguistics,* Illinois, Southern Illinois Univ. Press
CARDENAS, D. N. (1960), *Introducción a una comparación fonológica del
español y del inglés,* Oxford Univ. Press
DEFERRARI, A. E. (1967), *The Phonology of Italian, Spanish and French,*
Washington, D.C.
GIFFORD, D. (1973), 'Spain and the Spanish Language in Spain', in *Spain.
A Companion to Spanish Studies,* ed. P. E. Russell, London, Methuen,
1–39
LAUSBERG, H. (1965), *Lingüística románica,* Madrid
MACPHERSON, I. R. (1975), 'Delateralization and Phonetic Change: the Old
Spanish palatals [ʎ], [ʧ], [(d)ʒ]' in *Studies in Honor of Lloyd A. Kasten,*
Madison, 155–64
MALKIEL, Y. (1975), 'En torno al cultismo medieval: los descendientes
hispánicos de DULCIS' in *NRFH,* XXIV, 24–45
PENNY, R. J. (1972), 'The re-emergence of /f/ as a phoneme of Castilian' in
Zeitschrift für Romanische Philologie, LXXXVIII, 463–82
—— (1976), 'The Convergence of B, V and -P- in the Peninsula: a reappraisal'
in *Medieval Hispanic Studies Presented to Rita Hamilton,* ed. A. D.
Deyermond, London, Tamesis, 149–59
VON WARTBURG, W. (1952), *La fragmentación lingüística de la Romania,*
trans. M. Muñoz Cortés, Madrid

INDEX

Except where otherwise stated, references are to chapter and paragraph numbers. Phonetic symbols are placed at the end of the appropriate letter section.

WORD LIST

In this list of Spanish words cited in Part II entries are spelled as they appear in the main text: thus *fallar, massa, lexos* are alphabetized under their Old Spanish spellings. References are to chapter and paragraph numbers.

a, 12.13
abad, 13.12
abeja, 17.10
abrir, 17.8a
abuela, 12.10
acebo, 13.11b
açor, 17.18, n.
agua, 15.13c
águila, 15.13b, 17.5
ala, 12.12
albo, 15.12
algo, 15.13b
alma, 17.13
almuerço, 14.10, n.3
alto, 12.8b
ama, 13.9b, 14.3
amabais, 14.5
amáis, 13.9, n.1, 14.5
amarillo, 17.1
amasse, amas, 13.12, 14.8
amigo, 15.5
amistad, 17.7, n.2, 17.18
amizat, 17.18
amos, 15.12a
ampliar, 16.4c
ancla, 17.22c
ancho, 16.4c
ángel, 17.5
ángelus, 14.6
anillo, 13.4a
antigua, 15.13c
añadir, 13.12
año, 16.3d, 16.5b
apendicitis, 14.5, n.2
apóstol, 17.5
aprisco, 13.4b
araña, 16.3a
árbol, 17.5
arce, 17.8c
arte, art, 14.2, 14.8
arrojar, 17.11
asa, 12.9, 15.12d
aspid, 14.5, n.2
Asun(ción), 14.6
ave, 14.2
avispa, 13.4b
ayuno, 16.7d
azufre, 12.5, 12.11

balaj, 14.8

balanza, 15.6
baño, 16.3a
barba, 12.10
barrer, 12.10
basura, 12.10
baxar, 16.6b
baxo, 12.7, n.1
bebdo, 17.20
beber, 12.10
benigno, 16.3c, n.2
bermejo, 12.10
berza, 12.4a, n., 12.10, 14.10, n.3
beso, 12.7
bicis, 14.5, n.2
bizma, 15.9
blando, 15.11a
bobo, 12.8b
boca, 12.10, 13.12
boda, 12.10
bodega, 15.9
bodigo, 12.10
boj, 14.8
bondad, 17.21
borraj, 14.8
brazo, 15.11a
bronquitis, 14.5, n.2
bueno, 12.1, 12.10, 13.1
buey, 14.5
buitre, 16.4b, n., 17.22d

caballo, 12.13, 16.2c
cabo, 13.9c
cabra, 15.11b, 17.6
cacha, 17.12
cada, 12.9, 13.9c
cadena, 13.9c
calandria, 15.14
caldo, 17.21
caliente, 15.12
cáliz, 17.5
calza, 12.8b
calle, cal, 14.8
cambiar, camiar, camear, 15.12a
cambuj, 14.8
campus, 14.6
canal, 15.5
candado, 17.2, 17.6
cansar, 15.14
cantallo, 16.2c, n.
cantan, 14.3

derecho. 16.4a, n.4
dezildo, 17.11, n.2
dezir, 14.11, 18.5
dice, 14.2
dicho, 16.4a, n.2
diestro, 15.14
digno, 16.3c, n.2
dijeron, 13.4, n.2
dios, 13.4, n.1
dixe, dix, dixo, 14.8, 16.6a, 18.7
dize, 14.10b
do(y), 14.5, n.1
doble, 15.11b
domar, 12.13
domingo, 17.7
don, 13.6
doze, dodze, 17.19b
dragón, 15.11a
dueño, 13.6
dulce, duce, duz, dulz, 12.5n., 14.8
durazno, 15.2
durmamos, 15.8b
duro, 12.13

echar, 16.4a, 16.7d, n.2
egual, igual, 15.8a
elle, el, 14.8
encina, 15.9
enchir, 16.4c
ende, 14.2
enebro, 16.7d, n.2
enero, 16.7d, n.2
engendrar, 17.2, 17.13, 17.17
engeño, 16.3a, n.
enjullo, 17.9a
ensayo, 16.7c
ensemble, 12.12
ensiemplo, insiemplo, enxiemplo, 15.8a,
    16.6c
entrar, 15.14
entre, 12.9, 12.11
enxalma, ensalma, 16.6c
enxeco, enseco, 16.6c
enxugar, ensugar, 16.6c
enzía, 16.3b, n.
esbelto, 18.10c
escaldar, 15.14
escama, 15.13a
escapar, 15.14
esconder, 15.14
escrito, 12.2, 15.12c
escuchar, 16.4b
escudilla, 15.10
escuela, 15.10
espada, 15.10
espalda, 17.11, n.2
espectáculo, 17.5
espejo, 15.10, 17.2, 17.11, n.1
espesso, 13.12
esse, 13.12, 15.12b

estable, 17.9a
estaño, 16.3c
estar, 15.10
este, est, 14.8
Esteban, 13.11b
esto(y), 14.5, n.1
estrado, 15.10, 15.14
estrecho, 16.4a, n.4
exe, 16.6a, n.1
extraño, 16.3a, 16.5b

fablar, 18.3
façes, 14.11
facundo, 13.11, n.2, 18.3
falso, 13.11a
falta, 13.11a, 17.7, n.1
fallar, 13.11, n.3, 16.2b
famélico, 18.10d
fazes, 14.11
fe, 13.11a, 14.7
fecho, 18.1, 18.3
femencia, 12.10, n.
fenchir, 13.11, n.3, 16.4c
fértil, 13.11, n.2, 18.3
fiar, 13.11a
fiebre, 13.11a
fiel, 12.12, 14.2
fiero, 13.11a
fiesta, 13.4b
fijo, 18.1, 18.7
fin, 14.2
finchar, 13.11, n.3, 16.4c
fingir, 13.11, n.2
finojo, 14.12, n.3
fito, 16.4a, n.2
fize, 12.4a
flaco, 16.2a, n.2
fleco, 13.5
flema, 16.2a, n.3
flexible, 16.2a, n.3
flojo, 16.2a, n.2
flor, 16.2a, n.2
forma, 13.11, n.2
franzir, 16.3b, n.
frañir, frañer, 16.3b
freno, 15.11a
frente, 13.4, n.3, 13.5
frío, 15.11a
fuego, 13.1, 13.9c, 13.11, n.1, 18.3
fuelle, 13.11, n.1
fuente, 13.6, 13.11, n.1
fuero, 13.11, n.1, 18.3

gallo, 12.13
gente, 14.12, n.2
genio, 14.12, n.2
giro, 14.12, n.2
glotón, 13.12, 15.11a
golpe, 17.7, n.1
gordo, 15.12